The Great Jobs Deception

Why More Workforce Education
Will Not Solve the Problem of Inadequate
Jobs

Brynne VanHettinga,
J.D., M.P.A., Ph.D.

Dedication

To every person who has made investment and effort to improve themselves and the world.

Other Books by this Author

Full Length Books

Why Assholes Rule the World (2019)

Good People, Evil Society: A Philosophical and Moral Inquiry (2021)

EBooks

The REAL History of Labor Day and the War on American Workers

Campaign Finance Reform: The Shifting and Ambiguous Line Between Where Money Talks and Speech is Free

Survival in the Gig Economy or get it **Free** by visiting www.books4thinkers.com

Acknowledgements

No work of this magnitude is possible without the assistance of others. While the writing and editing of this book (and any errors therein) is entirely my own, I would not have been able to collect, analyze, and interpret the data for the study that underlies the premise in this book without input and support from the following persons.

The anonymous respondents who completed the lengthy survey questionnaire on underemployment and the individuals among these who were willing to share their stories.

The members of my doctoral dissertation committee, Dr. Kristen Dailey, Dr. Raj Singh, and Dr. William Benet. Without their advice and encouragement, the study that formed the basis of this book would not have been possible.

Dr. Linda Day and Dr. Louis Milanesi, who contributed their thoughts and insights.

The individuals and organizations who made the surveys available to their members: Les French and the Washington Alliance of Technology Workers, Richard Tax and the American Engineering Association, Annette Ferebee and The American Public Health Association, Larry Houchins and the Mississippi State Bar, and Jordan Yochim and the Kansas Bar Association

My beloved husband Vic, who always stood with me when speaking truth to power, encouraged me through dissertation, and was called home by God before he would see this book.

Table of Contents

Introduction

THE SUBJECT OF JOBS IS A CONCERN FOR EVERYONE—from Presidential candidates to anyone struggling to make ends meet or find their calling in life. In the 2016 election, for many people candidate Donald Trump was personally unlikeable and he had a history riddled with questionable ethics, yet his promises to bring jobs to struggling communities resonated with voters. While people do not agree on how to fix the jobs problem, most everyone agrees that we have a problem with jobs.

Conservatives traditionally take a supply side approach; that is, if we give tax breaks to corporations and wealthy individuals they will hire people. The actual evidence suggests otherwise, as unemployment was lowest during the period when marginal tax rates were highest (1945-1973). Conversely, liberals typically argue that the problem of insufficient jobs involves lack of demand. The suggested fix here is that the government should "create" jobs for the unemployed, which potentially appeals to conservatives as well because recipients of public welfare would now be required to earn it. During the Great Depression, the Civilian Conservation Corps and the Works Project Administration provided paid employment to thousands of out-of-work and desperate men while rebuilding national infrastructure. Thus, there is some evidence that public "demand stimulation" can alleviate a lack of employment in the short term. Yet, even many who agree that public employment may be a viable solution in the short term also acknowledge that it should only be used as a temporary stop-gap until the economy recovers and begins to create jobs again.

Economists have somewhat more sophisticated theories on the problem of unemployment. One set of theories focuses on foreign exchange rates and trade deficits. That is, when the United States imports more goods and services than it exports, or foreign goods become cheaper relative to domestic goods, American jobs will suffer. Another set of theories involves attempts by the Federal Reserve to either stimulate or slow down the economy through the setting of interest rates. The premise behind monetary policy is that there is a zero-sum trade-off between inflation and unemployment: If you create too many jobs, prices will rise, thus offsetting any wage gains from increased employment.

What all of these theories fail to address is whether or not jobs are working for jobholders. It is not simply a matter of an insufficient number of jobs, but whether or not available jobs are fulfilling human needs. With respect to individual jobholders, many jobs (even here in America) do not even provide the basics of subsistence, let alone fulfill higher order needs for accomplishment, community, and meaning. With respect to society in the aggregate, we are losing the productive capacity of unused talent, skills and education. *The Great Jobs Deception* proposes that it is the fundamental structural problems of the "job market" and even the design of individual jobs themselves that must be remedied before we will ever be able to fix the problem of inadequate jobs. Indeed, I am making the revolutionary proposal that we must move away from the idea that everyone has to have a "job" and toward a society that fosters the creation of individual livelihoods.

The Great Jobs Deception is based on a study about underemployment experienced by highly educated and skilled Americans. In spite of all the political rhetoric about a so-called skills shortage, Americans are spending huge amounts of both time and financial capital to better themselves, but they are not receiving a corresponding return in the workplace. Workers with college and even post-graduate degrees find themselves either unemployed or forced to accept jobs that do not require their level of skills and education solely to survive. At the same time, public resources are directed to worker training and "job readiness," primarily targeted to workers lower in the job hierarchy (e.g., workers with less education, immigrants, or persons recently released from prison). The conventional premise is that the workforce is what needs to be fixed, while seemingly no attention is paid to the fact that the job market will likely be inadequate to absorb everyone with credentials. By focusing solely on job market inadequacies experienced by highly educated workers, *The Great Jobs Deception* analyzes the evidence and concludes that there is greater dysfunction with the job market than with workers.

The analytic foundation for *The Great Jobs Deception* is a doctoral dissertation study on professional underemployment. A review of the academic literature strongly suggests that credential and skill underemployment (that is, employment that does not utilize a worker's highest skills and education) has existed as a structural feature of the U.S. labor market for decades. However, national databases (e.g., the Bureau of Labor Statistics and the Current Population Surveys) are failing to capture this form of underemployment. Both recessions and presidential elections bring enhanced public discussion about the need to create jobs and raise the minimum wage. However, what is missing is a true measure of the scope and depth of underemployment—what economists sometimes term *labor disutility*—as well as a better understanding of how existing labor market structures and socio-political ideologies may actually facilitate underemployment.

The Great Jobs Deception is based primarily on academic research, but it is not intended solely for academics, labor economists and workforce development analysts. It is written for critically thinking lay audiences, particularly anyone who has always thought that something was wrong with the "job market" but could not articulate what or why. Indeed, the common response of persons who lose a job through no fault of their own is to blame their former

3

employer, a recessionary economy, or globalization. While all of these can certainly play a major part in a world besieged by downsizing and layoffs, there are less obvious but more troublesome issues. The hope for this book is that un- and under-employed citizens will gain a better understanding of both economics and the hierarchical power structures that govern the labor market. When this happens, un- and underemployed workers will stop blaming either themselves or inevitable market forces and demand (or create) real reform.

As the study found, a college or post-graduate degree does not inoculate someone from experiencing un- and under-employment. Young people with new degrees soon find out that they need to gain experience somewhere, but they are spending greater portions of their careers in either unrelated "entry-level" positions that don't require their education or (surprisingly competitive) unpaid internships. Laid off workers—even educated ones with experience—can search months or years before they find subsequent employment, and the next job often pays less than the previous one. Job changes are becoming more frequent and time in-between jobs lengthier. More people are having to make ends meet in a "gig" economy—driving for ride-sharing services like Uber or cobbling together freelance projects.

A few enterprising individuals have actually been able to make a modest living in the gig economy, since alternatives in the regular job market are often not much better. Because most people (especially Americans) want to make the best out of a bad situation, un- and underemployed workers frequently return to school and gain new skills and credentials (or upgrade old ones). Although there are some of us who actually welcome a culture of lifelong learning, this constant upgrading always seems to come out of our own pockets and never seems to produce a corresponding reward—not just in terms of salary, but even in terms of meaningful work.

4

Paradoxically, the proposed policy solution from the political establishment is to get more of the workforce trained, particularly for projected in-demand technical and health care occupations. Proponents of the brave new "knowledge economy" believe that the majority of jobs in the future will require specialized skills and training that cannot be learned on-the-job. According to the U.S. Bureau of Labor Statistics (BLS), projections for growth in the top ten occupations by absolute numbers are in jobs that do not, for the most part, require a college degree.[1] The highest projected job growth by percentage is for home health aides (38.1%), personal care aides (25.9%) and medical assistants (23.5%), with median annual wages ranging from $20,440 to $29,000. Although significant growth is also projected in a few higher skilled (and better paying) occupations such as computer systems analysts (20.9%) and software developers (18.8%), these occupations are fewer in absolute numbers.

What is being ignored is the number of workers who already have existing training and skills (or at least arguably transferable skills that would require minimum upgrading) who are un- and underemployed. Many of these workers are deliberately being replaced by cheaper foreign and younger workers. From a purely supply and demand standpoint, training more people will operate to lower wages in these occupations in an economy where most workers' wages are already stagnant. From an economic policy perspective, spending public funds on worker training while workers with credentials are underemployed represents an inefficient use of resources. From a more general policy perspective, when training and credentials do not produce returns for workers (either in the form of better pay or more secure work), such a situation creates a violation of the social contract.

Many Americans were raised on the admonition that if you worked hard and did well in school, you would be able to get a good job—or at least a job where you would be able to work your way up. In the middle of the past century, the United States committed to providing all citizens with 12 years of free public education, along with heavily subsidized public colleges and trade schools in order to broaden access to the American Dream. Persons who availed themselves of educational opportunities and applied them at work could be assured of a comfortable middle-class lifestyle, reasonable job security, the ability to build a better life for themselves and their children, and retirement in relative comfort. When the promises of education and hard work no longer deliver for the majority, this presents the possibility of social unrest and civic discord.

A post-Great Recession economy and anemic "recovery" in the job market have generated political concern for the creation of jobs. However, this concern appears to be focused solely on job quantity without concern for job quality. The last two recessions have resulted in the anomaly of so-called jobless and wageless recoveries. Indeed, wages have been stagnating for decades, notwithstanding increases in GDP as well as average educational levels across all demographic groups. However, politicians and economic development experts (usually associated with national or local chambers of commerce) continually tout the requirements of a brave, new "knowledge economy" and a pressing need to solve a skills shortage crisis.

In the United States, official unemployment is defined narrowly—that is, as how many people are actively seeking work compared to how many people are working. There is no official measure of workers who have taken a job as a means of subsistence that does not fully use their skill level or educational credentials. This underutilization of skills, education, and training represents a waste of human capital, or the combined public and private investments applied for the development of these skills. Although the sporadic academic studies that have analyzed underemployment and overeducation have found that some level of this has existed in the labor force for decades, it is not being captured in official (BLS) labor market data. Whether this neglect is due to lack of political will (no administration wants to see unemployment data look worse) or lack of analytical capacity remains to be answered.

During these same decades, there has been a paradigm clash between those who argue that the new knowledge economy requires an ever-increasing and perpetual upgrade of worker skills and those who argue that jobs are deliberately being degraded/deskilled and cheapened. In Chapter 3, the theoretical foundations of this paradox are examined in detail. Historically, in the beginning of the Industrial Age, craft production that once was performed by one person was broken into a few select higher level (and higher paid) functions and a mass of lower level (and lower paid) functions, which operated to reduce the costs of production overall.

A primary motivation behind the deconstruction of work was to disempower the majority of workers by bifurcating executive (decision-making) and production functions. Combined with bureaucratic organization of work and hierarchical chains of command, this served to not only limit the workers' knowledge, but operated to limit avenues of upward mobility. As the masses of workers began to realize that avenues of upward mobility depended on education, there was increased public demand to broaden access to education, particularly higher education. However, in spite of the increasing aggregate knowledge of workers—and even the technological upgrading of many jobs—the economy does not generate a sufficient number of higher level jobs to accommodate all workers with higher education.

One line of theory (the neoclassical paradigm) begins with the work of Adam Smith, which argues that the wealth of a society is comprised as much from the skills, knowledge and abilities of its citizens (i.e., the "improvement in the productive powers of labour")[2] as it is comprised of physical and financial capital. In Smith's time, European observers of the new American nation were amazed at the productivity of American citizens. This can be attributed to a number of factors. First, nearly every citizen (which at that time included only property-owning white males) owned his own land and small capitals, i.e., a farm, a shop, or tools of a trade. The American citizen was also able to reap all the benefits of his own labors, in contrast to Europeans who were just emerging from feudalism, where inherited nobility owned most of the land, and the majority of people who worked the land were required to pay a portion to the land "lord" in exchange for protection. The typical American freeholder had control over his own land, labor, and affairs, and there was also a built-in limit to ownership. That is, there was no incentive for anyone to acquire more land than a man and his family could work by themselves. Under such a system, where citizens owned their own labor but not the labor of others (women, slaves, and other non-citizens excepted), the laws of Adam Smith's "free market" worked efficiently as described.

The modern extension of Smith's theory on the creation of national wealth is human capital theory. Human capital theory was developed primarily by the Chicago School economist Gary Becker (1964), and proposed that both individual well-being and national wealth (GDP) were correlated with increasing investments in skills and knowledge. Becker realized that the concept of "human capital" could be exploitative, but there was a humane side of the concept that was equally important. Worker productivity is enhanced as much by worker well-being as it is by the acquisition of skills. Thus, Becker's theory served as a foundation for progressive developments in the form of employer-provided health insurance and retirement plans, as well as more modern amenities such as on-site gyms and day care. According to human capital theory, the antidote to low economic growth, as well as un- and underemployment, is more skills, training and education in the workforce. Although human capital theory has extensive empirical and experimental data to support it, it provides no explanation for underemployment of educated and skilled individuals. It also cannot explain stagnating wages at the same time both GDP and aggregate educational levels are increasing.

8

Nearly one hundred years after Smith's *Wealth of Nations* was published, a German economist named Karl Marx observed a vastly different system in the way that work was structured. Marx's observations covered the initial period of industrialization, as goods were increasingly produced in collectivized factories rather than by individual craftsmen (they were almost invariably men). For the factory owners, there were efficiency gains from having a single worker perform a narrower range of functions and therefore get better at them (as described by Adam Smith). However, Marx argued that the real goal was to disempower the craftsmen and cheapen their labor by separating the worker from control over the work.

Although Marx's work was discredited in capitalist countries as being only applicable to low-level industrial production (i.e., it had no relevance in modern "knowledge" economies), Harry Braverman (1974) applied Marxian deconstruction processes to modern office work, which came to be known as "labor process theory," or alternatively, the "degradation of work." In a world where work at all levels was increasing in technical content, Braverman's model suggested that it was not so much that individual jobs were being fragmented, but that labor processes were operating to divide work into a few "good" jobs (which did require higher level technical and managerial skills) and "bad" jobs that were occupied by a much larger low-paid and fungible work force.

The works of Adam Smith and Karl Marx split into two divergent theoretical frameworks and indeed two divergent political ideologies. The problem with this is that both theories are correct, if only partially correct. Here in the United States, Marx's work and labor degradation theory are either met with outright hostility or ignored. Political attention is rightly focused on finding ways to reduce the cost of higher education and upgrade the skills and training of workers at the bottom of the occupational hierarchy. However, the skills that go wasted because educated workers can't find jobs that require their education do not even get measured. This is a result of more than a clash between competing theories, but rather suggests a convenient bias. That is, if we attribute un- and underemployment to deficiencies in the workforce or in individual workers (a "blame the victim" worldview), then no one has to acknowledge the real deficiencies in the job market—or do anything about it.

In addition to the paradigm clash between human capital and labor process theories, a third force (independent of labor market economics) has exerted an even greater influence on organizational structures. As organizations—both corporate and government— became larger, the new science of management theory was born. In the corporate sector, this was often referred to as the "principle-agent" problem, and the objective was to either break or manipulate the will of the workers in order to manage them efficiently for production. In the public sector, while efficiency was also a goal, the same phenomenon was termed "bureaucracy," and the objective was to insure the accountability of unelected public officials.

As both public and private organizations grew larger in size and scope, they tend to become characterized by top-down, command-and-control hierarchies. Although there has been much debate about the purported dichotomy between private enterprise and government, many of their organizational structures and functions are the same. The major difference is that private organizations exert control for the purpose of profit while public organizations exert control for the purpose of accountability. Max Weber was one of the primary thinkers in the development of this so-called "theory of bureaucracy." While Weber predicted that bureaucratic organizations were the way of the future, he also warned that hyper-rationalization, taken to extreme, could become counter-productive and even dehumanizing.

This book is adapted from a doctoral dissertation study[3] that analyzed underemployment among professionals in the STEM (science, technology, engineering and math), health care, legal, and academic professions. The rationale for focusing this study on

10

professionals with college degrees or higher was to challenge the premise of human capital theory as well as to provide evidence that labor market statistics were grossly under-measuring this form of labor disutility. In this study, survey respondents were to consider themselves underemployed only if, after having obtained their highest level credential, they found themselves involuntarily (1) unemployed, (2) part-time, or (3) working in a job that did not expressly (per the job description) require their degree. This was intended to define underemployment/overeducation as narrowly as possible. Thus, the study did not even take into account cases where a professional had been laid off and then rehired in a job that, even if it required the same education, did not require the same level of experience and skills. So, a manager with a college degree and 10 or 15 years of experience is laid off and ends up taking a job that also requires a college degree but only one or two years of experience and no management duties (and pays less) is still underemployed, but would not be considered underemployed for purposes of this study.

One purpose of the study was to challenge the basic premise of the skills shortage alarmists, as well as to determine if underemployment had different manifestations in different professional categories or even among different types of professionals. The media and politicians are everywhere touting the need for more skills training in the STEM and health care occupations. There are predictions of dire skills shortages in these areas, leading to the impression that persons who have these skills should be able to find employment—even well-paid employment. Conversely, media stories about legal professionals tend to focus on the fact that there are "too many lawyers" and the struggles of recent law school graduates searching for legal work or having to accept non-legal jobs. The economic anomaly here is that an oversupply of lawyers (according to conventional economic theory) should drive the cost of legal services down. Yet, many working and middle-class people cannot afford a lawyer. The situation with academic and teaching jobs appears to be bifurcated. That is, the expansion of education has created institutions characterized by a small cadre of high-paid faculty and administrators alongside an increasing number of overworked and underpaid adjunct instructors at the college and university level.

In addition to having a college degree or higher, survey respondents had to also belong to one of 28 specifically defined occupations that are commonly considered to be "professional" (e.g., engineers, scientists, doctors, nurses, lawyers, teachers, etc.), so respondents' credentials were more occupationally specific than a general liberal arts or business degree. Prior studies of underemployment have generally either analyzed the workforce as a whole or examined a specific occupation. This study differs from prior studies on underemployment in that it both delimits the type of underemployment examined (professionals with college-level education or higher employed in jobs that do not require their degrees) and expands (four broad professional occupational categories) the population subsamples. The reason for this was to determine whether higher levels of underemployment exist in occupations where there might be a temporary oversupply of specific skills and particular workers, or whether it might be a manifestation of more fundamental, structural deficiencies in the U.S. labor market.

Chapter Two summarizes the literature on underemployment over the past four decades and analyzes the sufficiency of current labor statistics. Chapter Three analyzes the foundations and paradigm clash between human capital theory and labor degradation theory. More modern economic models of the labor market are analyzed in Chapter Four. The findings of the study with respect to the survey population as a whole are described in Chapter 5. Chapter 6 provides additional detail about how underemployment dynamics compared across the four occupational categories. In Chapter 7, the process of how career choices are made is explored. Chapter 8 looks at how education has been rationalized, how this may impact career decisions and the quality of labor market information, and even the mutually reinforcing processes between the educational system and labor market "demand." In the final chapter, these issues are explored from the standpoint of broader social forces, and what might be done to attempt to address them.

For me, underemployment is more than an interesting topic for a dissertation study: I have been literally observing, studying (and living) underemployment since the 1980s. In the early working years, I experienced the "working poor" variety of underemployment—a string of low wage and irregular jobs that had no future. It was obvious that education was the only way out and up, so classes had to be squeezed into job schedules. It took me over 10 years to earn an undergraduate degree, although I admit that some of the problem was frequent moving and my own inability to settle on a major. I finally decided on economics, because I sensed that, long before former President Clinton said so in a campaign speech, most of us were working harder for less. I wrote my first paper on underemployment as an undergraduate, when Teresa Sullivan's *Marginal Workers, Marginal Jobs*[4] provided the first foundational framework for describing underemployment.

While pursuing my undergraduate degree, I worked in a retail store. Fortunately, this was a family-owned enterprise and not a corporate chain, and they were willing to accommodate my class schedule. One of my co-workers was a prime example of underemployment—a woman who had a Masters in geology which she had earned in Brazil, and who was fluent in English (her native language), German, and Portuguese. As I wrote the paper at the end of the Reagan era, I found many similar dynamics that were documented in my dissertation some 25 years later. In the interim, the "baby boom" generation was entering mid-career, at the same time the labor market was experiencing massive corporate downsizing. I discussed the so-called service economy, the (even then measurable) diminishing returns to education, and the myth of unlimited opportunity. While writing the paper, strangers everywhere were willing to tell me about their work life, echoing the same kinds of angst I would hear in interviews over two decades later:

> *"I knew there was no future in my job, but I got a family to support. So I bust my a— and get a degree in business while I'm still working, and [the company] finally promotes me to management. Now I work even longer, crazy hours, have responsibility for a million-dollar store, and they pay me $16,000 a year! By the time I pay on my school loans, I'm not much better off than before."*
>
> Manager, retail sporting goods chain outlet.

> *"I tried working lower-level jobs, but they just never seemed to work out. One boss flat out told me when he fired me that I just didn't 'fit in.' All my experience counts for nothing! These 'management trainee' positions always hire the young studs—they figure the kids will swallow the company loyalty bulls---."*
>
> Unemployed over-40 executive pursuing an MBA.

> *"As a new employee with a college degree, I feel my contributions will be better recognized in another company where creativity, risk, ambition, and marketing are recognized as key components for success."*
>
> Lower-level supervisor for a public utility.

> *"You ain't got a decent job, you ain't got nothing."*
>
> Veteran spot-welder who took a $6-an-hour pay cut in order to keep his job.

> *"If I'm told one more time I ought to be glad to have a job, I'll scream!"*
>
> Survivor of a corporate merger.

Because economics could not explain what I was seeing in the job market, I went to law school. Maybe the problem of inadequate work had a legal solution. While in law school, I served as a volunteer advocate at a legal clinic sponsored by the San Francisco-based Employment Law Center. Most of the clients were ethnic minorities or immigrants who were subjected to grossly unfair (and sometimes actually illegal) treatment at work. Often we were unable to help them, and the regulatory infrastructure to protect labor rights appeared to be underfunded and inadequate. Later, as a practicing attorney myself who represented employees, I was saddened and demoralized at both the toothlessness of labor rights laws and outright hostility of some members of the judiciary to employment cases and employees.

So, I went back to school for a Ph.D. in public policy and administration. This is not so much that I actually believed that bureaucracy could fix the broken labor market, but maybe if I understood how "the system" worked, I would have a better idea about how to create solutions that actually worked for workers. Ironically, in a world where workers cannot realize gains from their own education, we may need to have even more education (albeit with a different orientation) in order to address the problem. When I completed dissertation I therefore was not surprised to be confronted with difficulty finding work. I was too broke to pay the fees to activate my bar license (although I had successfully passed the state bar exam before starting on the Ph.D). I had no teaching experience, which made academic jobs out-of-reach, even if I had been willing to work at poverty adjunct wages. I was told I was overqualified for many other jobs, and was even urged to leave some education and experience off my resume, which then created "gaps" that most employers deem unacceptable. Thus with few options and no real plan, I started attending several job clubs in the Austin, Texas metropolitan area.

To read the headlines, one would expect that finding a job in the "booming" Austin economy would not be too difficult. Even in a post-recession economy, Austin is among the top metropolitan statistical areas for its job creation numbers and low unemployment rate. Texas politicians were constantly in the media, lamenting a skills shortage and the need to increase workforce training to fill all the great new jobs. Yet, at every single one of the job clubs were dozens of unemployed professionals, including those with purportedly in-demand skills such as IT, systems engineers, project managers and web developers.

What most of these unemployed workers had in common was years of experience and gray heads. Even the workforce development caseworkers grudgingly began to admit that age discrimination was real. While age discrimination seems like a logical explanation, it probably has as much to do with money. Better to lay off the older workers (who have experience) and hire the millennials with "fresh" degrees who are pouring into the region and willing to work for much lower salaries. Indeed, some of the laid off job club professionals were only able to find work (at lower pay) after they completed classes for "newer" credentials. In essence, these professionals had to pay to update existing skills for work that paid less. A number of these professionals found themselves cycling through the job clubs for second, third and more times due to a constant series of layoffs and rehiring.

So, it is not just research and not just data, but real life and real time observations that suggest serious structural deficiencies in the U.S. labor market. These deficiencies are not being captured by labor market statistics, which increases the angst of un- and underemployed workers who are bombarded with apparently optimistic employment numbers. While a post-Great Recession economy has made the situation worse, it is not the sole cause of a dynamic that has existed for decades. This study attempts to better understand some of the complex factors that are associated with underemployment in the context of competing and alternative theoretical frameworks. Our economy did not get to the place it is now overnight, and there will be no quick fixes. Yet, continuing with business as usual is obviously not the correct solution.

Notes

1 http://www.bls.gov/emp/ep_table_104.htm

2 Smith, A. (1776). *The wealth of nations*. Cannan, E., (Ed., 1904). New York, NY: Bantam Dell/Random House (2003 Edition), p. 9.

3 VanHettinga, B. (2015). Professional reserve armies: Underemployment and labor degradation in professional occupations. (Doctoral dissertation). http://search.proquest.com/docview/1655360861.

4 Sullivan, T. (1978). *Marginal workers, marginal jobs: The underutilization of American workers*. Austin, TX: University of Texas Press.

Chapter One
The Nature and Purpose of Work

*"The property which every man has in his own labor,
as it is the original foundation of all other property, so it is the most
sacred and inviolable."*

Adam Smith, *The Wealth of Nations*, 1776

IS WORK A GOOD OR A BAD THING? Some people, particularly those who work in religious, public service, or non-profit settings, regard their work as tantamount to a spiritual "calling." Others respond with the contrary observation that "work is a four-letter word." However, until the late 19th and early 20th century, there was little argument about the purpose and meaning of work. Most of us have to work to survive, and indeed it has been thus since the dawn of humanity. When work was closer to everyday subsistence— plowing the field, tending the garden, milking the cow, spinning and weaving cloth—there was no need to question the "why" of work. Although it cannot be said that most people enjoy their work in subsistence economies, it at least gives them a purpose and a place in their families and communities.

While modern work is not as physically strenuous and dangerous as in times past, there seems to be more angst associated with it. Everyday tasks and functions are more specialized (and usually mediated by some form of technology), so there is not an immediate connection between what one does and an ultimate objective or higher mission. The irony is that modern work holds the promise of developing our higher-level skills and talents in pursuit of goals more advanced than basic survival, yet it often doesn't seem to deliver on either. The academic literature has documented rising aggregate levels of knowledge and education concurrent with increasing inability to find suitable employment, notwithstanding increases in GDP and technological advancement, and this trend has been occurring over at least the past several decades. Yet, one seldom hears of this phenomenon in the popular media or conventional labor statistics.

Work as a Moral Dilemma

The Bible, particularly the Old Testament, seems to argue against the principle that human work is something inherently "good." When God rested from the labors of creation on the seventh day, this was the day that was made holy (Gen 2:2). The necessity of work to sustain subsistence was God's curse as punishment for the disobedience of original sin: "In the sweat of your face you shall eat bread" (Gen. 3:19). The New Testament is somewhat more ambiguous in taking a position on whether work is good or bad. There are references to "good works," or work that is done in the name of God or Jesus. We are told that one cannot have faith apart from works (James 2:18-26). Yet we are also told the story of Mary and Martha. When Jesus visits the two women, Mary sits quietly at Jesus' feet to learn, while Martha bustles busily about tending to Jesus' (and possibly others) material comforts. When Martha complains to Jesus and argues that Mary should be helping her, she is admonished by Jesus to get her priorities straight (Luke 10: 38-42). This suggests that, in the view of the Mosaic tradition and early Catholic church, while "work" to maintain physical subsistence is necessary, it is more important to attend to spiritual, or Godly things.

This worldview began to change during the Protestant Reformation, which is generally described as occurring between 1517 (Martin Luther's 95 theses) and 1648 (Treaty of Westphalia). The Reformation was followed soon thereafter by the so-called Age of Enlightenment (1620s to late 1700s), which emphasized reason, individuality, and challenge of traditional authorities. Many of the early settlers in what eventually became the United States were members of Calvinist Protestant sects (Puritans, Quakers) that believed hard work and frugality were a sign of moral virtue, where indolence and sloth were regarded as sinful. A popular idiom, "the devil finds work for idle hands" suggested that work could keep one out of trouble and away from sin.

European visitors to America in the early 1800s were amazed at the transformation of what had been essentially wilderness. Early American settlers had built a civilization upon a "work ethic," which had taken on a form of morality. From the idea that a moral life was devoted to work grew a corollary concept that material wealth represented a sign of God's grace. Writers in the early 20th century such as Max Weber[1] noted empirical connections between hard work, economic progress for society, material prosperity for individuals, and a capitalist economic system. These interrelationships were further connected to moral superiority, reinforcing popular narratives that correlated capitalism with both American exceptionalism and God.

What these early writers and thinkers did not explore in depth was the fact that early Americans were free of the class system that dominated Europe, and most citizens (who were mainly free, white and male) worked for themselves as small farmers, shopkeepers and tradesman. That is, in the words of Karl Marx, they were able to enjoy the full benefits of their own labor product. In the early days of America, hard work produced tangible wealth and social standing for the average citizen.

What early economic writers such as Adam Smith did not (and could not) foresee was the development of the modern corporate state. In the days of Adam Smith, the economy was dominated by small individual and family producers, none of which could dominate markets any larger than the immediate locale. The so-called "invisible hand" worked because the connections between consumers and producers provided immediate regulatory feedback. No one would last either in business or as a welcome member of the community who was selling tainted goods or whose activity was detrimental to the community at large in some way. That is, the people who lived in communities had some control over the human events that constituted their everyday lives.

The story of Jesus itself suggests that one's calling is not necessarily the same as one's occupation (that is, the work one does to sustain physical survival). The story centers primarily around Jesus' birth as fulfillment of prophecy and his ministry. Information about the intervening 33 years of Jesus' life is somewhat sketchy to practically nonexistent. We are told that from the age of 12 years Jesus advanced in wisdom and God's favor (Luke 2: 42-52), and later that he performed work as a carpenter (Mark 6:3, Matthew 13:55). We do not know if Jesus was a great carpenter or a mediocre one. We presume his skills were sufficient to support him until he was able to begin his ministry. However, all the things that are so important to our identities today—where we went to school, what we studied, our job histories—are considered irrelevant in Jesus' story. In a culture that practically defines us by what we do, this seems either quaint and outdated or radical. Indeed, some of us might take comfort from the message that what we do for a living (our "survival" jobs) may have nothing to do with our God-purpose in life other than to keep body and soul together.

A lesser known passage in the Old Testament Bible describes what work would be like in the kingdom of God's promise—what some interpretations term the "millennial" times, or the "new heaven and new earth." In the Book of Isaiah, Chapter 65, the Prophet begins with a condemnation of exclusionary religious practices and self-righteousness before transitioning to a description of the inheritance which God promises to his servants, where "the voice of weeping will no longer be heard." The passage that specifically addresses work says:

"They shall build houses and inhabit them; they shall plant vineyards and eat their fruit. They shall not build and another inhabit; they shall not plant and another eat; for as the days of a tree so shall be the days of My people, and My elect shall long enjoy the work of their hands. They shall not labor in vain…"

Isaiah, 65: 21-23.

The message implies that when God's Kingdom arrives and perfect justice reigns over the Earth, people will still need to work, but their work will provide them sufficient subsistence to live peacefully, healthfully and abundantly. In this world, people will not have to struggle to find their place nor be consumed with the constant worry about how they are going to meet their needs of tomorrow. In our world of today, where the oxymoronic "working poor" and the phenomenon of underemployment is an ever-increasing reality, this passage suggests that God him (or her) self prefers that workers be allowed to retain and enjoy the produce of their own labor rather than having it extracted for the enrichment of others.

Human Work through the Ages

As societies evolved, so did economies and the world of work. One of the earliest forms of human social organization was the hunter-gatherer tribes. These were bands of humans who wandered the land in search of subsistence and performed a variety of tasks. There was also the application of rudimentary knowledge, as members came to learn how to catch fish and game, which plant foods were poisonous, and rudimentary toolmaking. For the most part, people took part in collective self-provisioning and did what was needed without the formal division of tasks. However, even in this early stage there was a form of status sorting. Hunting and protection, which was performed primarily by men, had a higher status (presumably because it was a more dangerous activity) than the gathering of fruits and the raising of children, which was performed primarily by women.

As nomadic hunter-gathering peoples gained skills, they began to settle in more permanent places. Communities began to fence in land, which allowed them to grow food (both plant and livestock) without having to be on the constant move in search of it. In the early days, the land used for food production was owned and worked by the community, but the concept of private property gradually took root. Individuals asserted ownership rights over particular parcels and livestock, and work was transformed into individual (or family) self-provisioning. Those who were able to provide protection could assert dominion over the land and the people who worked it. These so-called "land-lords" could demand a portion of the produce of land in exchange for this protection, which operated to divide society into owners and workers (serfs). As the lords entered into a series of agreements and alliances, the collection of produce from the serfs became institutionalized. Thus was born the early foundation of the nation-state and a system of taxation.

As Europe began to emerge from a feudal system into modern nation-states, economies were also evolving beyond simple self-provisioning. The primary form of wealth in these emerging economies was land, as it was the land from which most people still obtained subsistence. However, anyone who owned or controlled more land than he could work himself had to engage the assistance of others. Sometimes this assistance was voluntary, and other times people were conscripted into labor against their will. The era of European colonization and empire included the dark side of slavery and the "trade" of human beings for labor. As more land came under the control of other humans, it became harder for even freemen to find land they could call their own and secure sufficient resources to support themselves and their families.

In 18th century Europe, a confluence of material and intellectual progress produced what historians term the "Age of Enlightenment." The Age of Enlightenment was characterized by revolution in ideas as much as it was by scientific progress and intellectual development. Among these ideas were that social progress depended on individual liberty, scientific empiricism, and social tolerance. It challenged the authority of both kings and church, as well as the idea that only certain individuals were endowed by divine right to rule others. It is in the context of the Enlightenment that early settlers came to America, where here they could own their land as freeholders and enjoy the fruits of their labors. While early America remained a primarily agrarian economy, it (as well as the rest of Europe) was shifting into an economy of craft production. As people settled into towns, they became more skilled at making things. A single craftsman could produce more than he needed for himself and his family. As simple technologies developed, people were now able to make not only more things, but a broader variety of things. The emergence of a craft production economy permitted some persons the ability to earn a living without making anything at all, but by trading the excess production of communities with other communities. This developing craft and mercantile economy is what existed at the founding of America and at the time Adam Smith wrote *The Wealth of Nations* in 1776.

Frank Trentmann documents the historical transition to a consumer society from the 15th to the 21st century, including an alternating cycle of debate about whether increasing consumption served to increase freedoms (particularly choice) and blur the lines of class distinction, or was creating a society of perpetual indentures and ripping apart the fabric of society and moral life.[2] Trentmann cites historians in the 1770s who lament the "industrious revolution," and the constant busyness of household life ("you see the wheel going at almost every door"), not because people wanted to work, but because they had become "slaves to their own wants."[3] It was not only home-made goods that were driving the new materialism, but the expansion of mercantilism and empire allowed access to foreign novelties such as tea, coffee and sugar, which served to increase both the quantity and scope of demand.

Others argued that industriousness was a "prescriptive ideal" brought about by liberalism and imperialism, and that most people did not really have much choice but were forced to work harder due to rising prices and a "tough labor market."[4] Additionally, people began moving into towns and larger cities, where they were able to instantly upgrade their status with clothing and the display of other external objects because they were unlikely to encounter someone who knew them.[5] Indeed, today's job-seekers are advised to use the same status-signaling strategies—even if you have never owned a Brooks Brothers suit or paid for a $400 haircut, you might have to do these things if you hope to compete for a better job.

Trentmann also documents the cycles of moral conflict surrounding the increase in work and material wealth. This was especially apparent in lifestyle changes occurring in African tribes alongside an active trade in African slave labor. Most of us are familiar with the arguments against slavery, but the conditions of "free" colonial Africans were no less a subject of controversy. Even Christian missionaries were split between those who viewed the consumption of European goods by Africans as liberating and those who expressed concern about the destruction of "the spirit of tribal kinship," with its ethic of mutual support and interdependence.[6]

In America and Europe, the new consumerism gave birth to Consumer Leagues and other societies, who provided information about how goods (particularly imported goods) were produced, and advocated boycotts of things that were produced from the blood labor of slavery and sweatshops. Because most of these consumer advocates were women, Trentmann suggests that this consumer activism gave rise to the suffragette movement and an increase in political rights and social citizenship generally.[7]

Nearly 100 years after the publication of Smith's *Wealth of Nations,* economic life had undergone yet another radical transformation. Instead of land, the new form of wealth consisted of the ownership of collective production, i.e., industrial factories. Just as feudal lords had consolidated power and wealth in the form of land, power and wealth was now being consolidated in the form of factories, which involved both ownership of material wealth and the labor of others. While goods could now be made faster and cheaper, the old ways of craft production (as well as the old skills) were replaced by armies of workers who performed a few simple repetitive tasks over the course of the day.

In addition to fragmenting production and subjecting the majority of workers to a system of command-and-control, the new forms of work imposed the tyranny of measured time and quantitative production quotas. Work was no longer defined by the completion of a particular job, and work itself was no longer governed by the natural rhythms of life, but by the dictates of external timekeepers and mechanical bells and whistles. Moreover, as more people began moving into cities, they could no longer afford a plot of land upon which to establish a homestead. The old ways of self-provisioning were eventually lost, as people became more dependent on industrial production for both the provision of everyday goods and for a livelihood.

As the new forms of production gained ground and replaced the older economies, they required ever larger scale and control over supply chains to be competitive. As firms became more fixed on growth and market domination, it became more difficult for small producers to earn a living. This created a feedback loop in which livelihoods became more dependent on narrow and specialized corporate "jobs" rather than managing an independent family farm or business. As firms grew larger, it became necessary to secure ever greater amounts of capital in order to establish a business. Thus more persons were pushed out of independent livelihoods and required to submit to employment for others in order to earn a living. At the same time, the economy was again transformed from one being based on industrial production to an economy based on money capital and finance. Technological and financial transformations, as well as the increasing complexity of managing much larger organizations, required new skill sets. These newer skills involved the understanding and application of abstract information. That is, they were not the sort of skills one could learn simply by doing the work or through an apprenticeship.

Jobs, Skills, and the Myth of Meritocracy

As more specialized and technical skills became necessary to earn a livelihood in the evolving economy, developed societies recognized the necessity of providing higher levels of education to the majority of citizens. While these avenues of upward mobility were always more accessible to those of means and privilege, the general trend was to provide ever higher levels of publicly supported education to a broader population base. In early America, most schooling was private, but by 1870, all states had free elementary schools. A reformer named Horace Mann brought the European concept of "common schools" to Massachusetts in 1848, which included the provision of education to train the teachers. The common school concept was based on the premise that education should be universal, free, and non-sectarian.

The purported objectives were to produce graduates who not only had basic literacy and numeracy skills, but were imbued with moral character and civic virtue. However, Mann also touted a system of public education as a way to control "undisciplined and unruly" children. Thus, even from the beginning, schools have been characterized as a means to produce better citizens, a pathway for upward mobility, and as a formalized control of the lower social orders. This paradox of the dual purpose of schooling has been greatly expounded upon by the modern academic critics Samuel Bowles and Herbert Gintis.[8]

The expansion of education along with the hubris of American exceptionalism paved the way for an ideology of meritocracy. That is, anyone could make it in America because of a combination of individual freedoms, seemingly limitless natural resources, and broad-based access to opportunity. Indeed, this might have actually been the case for early Americans who were free, white, male, and owned some form of land, property, or other means of producing income. Although it took until past the middle of the twentieth century, avenues to economic mobility were gradually expanded to include racial minorities and women, although this was not without conflict.

It is at the intersection of schooling and work that holds the greatest promise of meritocracy. The standard proposal is that a combination of intellect, ambition and hard work will permit the best and the brightest to rise in the social hierarchy, where they will not only do well for themselves, but make contributions to the larger society. For many of us, however, work is where we see the greatest disconnect between effort and reward. We go to school—and then go back to school or participate in continuing education—either in the hope of advancing in our career or staying up with the ever-changing needs of the labor "market." We work hard, sometimes sacrificing time with family, friends and community, only to find ourselves on the wrong side of a layoff. Those who survive a layoff double down on working, but even this may not immunize them against another round of layoffs.

Alternatively, the CEOs and corporate executives whose decisions result in layoffs or even the collapse and bankruptcy of the entire company are rewarded with "golden parachutes." The people who did their jobs lose their jobs, and those who failed at their jobs and bring an institution and perhaps an entire industry to the brink of ruin are bailed out. Those who are laid off frequently have to either accept a lower level job or go back to school for additional credentials—regardless of years or even decades of professional-level experience. Very often, the new job pays less than the previous job, and there is little to no expectation of upward mobility. Thus it seems that individuals who subscribe to the ideal of meritocracy are constantly bettering themselves but finding ever fewer decent jobs with any kind of future.

Drs. Stephen J. McNamee and Robert K. Miller, professors of sociology at the University of North Carolina-Wilmington, challenge the meritocracy myth,[9] or the ideology that proclaims where you end up in the socio-economic hierarchy is a direct function of your own effort and abilities. The professors define "merit" as a combination of innate talent, hard work, high moral character and integrity, and the "right attitude." They then present data that suggest that the touted correlation between "merit" and economic success is vastly overestimated. Moreover, a combination of "non-merit factors" actually operates to negate true merit and create barriers to individual mobility. From a mathematical standpoint, there is no logical reconciliation between the grossly skewed distribution of income and wealth and a purportedly "normal" (represented by the typical bell curve) distribution of individual merit.

The professors first describe a lack of direct correlation between intelligence as measured by IQ tests and income differences between individuals. They then do the same with respect to "hard work" and even point out that those who actually work the hardest physically are the most poorly paid, while the really big incomes in America derive from investments (where no work is actually done) rather than jobs. They next examine the more nebulous concept of "attitudes." A standard establishment explanation for the "cycle of poverty" is that the poor are anti-school, anti-work, anti-family, and anti-success. This is a variation of the Calvinist proposition that people are rewarded (if not by God, by the almighty and infallible market) in accordance with their just deserts. However, they argue that the poor value work, school and family as much as anyone, but they learn to adjust their ambitions and expectations based on a more realistic assessment of their limited life chances. The final argument addresses the fallacy of any connection between moral character and integrity and economic success. The professors cite already well-known corporate and political scandals and suggest that those who actually play by the rules can restrict their own opportunities for upward mobility.

So, if "merit" is only partially implicated in career success, what are the factors that have the greatest impact in the race to advance? Professors McNamee and Miller suggest that probably the biggest determinant of where one ends up is the effect of inheritance, or the place where one starts. Obviously, individuals born into wealthy families are going to have access to more resources and opportunities—including opportunities to identify, cultivate, and apply their natural talents. In addition to providing better opportunities and insulation from the vagaries of misfortune, individuals from wealthier families have access to higher levels of social and cultural capital. That is, they have greater access to social networks of wealth, power, and privilege as well as the expected behaviors, attitudes and demeanor of those in the upper classes. The biggest advantage of inheritance is access to elite education, which serves as a gatekeeper to better jobs and positions of power and privilege. Citing the works of Samuel Bowles and Herbert Gintis, the professors describe the pipeline of elite prep schools to elite universities, and the benefits of "legacy" admissions over poor and middle class students who have earned good grades but can only attend with scholarship or other public financial support.

Professors McNamee and Miller also discuss non-merit barriers to mobility that are directly connected with work: discrimination, a loss of self-employment, and simple bad luck. Indeed some form of these barriers were demonstrated in the survey sample of underemployed professionals. Race and sex discrimination have been the most pervasive forms of discrimination in America.[10] Although these have declined significantly (mainly due to legal mandate), there are still inertial effects of past discrimination that continue to create present disadvantages. However, discrimination itself has morphed into more categories, now including age, religion, disability, national origin, sexual orientation, and even physical appearance generally.

Discrimination has always also included a more subtle elitism, and these forms of status sorting were experienced by some of the survey participants. A loss of self-employment along with an increase in the size and dominance of corporations has also created non-merit barriers to avenues of upward mobility. This phenomenon also had a definite negative impact on some of the survey participants, who either had to accept substandard work in corporate hierarchies or struggled to earn a livelihood in a small sole proprietorship.

So-called "bad luck" happens when a worker is laid off from a job that he or she is very good at, or when an individual spends many dollars and many years preparing for a job or career which is no longer in demand. In essence, anyone who is preparing for a job must be able to accurately predict which skills and experience are going to be needed in the labor market of the future. A portion of this study examined the inadequacies of labor market information even as students were pursuing their professional education. Anyone who is currently looking for a job is also likely to be frustrated with real-time information about such things as organizational culture (including ethics), avenues to upward mobility, and other "environmental" factors unrelated to the actual job description. However, generally available information about corporations usually is produced by the corporation itself with very little independent vetting or oversight. Job seekers are constantly being exhorted to tweak their resumes, beef up their social media presence and research, research, research companies and network, network, network in the hopes of meeting those individuals who can get them past the job gatekeepers. In some respects, the ability to game the job market can have a greater impact on job outcomes than actual skills or talent.

Thus, for underemployed professionals, the disappointment manifests on two levels. The first is personal: You have spent years of your life and probably gone into tens (if not hundreds) of thousands of dollars in debt, and yet the promise of even a middle-class lifestyle remains elusive. The second is aspirational: You likely entered graduate or professional school with high hopes of contributing to society and making a difference. Yet, you may find yourself as a mid-level functionary in a corporate hierarchy whose sole purpose is to make money for someone else. You may even experience a form of angst usually associated with the working class. You did what you were supposed to do and paid the price to obtain professional credentials, but yet you receive no respect at work and the work itself seems to have no meaning or higher purpose.

Work and Democracy

In early America, work was complementary to a robust civic life. Although both paid work and politics were almost exclusively the domain of white men, citizens were able to incorporate both work and civic engagement into their daily routines. Today, many people spend the greater part of their waking lives commuting to and working in jurisdictions where they are not even allowed to vote. In the place where one lives and votes, the main objects of concern are likely to be related to public schools, public works, or local development projects. The political issues that never appear on anyone's agenda are the relationships between our work, our lives, and a democratic society.

Most people realize that work is not a democracy. You do what the boss tells you to do, even if he is wrong or the activity is potentially illegal. What many people do not realize is that, if you work for a private employer, you enjoy absolutely zero constitutional rights. You can be fired with impunity for speaking the truth (just ask any former whistleblower) and your employer is free to search your belongings and spy on your activities. Working for "the man" is a constant struggle between freedom and control, a struggle that is familiar to the stereotypical American working class. Professionals have typically

33

aligned with the owners of capital, but now experience many of the same disempowering and alienating features of modern work themselves. How this is resolved is yet to be determined.

Those who benefit from the dominant ideologies that support the status quo will not welcome challenges. For an inegalitarian system to remain stable over time, those in power must develop ideologies that convince everyone else the system is fair. In modern society, conversations about job markets are based on the premises of neoclassical economics. Research on work "socialization" is primarily conducted by management think tanks, whose objectives are to conform workers to corporate culture and/or get them to work harder for less without the workers' realization that they are being manipulated. This system is not solely about bad bosses or greedy corporate executives as it is about a complex and interconnected public discourse that is deliberately contrived to circumvent questioning.[11] It is not that people are afraid to say that the Emperor has no clothes, it is that the fact the Emperor is naked is viewed as the natural world order.

The purpose of the study upon which this book is based was to suggest that there is a lot of human talent out there that is not being fully utilized. This talent can be viewed as either an asset or a liability. Like capital reserves, it can be tapped for all manner of projects that could make the world better in some way. It also represents a form of economic waste. Yet, the popular media almost exclusively focus on official unemployment numbers—data which fails to capture the full range and depth of labor disutility. Politicians, corporate think tanks and chambers of commerce have hijacked public discourse, creating a discussion about rationalized labor "markets" rather than human livelihoods.

In this ideological framework, the workforce is what needs to be "fixed." The solution to un- and underemployment is more worker training, but it is a very specific type of training. That is, educational objectives are to prepare a workforce that has all of the just-in-time corporate technical skills but without the critical thinking skills necessary for a democratic civil society. What this study (and the numerous other studies that provided its foundation) suggests is that the labor market itself is what is grossly deficient, and training workers at the bottom of the job hierarchy will not cure the fundamental problem. In essence, this research needs to get out of academia and into policy discussions about what all of us do for a living.

Notes

1 Weber, M. (1905). *The protestant ethic and the spirit of capitalism.* London/New York, NY: Routledge Classics (1992). http://www.d.umn.edu/cla/faculty/jhamlin/1095/The%20Protestant%20Ethic%20and%20the%20Spirit%20of%20Capitalism.pdf

2 Trentmann, F. (2016). *Empire of things: How we became a world of consumers, from the fifteenth century to the twenty-first.* New York, NY: HarperCollins Publishers.

3 *Id.* at p. 75.

4 *Id.* at p. 76.

5 *Id.* at p. 94.

6 *Id.* at pp. 134-134.

7 *Id.* at pp. 156-157.

8 Bowles, S., & Gintis, H. (1976). *Schooling in capitalist America: Educational reform and the contradictions of economic life.* New York, NY: Basic Books.

9 McNamee, S. & Miller, R. (2004). *The meritocracy myth.* Lanham, MD: Rowman & Littlefield Publishers.

10 However, recent studies suggest that age discrimination (which is harder to prove) is probably more widespread in the job market, although it is aggravated by other discriminatory factors, particularly gender. Matthews, S. (2015, October 26). Here's proof that age discrimination is widespread in the job market. Bloomberg online at: http://www.bloomberg.com/news/articles/2015-10-26/here-s-proof-that-age-discrimination-is-widespread-in-the-job-market

11 Indeed, a recent (2016) book by Ari Rabin-Havt and Media Matters, *Lies Incorporated: The World of Post-Truth Politics*, documents how a powerful and highly interconnected network of politicians, lobbyists and corporate-funded think tanks has resulted in legislation and policy agendas that are contrary to the public interest. This same dynamic is even more insidious, because it influences our worldview and even infects our collective morality.

Chapter Two
How Bad is Underemployment?

THE SHORT ANSWER to this question is that underemployment is worse than we think it is. How much worse is harder to determine. Current measures of labor force disutility focus primarily on unemployment. That is, the way data is collected in the United States assumes that simply having a job is sufficient. There are more recently developed measures that take into account whether or not someone is employed full time versus part-time, but no measurements exist that are designed to capture job quality or job match—or lack thereof. This lack of measurement not only fails to capture whether or not work is "working" for workers, it also fails to capture huge amounts of education, skills, and training that are essentially being wasted.

Academic researchers seem to have a better handle on underemployment than labor economists and statisticians, but their studies are conducted in a piecemeal and fragmented manner from which it is difficult to establish either a baseline or long-term trends. Moreover, underemployment is examined by academics in a wide range of disciplines—economics, labor relations, sociology, psychology—each having its own theoretical frameworks. Thus, although there is general consensus among academics that underemployment is a real problem that is not being adequately measured or addressed, there is no agreement on how bad it actually is, the best way to measure it, or what to do about it.

In 2011, Douglas Maynard, an academic psychologist at the State University of New York, and Daniel Feldman, Synovus Chair Professor at the Terry College of Business, University of Georgia, conducted a comprehensive review of the academic literature on underemployment. Maynard and Feldman analyzed under-employment from the standpoint of economics and behavioral science, as well as its effect on various populations. Maynard and Feldman conclude that underemployment is a "pervasive problem" with "serious and significant" negative consequences about which "there is much we don't know."[1] Other researchers lament the lack of a "unitary framework"[2] or a "strong guiding theory."[3] Several researchers have noted that national data sources are inadequate to sufficiently inform labor policy decisions.[4] In summary, academics who study underemployment say it is a big problem, but they still don't have a handle on explaining it, and we aren't collecting the data we need to understand it, let alone do something about it.

As some researchers suggest, a large part of this problem is that the United States (and most other countries as well) has not developed good ways to measure underemployment. Underlying the problem of inadequate measures are inadequate definitions. The concept of underemployment contains overlapping constructs of skill, time, and wages. For example, someone who works full time at poverty level wages is underemployed with respect to income. If the same person is only working part-time, he or she is underemployed with respect to time, and may or may not be underemployed with respect to income or skills. Another example is the paradox of underemployment and overwork. That is, a person who works multiple part-time jobs just to make ends meet may be both over- and underemployed with respect to time, and is likely underemployed with respect to income.

Additional confounding factors create measurement validity problems when attempting to link a worker's skills to wages. Wages are not always directly correlated with skills, as social biases (discrimination) and power relationships (union-busting) impact how skills are valued and rewarded in society. Not only does discrimination affect wages directly,[5] it affects wages indirectly when some workers are less likely to receive on-the-job training or have access to social networks.[6] Moreover, exogenous macroeconomic factors (i.e., wage stagnation) and labor market anomalies unrelated to worker skills also affect wages. These market anomalies take the form of bifurcated (two-tiered) labor markets or winner-take all markets, in which a few workers are paid much more than their marginal product while most others are paid much less.

Credential underemployment is referred to in academic literature as "overeducation." Many of the studies on overeducation approach it from an economics cost-benefit analysis, or measurement of rate-of-return on educational expenditures. From the standpoint of the individual, the cost of education is skyrocketing, while the returns in the job market are modest, at best. However, failure to "invest" in any post-secondary training virtually guarantees a lifetime of bare subsistence and financial struggle. A college education (or alternative post-secondary trade skills training) is required simply to keep one out of poverty, but it does not guarantee that the degree-holder will attain a comfortable middle-class status or lifestyle. Education has become one more thing for which most of us are paying more and getting less.

This inefficiency is not limited to the effects on individuals, but extends to the rest of society as well. In addition to tuition paid by the student (or her family), public colleges and universities are supported by state and federal tax dollars. Private universities are also indirectly supported by tax dollars, most commonly in the form of federally subsidized student loans or research grants. When graduates are unable to secure appropriate employment, society also loses the full benefit of tax dollar investments in their education and training.

While education continues to cost more and deliver less, ironically the political debate about jobs in the United States has been captured by those who claim that the way to solve un- and underemployment is through more worker education and training. These "skills shortage" alarmists are generally represented by corporate and employer interests, although they have allies among progressive groups who advocate for minority and other economically disenfranchised populations. A primary purpose of this study was to demonstrate that underemployment exists in higher-skill occupations and not just in low-skilled work, or even just for those workers displaced from traditional middle-class manufacturing jobs. While workers on the low end of the labor hierarchy should have the opportunity to better themselves through education, what the skills shortage worldview ignores is the amount of skills, training, and education that is going to waste. The big unanswered question is that if we (as taxpayers) "invest" in getting everyone "trained," will there be sufficient jobs. Included in this question are whether there will be not only just a sufficient number of jobs, but jobs that provide a decent quality of life—jobs that permit workers to raise families and be active in their communities outside of work.

By focusing only on credential (and to a lesser extent, time) underemployment, this study avoided the definitional and construct validity issues associated with skill measurement and the determination of a "fair" wage. That is, this study deliberately avoided issues involved with whether professionals were receiving an adequate return for their investment in education and training. It also avoided issues around whether or not professionals were receiving adequate compensation for their skill level. In essence, this study looked at the simplest (and most unambiguous) construct of credential underemployment: Study participants were considered to be underemployed if they were unable to find full-time employment that expressly required their highest educational degree.

Evolution of Modern Measures of Labor Disutility

The primary method of measuring labor market disutility in the United States is the official rate of unemployment. The official unemployment rate is produced by the U.S. Bureau of Labor Statistics (BLS), which derives its measures of employment and unemployment using the Current Population Survey (CPS) and the Current Employment Status (Payroll) Surveys that are conducted monthly by the United States Census Bureau. The CPS covers a rotating sampling of 60,000 households (approximately 110,000 individuals) and measures unemployment based on the United Nations' International Labor Organization (ILO) definition. The Payroll Survey covers a sampling of 160,000 businesses and government agencies that represent 400,000 individual employers. These two sources have different classification criteria, and usually produce differing results, which must be reconciled before the "official" unemployment rate is determined.

The official rate of unemployment is defined as a ratio (or percentage) of persons able and willing to work but do not have a job to the total civilian labor force. The "total civilian labor force" in turn is defined as the sum of all persons who have a job—any job—plus those who are actively seeking work. Persons who work only a few hours per week, or work without pay for 15 or more hours per week in a family-owned business are counted as "employed." People who are neither employed nor counted in the officially "unemployed" are simply not included in the total civilian labor force. This form of measurement is based on the logical fallacy that only people who are working or actively looking for work "count," and everyone else who is not working is doing so by choice, and therefore not un- or underemployed. Indeed, at least one Nobel Prize[7] was awarded to an economist who has constructed a model demonstrating that work and leisure are substitutes, or voluntary "trade-offs."

This official unemployment measure, along with the number of jobs being lost or created, is regularly reported in the popular media and is fraught with political implications. The political party in power generally touts positive trends in the job market: an increase in the number of jobs being created, or a decrease in the rate of unemployment, as compared to previous reporting periods. Conversely, the "opposition" party tends to argue that the numbers do not give a true and accurate picture of the job market. As this study finds, these "contrarians" are more likely to be correct—regardless of whether they are Republicans or Democrats.

Early U.S. census measures were concerned only with the question of whether or not a worker had a "gainful occupation," which was defined as any usual profession, occupation, or trade that produced income, regardless of whether the worker was currently engaged in work.[8] For example, someone who had carpentry skills and periodically performed carpentry work for pay was classified as a carpenter, even if the person had no carpentry work at the time he was surveyed. Following the Great Depression, census measures were revised in 1937, where the primary concern now was to determine whether or not a person was entitled to taxpayer- subsidized "work-relief" payments. The new survey asked workers whether they currently had a job or were actively looking for work, and these questions continue to form the basis of unemployment measures today. In essence, the focus of policy concern with unemployment is its impact on public welfare expenditures such as unemployment insurance (UI) and other tax-funded social support programs. This concern is operationalized at state-level workforce development agencies, whose primary objective is to get UI recipients into jobs— any jobs. Whether these jobs are full or part-time, or even pay enough to fully remove the worker from public subsidy, is of secondary concern.

A subset of unemployment (which represents a 100% labor disutility for that worker's skills and training) is involuntary part-time employment (which represents a partial labor disutility). While some workers (mainly students and mothers) have traditionally chosen part-time work in order to accommodate other lifestyle needs, not everyone who works part-time has chosen to do so. Beginning in the middle 1970s, several researchers found that rates of involuntary part-time employment virtually tripled between 1970 and 1990.[9] Not surprisingly, involuntary part-time employment more than doubled during the Great Recession.[10] The BLS has also documented a sharp increase in involuntary part-time employment beginning in 2008, and this is expected to increase again as employers restructure their work force to avoid payment of health insurance benefits under the recently enacted Patient Protection and Affordable Care Act.

In 1994, the U.S. Census Bureau updated the CPS because of concerns that current measures were unreliable and likely underestimating the extent of labor underutilization.[11]   BLS now has developed a six-level measure of labor underutilization, which is expressed as a percentage of the civilian labor force. U-1 is the number of persons unemployed 15 weeks or longer. U-2 consists of persons who have just lost jobs as well as persons who have completed temporary job assignments. U-3 is a combination of U-1 and U-2 (there is some overlap), and represents the "total unemployed" or the federal official unemployment rate. U-4 is the total unemployed (U-3) plus "discouraged workers," which BLS defines as "having a job-market related reason[12] for not currently looking for work." U-5 is comprised of the unemployed (U-3), plus discouraged workers (U-4), plus the "marginally attached," which BLS defines as "neither working nor looking for work but indicate they want and are available for a job and have looked for work sometime in the past 12 months." U-6 includes all persons included in U-5 plus all persons employed part-time for economic reasons (the involuntary part-timers). However, the "official" unemployment rate is reported at the U-3 level, which can under-report labor underutilization according to the U-6 measure by as much as 200%.

Although BLS has added factors to account for the so-called "involuntary part-timers" and "discouraged workers," these factors are not included in the officially reported unemployment rate. Moreover, there is no measurement, either officially reported or otherwise, that captures skills, knowledge and education that a worker possesses above and beyond the requirements of the job description. In essence, unemployment measures have no way to account for a downsized manager (perhaps with years or even decades of experience) who is now working as a Walmart sales associate, or a person with a Master's degree who can only find a job that requires a Bachelor's degree (or less). As far as the statistics are concerned, these workers are fully employed.

Part-Time Underemployment and the Unique Status of Professionals
In 1938, the Fair Labor Standards Act (FLSA) became law, although it met with vociferous opposition from employers. The FLSA established a national minimum wage (at that time 25 cents per hour), an 8-hour workday and a 40-hour workweek. Employees who worked in excess of the federally defined workweek were required to be paid at one-and-one-half times their regular wage rate. One purpose of the FLSA was to lessen he amount of "overwork" that was ruining the health of workers and fracturing families (it also outlawed child factory labor, although children could still work on family farms or in small family businesses). However, a secondary purpose of mandated overtime was the creation of jobs. It was presumed that employers would be more willing to hire additional workers rather than pay existing workers the overtime premium. The great promise of the FLSA was that it would alleviate poverty, reduce the incidence of overwork, and create jobs.

Over seven decades later, it is obvious that the FLSA has not delivered on its promise. One of the main reasons for this is that the majority of jobs in the United States are classified as "exempt," that is, they are not covered by FLSA protections. The first test for exemption from overtime rules is the income test. In order to be classified as "exempt," the job must pay at least $23,600 per year. [13] Recent rule changes at the U.S. Department of Labor (DOL) have doubled the exemption threshold to $47,476 per year, which was originally scheduled to take effect December 1, 2016.[14] The second test for exemption is the job duties test: The job itself is exempt from FLSA if it involves "executive" (i.e., managerial), "administrative," or "professional" duties. These duties tend to be defined broadly; thus, a single clerk working in a convenience store, who is for all appearances is "in charge" of the store, is likely to be exempt, even if she spends most of her shift stocking shelves and serving customers. The new DOL regulations have made no changes to the job duties test.

"Professional" exemptions cover work which is predominantly intellectual, requires specialized education, and involves the exercise of discretion and judgment. This includes the traditional learned professions such as lawyers, doctors, dentists, veterinarians, pharmacists, teachers, architects, clergy, registered nurses (but not LPNs), accountants (but not bookkeepers), engineers, actuaries, and scientists. Consequently, like many other "exempt" employees, professionals are more likely to be overworked (with concomitant long hours, foregone vacations, chronic fatigue, and strained family relations) rather than underemployed in an involuntary part-time professional occupation. Indeed, studies have confirmed that overwork is more common among professionals than lower income workers.[15]

A recent study of professionals in Norway[16] found that relatively few professionals were underemployed on the basis of hours, or involuntary part-time, although part-time underemployment among professionals does exist. Rather, professionals were three times more likely to be "overemployed," working more hours than they preferred. Rates of both under- and overemployment varied, with underemployment being highest for schoolteachers and higher for women, although there was relative gender equality of underemployment among physicians, economists, and engineers. However, the major contribution of this study was the recognition that the relationships between professionals and their employer is independent of the relationships between professionals and their profession. For example, employment status (full or part time) had a greater effect on professional commitment, while job security and income had a greater effect on organizational commitment.

The Norwegian study also examined the dual nature of professional to profession and professional to employer relationships in the context of labor degradation (to be more thoroughly discussed in Chapter Three), more specifically in the context of role conflict. Role conflict is created when the demands of an employer are in conflict with duties to clients or professional norms. Some professions (especially law) require a duty of loyalty tantamount to a fiduciary, where the professional must put the clients' interests above his or her own. Many professions require some form of "diligence" standard, where the professional must do his or her absolute utmost to achieve the client's goals or maximize the client's benefits from the professional's services. These standards can clash with organizational dictates when the professional is assigned more work than can realistically be handled with competence. This typically occurs in private organizations who may sacrifice quality and service to increase profits. However, the same can occur in public organizations as well, especially if they are caught in the double squeeze of reduced budgets and increased public demands.[17]

Evolution of Research on Overeducation

In the 1970s, a demographic confluence of coming-of-(working)-age of the Baby Boom cohort (generally defined as persons born between 1946 and 1964), veterans returning from Vietnam using GI bill benefits to obtain a college education, and the post-feminist entry of women into higher education and the professional work force generated concern that the job market was unable to absorb all of the new workers with college degrees. This phenomenon was first introduced in *The Overeducated American,*[18] and was deemed to be a social issue worthy of academic attention.[19] Later studies termed the imbalance between job specific demand for labor and schooling level supply "mismatch," and proposed methods to measure the phenomenon using current social indicators.[20]

In 1978, Teresa Sullivan,[21] then a young academic at the University of Texas, applied a labor utilization framework (LUF) analysis of underemployment using U. S. Census and other national survey data. Sullivan first proposes that the forms of labor underutilization increase with greater heterogeneity of economic organizations.[22] Sullivan further proposes that, in advanced economies characterized by a high degree of differentiation (separation of home and community from work, separation of production and consumption, and use of money and credit as exchange), so-called "inadequate labor exchanges" take four basic forms: unemployment (the most extreme), inadequate income (the working poor), inadequate hours of work (the involuntary part-time) and inadequate use of skills.[23] Sullivan then sets out to construct measures of these four labor market disutilities. Although Sullivan's underutilization index was criticized on methodological grounds, most subsequent studies have used some variation of Sullivan's basic four-part framework to analyze underemployment. Even Sullivan's critics[24] acknowledged that her study served a valuable purpose by focusing attention on "the neglected inquiry of labor inadequacy."[25]

A common theme among the overeducation literature is ongoing debate about how to define it and the best way to measure it. Some researchers attempted to derive an aggregate measure of underemployment for purposes of the ILO "decent work" framework, which combined both time and skill-related underemployment.[26] A Flemish study[27] tested models from prior research that focused only on measures of under- and overeducation, and found that results varied widely depending on whether the analysis was based on worker self-assessment scales, job analysis scales, or statistically derived measures. Moreover, notwithstanding an arguably better methodology, statistics that were derived from purely objective criteria could also be suspect if they were based on outdated national occupational databases.[28]

Most researchers now acknowledge that overeducation has both a subjective (workers' perceptions of skills actually needed to do the job) and an objective (match between worker skills and formal job description) component, and measures that exclude one or the other are likely to be deficient. Although objective underemployment is more straightforward to determine, subjective underemployment has greater negative impacts on job satisfaction,[29] which can ultimately end up affecting job performance, worker health, and commitment to the organization.[30]

Other studies found complex inter-relationships between perceived and actual underemployment that further confounded measurement: workers become underemployed as their productivity rises; poor local labor conditions both aggravate workers' perceptions of underemployment and actual underemployment; and perceptions of underemployment are influenced by worker characteristics such as education, age, race and gender.[31] Occupational mobility presented additional challenges, particularly in the absence of longitudinal measures on a national scale.[32] Even the more mainstream economic studies that attempted to discern whether workers were receiving an appropriate return from investments in education were further confounded by macroeconomic phenomenon such as wage stagnation and inflationary educational costs.

Research was expanded beyond the microeconomic returns to individual educational investments to the analysis of possible macroeconomic causes and impacts. Grégory Ponthière, a Professor of Economics at the University of Paris, developed a mathematical model that attempted to explain the persistence of underemployment in developing countries with expanding economies. Ponthière's equations included factors such as demographics (i.e., birth rates and longevity), and the effects of institutions that govern labor relations. Ponthière's analysis suggests that the balance of bargaining power between workers and employers is a "major determinant of short run and long run dynamics of employment, production and longevity," and "the form under which job quality influences longevity—through the real wage or the employment ration—has also a strong impact on the dynamics of the economy."[33] To paraphrase: the political power of labor affects job quality, job quality affects how well and how long people live, and this in turn affects the overall economy.

Upon review of all these technical parameters, one could easily conclude that the analytical capacity to fully understand underemployment is beyond the budget constraints of all but the most developed countries who have made a full commitment to it. The typical workforce development policy analyst at the state level could easily become discouraged. In an era of fiscal austerity and a constrained public sector, there is a legitimate argument that collecting and maintaining a sufficient amount of data capabilities to ever obtain a true measure of underemployment is impracticable, if not impossible. However, in the U.S., the CPS routinely measures educational levels, employment, occupation, and income. Adding one or two questions that address educational level and job mismatch would not add significantly to the cost of administering the CPS. Even if such questions did not fully satisfy the rigor requirement of academic economists, it could provide useful information to those responsible for the formulation of workforce development policy.

In 1999, David Livingstone produced a comprehensive analysis of what he termed "the education-jobs gap" using existing national data (mainly Canadian) on education and employment.[34] Livingstone's data was bolstered by interviews of workers living in "the gap." Livingstone quantitatively documents the huge amount of both formal and informal learning that has been accumulated by Canadian workers, and then qualitatively documents the inability of workers to utilize many of these skills on the job, as well as their frustrations with attempting to find appropriate work. Most importantly, Livingstone suggests that data may already exist to give us a truer picture of underemployment and/or overeducation, but that national governments lack the political will to address it.

Ironically, Livingstone finds that, "the common response of so many people to conditions of their own underemployment is to seek still more education."[35] There are several logical explanations for this phenomenon. First, when jobs—particularly "good" jobs—are scarce, the job market becomes an arms race in which workers are driven to constantly upgrade themselves merely to maintain their relative position in the job hierarchy. Second, in an era of layoffs and downsizing, some workers (including those with high levels of education and years of experience) have to obtain additional new skills, especially if their previous occupation or industry has become obsolete. A third, and related reason, is that in a rapidly changing market, no individual worker can predict which skill set is going to be in demand during any particular time frame, so the strategy is to accumulate as many skill sets as possible in order to be prepared for an unpredictable market. The result is a feedback loop of weak labor demand driving the accumulation of ever more skills and education.

The Skills-Job Mismatch

A less developed line of studies criticizes the concept of overeducation because (1) it does not take into consideration other forms of skills not provided by formal schooling, and (2) cross-sectional measurement did not accommodate the natural process of workers finding the best job match.[36] These studies suggest that overeducation is a temporary phenomenon, in which overeducated individuals likely lack other forms of human capital (e.g., work experience), and will eventually be promoted or otherwise absorbed into more education-appropriate employment as they gain informal job skills and experience.[37]

One researcher[38] even suggests that the typical "job hopping" and turnover of younger workers is not the wasteful activity it is usually portrayed to be, but rather part of the personal productivity growth continuum that is necessary to find (or create) the best job match. Other theories suggest that education itself is not delivering in terms of the same level of skills for the same level of credential. These critics argue that the political economics of education, which demanded both the broadening of access (resulting in the admission of "lower ability" students) and higher student-faculty ratios, is producing lower quality graduates and diluting the "value" of degrees.[39]

Some researchers argued that the use of nominal "overeducation" as a measure of skills mismatch between worker and job presents a number of problems with construct validity.[40] One problem is that simply comparing the individual's educational level and the educational level required by the job is too nonspecific. For example, an individual with a college degree in French literature who works at an advertising agency in a position that requires a four-year Bachelor's degree is technically "matched" according to this narrow definition. However, unless the agency happens to have clients in France, the worker is likely not using proficiency in the French language nor cultural expertise in daily tasks, and so from this perspective is overeducated or over-skilled. Conversely, the same worker may have no training or knowledge in marketing strategies, and so from this perspective is undereducated or under-skilled. Additionally, workers may voluntarily prefer to utilize certain skills in the workplace but not others. That is, a worker may have many skills (e.g., self-provisioning, home maintenance, hobbies, etc.) that are not used on the job, but the worker has voluntarily chosen not to do so.

While this alternate line of studies tends to blame the worker rather than the job market, it contains some elements of truth. It also supports the primary line of research on underemployment in calling for longitudinal national measures to provide a better data representation of the phenomenon. Many studies are based on cross-sectional measures of un- and underemployment, that is, they measure a worker's status at a specific point in time. When the next measurement is taken, it covers a different sample of workers (i.e., one does not know the status of the previous sample). Longitudinal measures cover the same sample of workers over several measuring periods, which can provide a more accurate assessment of inflow and outflow from the job market. Like unemployment, at the individual level skills mismatch is transitory, which, also like unemployment, can be affected by economic cycles and the worker's stage of work-life development. One study found that overeducated workers were indeed more likely to be mobile, although younger workers were more likely to realize wage gains from occupational mobility than older workers.[41]

Researchers have attempted to reconcile this transitory nature of overeducation. That is, whether and how much of it is due to occupational mobility, economic cycles, or deficiencies in the job market. One early study concluded that a certain degree of "marginal worker status" constitutes a "structural property of the U.S. labor market" unrelated to economic recessions or growth.[42] Notwithstanding the passage of several decades to allow absorption of the Baby Boom generation as well as a majority of women into the labor market, later studies indicate that overeducation continues to be a problem.[43] Moreover, the problem is not limited to recent college graduates, but extends to laid-off workers with years of experience, including particularly former executives.[44] A post-Great Recession Australian longitudinal study specifically examined the relationship between career mobility and overeducation, and found that more highly "over-skilled" workers were indeed highly mobile, but many of them continued to be underemployed in subsequent jobs, with a "sizable portion...exiting into unemployment."[45]

The skills mismatch analysis has been expanded to a broader concept of person-job fit, which is comprised of a demands-abilities fit, or how well the worker's knowledge, skills and abilities fulfill the formal job requirements,[46] and a needs-supplies fit, or how well the job environment fulfills the worker's goals, values and aspirations.[47] The skills mismatch line of studies thus recognized that there was more involved with finding the "best" worker fit than formal education, training, and experience, as well as the reciprocal needs fulfillment between workers and employers. The majority of existing research suggests that measuring skills mismatch accurately would involve extensive surveys, in addition to analysis of every individual industry and job classification to determine the skills that are actually necessary, as well as the degree of those skills that are actually possessed by the worker. This line of reasoning also assumes that both workers and employers can find the "perfect" match, so long as they can derive the right matching algorithms and have access to all the necessary data variables.

Underemployment and the Great Recession.

Labor market decline (in the form of involuntary part-time employment, wage stagnation, and overeducation) has been ongoing for decades. Not surprisingly, this is compounded by cyclical effects. Underemployment, like unemployment, is aggravated by economic recessions, which themselves seem to getting worse and lasting longer. In the past several decades, post-recession job recoveries have increasingly taken longer and been less robust. Following the recession of 2001, anemic employment growth gave birth to the expression "jobless recovery." However, the recession of 2001 (along with the prior recessions in 1980-1982 and 1990-1991) was relatively mild—both in scope and in depth—when compared to the Great Recession of 2007-2009.

The so-called "Great Recession," which likely originated in the United States (particularly on Wall Street and the financial sector), was global in scope and rivaled the Great Depression of the 1930s in its effect. Notwithstanding declarations from establishment economists and politicians that the Great Recession was officially "over" by the end of 2009, employment recovery continues to be sporadic. The Center on Budget and Policy Priorities estimates that some 8.7 million jobs were lost during the Great Recession, and to date the U.S. is still 2.4 million jobs short of pre-recession levels. [48] Additionally, the long-term unemployment rate, defined as the share of the labor force without work for 26 weeks or longer, has risen to historic highs of 37.3% of the officially unemployed, or nearly 4.5% of the total labor force.[49]

Here I will note that the data collection for this study of professional underemployment occurred during March through July of 2014. While not in the depths of the Great Recession, it is acknowledged that data was collected in what can be termed a "post-Great Recession" economy. For this reason, survey respondents were asked not only if they were currently underemployed, but also asked to identify periods of underemployment over the course of their professional careers (in two-year increments). This was intended to provide some of the benefits of a longitudinal survey in a study that, due to logistical constraints, had to be performed as a cross-sectional study. This was also intended to explore some of the causational questions raised by the academic literature: Were more people underemployed at the beginning of their professional career (when they had no experience)? Were more people underemployed during (or following) recessions? Or might there be some as-yet-undetected pattern?

As will be shown (and discussed more fully) in Chapter Five, underemployment in the survey sample occurred regularly over the course of professional careers, although there was a definite spike during the period 2008-2012. Indeed, respondents' most common explanations for their own underemployment were recession (26.7%) and lack of experience (23.0%). Moreover, some economists[50] allege that the post-Great Recession economy is being defined as the "new normal," especially as it pertains to a weakened labor market. Although the literature abounds with evidence that underemployment and labor degradation have been occurring for decades, the ability to differentiate between the extent that these phenomenon are directly related to the Great Recession and that which is part of a larger trend is beyond the scope of this study.

A post-Great Recession job market has generated interest in the fate of so-called "dislocated workers." That is, how long does it take for a dislocated worker to find another job and is the new job comparable (in terms of pay, title/prestige, use of skills, and opportunity to advance) to the lost job. Joseph McLaughlin and Mykhaylo Trubskyy (with Andrew Sum) of the Northeastern University Center for Labor Market Studies (whose research is discussed more fully in the following section) used BLS dislocated worker surveys and compared rates of underemployment in subsequent jobs for the years 2000, 2008, and 2010.[51] Not surprisingly, rates of underemployment in subsequent jobs nearly doubled between periods, rising from 4.8% in 2000 to 8.5% in 2008 and 15.3% in 2010. Also not surprising was that underemployment rates tended to correlate with state unemployment rates. There was some evidence of status sorting factors (which was also found in the dissertation study), with women and ethnic minorities experiencing higher rates of underemployment than white males. Rates of underemployment also varied with the sector, industry, and specific occupation of the lost job.

Although workers with Bachelor and Master's degrees, as well as those displaced from professional occupations, enjoyed a significantly lower probability of being underemployed, they suffered from a significantly higher reduction in median weekly earnings. In addition to problems of underemployment, the research found that not even 49% of workers who lost their jobs during the Great Recession had secured subsequent employment by 2010, which has created a significant labor force reserve—a pool of "hidden unemployed" who are no longer counted.

While the dissertation study was in progress, another study was quietly released by the Federal Reserve Bank of New York in early 2014.[52] The authors used information from the U.S. Dept. of Labor's Occupational Information Network and asked incumbent employees whether their job actually required a college degree. Jobs

55

were considered to "require" a college degree only if 50% or greater of job incumbents said it was necessary. Based on this standard, the authors found that the underemployment rate (i.e., persons with college degrees working in jobs that do not require them) has remained at a *fairly uniform rate of 33% over the past two decades*. Confirming similar findings in other studies, the authors also found that underemployment is consistently higher for new graduates, as they transition into the labor market and gain on-the-job skills. There is also variation of underemployment among majors, with engineering and science majors faring better, as well as those in "growing' sectors such as education and health care, than those with liberal arts and social science majors.

A more troubling finding is that the quality of jobs taken by the underemployed has declined since 2000. Job quality was determined by wage levels (examples of "good" non-college jobs were mechanics and electricians with annual wages of $45,000 compared to jobs with wages below $25,000) and whether the job was part-time or full-time. The authors found that the share of recent college graduates in low-wage jobs rose from 15% to 20% between 1990 and 2009. Likewise, the share of underemployed college graduates in part-time jobs rose from about 14% in the 1990s to 23% in 2011.

The authors conclude that underemployment, particularly among new college graduates, is not a "new" trend, nor is it solely the result of the Great Recession, although they could not suggest an explanation: "It is not clear whether these trends represent a structural change in the labor market, or if they are a consequence of the two recessions and jobless recoveries in the first decade of the 2000s."[53] Curiously, there is no mention of this study in the mainstream media or in national labor policy discussions.

<u>Underemployment and Inequality</u>

Andrew Sum, a Professor of Economics at Northeastern University and Director of the Center for Labor Market Studies, has compiled (with the assistance of academic colleagues)[54] a number of reports that examine post-Great Recession underemployment using existing BLS data. As enlightening as these reports are, they are constrained by BLS definitions of underemployment, which are limited to involuntary part-time, discouraged, and marginally attached workers. Like unemployment, underemployment rose dramatically during the Great Recession. The first and fourth quarters of 2009 tied for the highest rate of underemployment (as a percentage of the employed workforce) since World War II at 6.4%.

Broken down by demographics, underemployment was higher for younger workers, Blacks and Hispanics, and high school dropouts. However, small rates of underemployment were found for workers with Bachelor's degrees (3.5%) and post-graduate degrees (2.2%), as well as workers in STEM occupations: computer and mathematics, 1.5%; life, physical, and social sciences, 2.2%; and architecture and engineering, 2.3%. Although unemployment rates rose much faster for males in the Great Recession, the underemployment rates for males and females were almost the same (6.5% and 6.4% respectively). Moreover, every one percent increase in a state's unemployment rate increased the marginal probability of underemployment by about .5 %.[55] According to Sum and Khatiwada, college graduates, professional workers, managers, and government employees were "well protected from job losses" during the Great Recession.[56]

Sum and Khatiwada analyzed how un- and underemployment affected workers according to their position in the income distribution. They divided the American workforce into income deciles and analyzed their respective combined rates of unemployment, underemployment, and "labor force reserve" during 2009. The labor force reserve is what the BLS defines as the discouraged and marginally attached workers (workers who would take a job if one was available, have looked for work within the past 12 months, but who are not actively seeking work at the time of the survey). For the lowest income decile (annual income less than $12,160), Sum and Khatiwada found a combined labor underutilization rate of 50.2%, and for the second lowest decile (annual income between $12,160 and $20,725), this rate was 37.6%, which Sum and Khatiwada allege is comparable to rates characteristic of a true depression. Although workers at the top fared much better, they were not unaffected, with workers in the top income decile (annual income greater than $138,700) experiencing labor underutilization rates of 6.1%, while those in the fifth decile (annual income between $39,000 and $50,000) experienced labor underutilization rates of 17.1%.

In a related study, Sum and McLaughlin turn from an exclusive focus on labor underutilization to examine other measures of post-Great Recession recovery.[57] Specifically examined were changes in the following wage and employment indicators between 2009 and 2011: Payroll employment (no change); total civilian employment (down .5%); real mean hourly earnings of private sector wage and salary workers (down 1.0%); real mean hourly earnings of production workers (down .6%); real mean weekly earnings of private sector wage and salary workers (up .1%); and real median weekly earnings of full-time wage and salary workers (down 1.0%). Changes in real weekly earnings of full-time workers were also examined by wage distribution. While those workers in the 10%, 25%, and 50% segments of the wage distribution saw wage decreases of 1%, workers in the 75% and 90% of the distribution saw an even higher wage decrease of 2%.

Conversely, the Dow Jones Industrial Average was up 49.0%, the S&P 500 was up 45.8%, and corporate profits were up 40.8%. Sum and McLaughlin (2011) describe post-Great Recession reality as "both a jobless and a wageless recovery,"[58] and note the irony of celebration on Wall Street while the majority of U.S. workers tell pollsters that the country is still in a recession. The Northeastern University reports of Sum and his colleagues demonstrate the failure of the official unemployment rate to capture the full extent of labor underutilization. Their reports also demonstrate that the effects of recession and recovery are not distributed proportionally across the U.S. population and economy.

Although Professor Sum's analyses present a more accurate picture of economic reality than is generally presented by mainstream data reporters, they do not accommodate measures of credentialed underemployment, that is, workers who have jobs that may not be fully utilizing their education, skills and abilities. It is understandable that those at the bottom of the social-economic hierarchy are counted and measured—they are more likely to apply for unemployment insurance or be eligible for other forms of publicly funded income maintenance assistance. Additionally, their hardship and desperation are more acute, where the underemployed professional is likely able to find employment sufficient to provide subsistence, even if it does not fully utilize the professional's education and training. However, by failing to measure this form of underemployment, it is too convenient to simply presume that everyone who has a full-time job is adequately employed. It is also too convenient to look at the army of unemployed, undereducated workers and presume that getting them trained will somehow make them "employable" without addressing the problem of inadequate jobs.

Psychosocial Consequences of Underemployment

Like unemployment, underemployment has negative consequences for individuals, families, communities, and (sometimes) even employers. At the individual level, underemployment can negatively affect physical health when psycho-social stressors result in an increase of chronic disease[59] and overall poorer health,[60] as well as an increase in health-risk behavior such as alcohol abuse.[61] Irregular hours and unpredictable income associated with underemployment can lead to feelings of powerlessness and social alienation.[62] Lack of opportunity to utilize existing skills—or develop them further—can result in deterioration of existing skills, as well as negative implications for career development and future earnings.[63]

Overeducation (or underemployment) may have negative consequences for worker attitudes and job commitment. A number of studies have demonstrated a negative relationship between work attitudes and worker-job "fit" mismatches, with perceived overqualification producing stronger and more consistent negative attitudes than involuntary part-time employment.[64] Underemployed workers are also more likely to be less attached to their workplaces,[65] with lower levels of affective commitment.[66] Most studies have found the effect of overeducation on actual job performance is small; with some studies suggesting that workers may withhold full contribution of their skills in order to balance the equities between inputs and outcomes,[67] while others suggest that this is offset by minimal performance requirements and financial constraints required to keep the job.[68]

The negative effects of underemployment are not limited to individual workers, but can extend to families, friends, and communities. Not surprisingly, underemployment can strain marriages by either increasing financial stress and instability,[69] or changing marital power relationships when a spouse (usually the wife) must return to the labor force to supplement family income.[70] Workers who are underemployed after a period of unemployment tend to become withdrawn and socially isolated, as they do not want to impose on already strained relationships with friends and extended family.[71] Like unemployment, underemployment and general economic volatility has also been associated with community-wide effects such as higher crime rates[72] and lower rates of civic and political participation.[73]

Because credentialed professionals can usually find work somewhere, they are unlikely to experience the extreme material hardship experienced by less educated workers. However, professionals tend to self-identify with their work more so than their blue-collar counterparts, viewing their work as an extension of themselves and not solely as a means of subsistence. Moreover, they have usually made considerable investments in the attainment of their credentials in the form of tuition and other costs of schooling, as well as the opportunity cost of foregone employment during the period of educational investment. The Gallup-Healthways Well-Being Index[74] found that underemployment negatively affects life ratings of college graduates and post-graduates to a greater degree than less educated workers, and suggests that this might be due to their greater expectations in the job market.

Underemployment and Economic Ideology

As the concept of underemployment—and specifically overeducation—evolved, it was analyzed from the perspectives of disciplines other than economics, management, and industrial relations. Duke University Professor of Sociology Stephen Vaisey combined labor market and sociological analysis in a longitudinal study that examined the relationships between job dissatisfaction, political liberalism, and rejection of the work ethic narrative.[75] Vaisey's graphical analysis shows a distinct upward trend in the incidence of overeducation between 1972 and 2002, even when adjusting for economic cycles. Vaisey's analysis confirmed the findings in the majority of prior studies that showed higher returns to required (i.e., "matched") education than for overqualification. Although workers received increased income premiums for both "matched" education and overqualification, Vaisey attributed this (by way of other studies) to the increasing college wage gap and income penalty for underqualification. These findings alone provide a viable explanation for overeducation as a defensive necessity in a deficient job market.

61

Vaisey's study also found a significant relationship between increasing overqualification and decline in job satisfaction, which fell from a high of near 60% in the mid-1970s to 45% by 2000. Political liberalism, which is typically higher among better-educated workers, remained essentially unchanged. However, what Vaisey found to be "more perplexing" was that belief in the rewards of work and the "American Dream" had substantially increased.[76] What Vaisey's study demonstrates is that people who work are doing worse, but they maintain a hopeful belief in reward from self-improvement, regardless of evidence to the contrary. Moreover, Vaisey takes his fellow sociologists to task for essentially abandoning the research of overeducation to economists and human capital theorists when the predictions of "radicalized social discontent alarmists" in the 1970s failed to materialize.[77]

Professionals, as persons who occupy higher positions in the socio-economic hierarchy, generally share the ideologies of those who also occupy higher status; namely, a belief in the role of meritocracy and hard work in determining one's ultimate career and occupational outcomes, equality of opportunity, and legitimacy of "the system."[78] Brian Starks, Professor of Sociology at Indiana University, found that recent experiences of job loss (either the worker's own job loss or that of a family member, friend, or co-worker), occupational downward mobility, or job deterioration following organizational restructuring were positively correlated with a decrease in so-called "American Dream" ideology.[79] Although Starks' analysis found that nonstandard (part-time, contingent or free-lance) work and organizational change did not *per se* result in changed worker attitudes, when combined with more direct negative changes in job security or job quality, nonstandard employment also resulted in a loss of faith about economic opportunity.

The significance of Starks' findings with respect to professional underemployment is that professionals are the vanguards of system legitimacy, the manifestation of "proof" that anyone with ability and motivation can obtain credentials and move up in the social hierarchy. If overeducation and job degradation result in a loss of faith among professionals which becomes sufficiently widespread, American workers may abandon their perennial efforts at self-improvement because they perceive that there will be no forthcoming returns in the job market. When a majority of Americans "give up" on the essence of the American promise, they may become rootless and civically disengaged or, alternatively, radicalized and revolutionary.

Notes

1 Maynard, D.C., & Feldman, D.C. (2011). *Underemployment: Psychological, economic and social challenges*. New York, NY: Springer Science+Business Media, L.L.C., pp. 2-4.

2 Vaisey, S. (2006). Education and its discontents: Overqualification in America, 1972-2002. *Social Forces 85*(2), 835-864 at p. 838.

3 McKee-Ryan, F. M., & Harvey, J. (2011). "I have a job but...": A review of underemployment. *Journal of Management*, 37(4), 962-996 at p. 989.

4 Bell, D. N. F., & Blanchflower, D. G. (2013, August). How to measure underemployment? Peterson Institute for International Economics, Working Paper No. 13-7 at p. 13: "As the nature of work changes, the unemployment rate will become an increasingly unreliable metric for excess capacity in the labor market [but] the data necessary to compile an equivalent underemployment index in the United States is not available." Retrieved from: http://www.iie.com/publications/wp/wp13-7.pdf

5 Loury, G. (1998). Discrimination in the post-civil rights era: beyond market interactions. *Journal of Economic Perspectives*, *12*(2), 117-126.

6 Athey, T.R., & Hautaluoma, J.E. (1994). Effects of applicant overeducation, job status, and job gender stereotype on employment decisions. *Journal of Social Psychology, 134*(4), 439-452.

7 1995 Noble Prize to Robert E. Lucas for his work on the rational expectations hypothesis.

8 Card, D. (2011, February). Origins of the unemployment rate: The lasting legacy of measurement without theory. UC Berkeley and NBER. Retrieved from: http://davidcard.berkeley.edu/papers/origins-of-unemployment.pdf

9 Stratton, L.S. (1991, August). Reexamining involuntary part-time employment. University of Arizona Discussion Paper 92-2. Also Tilly, C. (1991). Reasons for the continuing growth of part-time employment. *Monthly Labor Review, 114*(3), 10-18. Retrieved from: http://www.bls.gov/opub/mlr/1991/03/art2full.pdf

10 Reynolds, J., & Wenger, J.B. (2010). Prelude to a RIF: Older workers, part-time hours, and unemployment. *Journal of Aging and Social Policy, 22*(2), 99-116.

11 Bregger, J. E., & Haugen, S. E. (1995). BLD introduces new range of alternative unemployment measures. *Monthy Labor Review, 118*(10), 19-26.

12 That is, not a personal reason such as illness or caring for a family member.

13 In 2014, the poverty level for a family of four was an annual income of $23,850; and in 2015 it is $24,250.

14 These updated overtime rules have been suspended indefinitely under the Trump administration.

15 Denniss, R. (2003). Flexible measures for a flexible labour market. *Australian Bulletin of Labour, 29*(2), 113-125.

16 Abrahamsen, B. (2010). Employment status and commitment to work in professions. *Economic and Industrial Democracy*, 31(1), 93-115.

17 The U.S. Constitution requires the state to provide "competent" legal representation for indigent persons charged with a criminal offense. The National Legal Aid and Defender Society says that 150 felony cases per attorney per year is the upper limit for an attorney to adequately handle a felony representation. Yet, in many jurisdictions, public defenders are being assigned

upwards of 500-800 cases, in some instances as high as 1,600. This results in so-called "meet-and-greet" guilty pleas in which the attorney has barely gotten to know the client, let alone investigate the case. Public defenders in states such as New York, Missouri, Washington, California and Florida have taken to protests at their state legislatures about the need for increased funding, with one Florida Supreme Court opinion going so far as to call the situation "unconstitutional." Public Defender Eleventh Judicial Circuit of Florida, et al. vs. State of Florida, et al. (May 23, 2013). Found at http://caselaw.findlaw.com/fl-supreme-court/1632060.html.

18 Freeman, R. B. (1976). *The overeducated American*. New York, NY: Academic Free Press.

19 Rumberger, R.W. (1981). The rising incidence of overeducation in the U.S. labor market. *Economics of Education Review, 1*(3), 293-314.

20 Clogg, C. C., & Shockey, J. W. (1984). Mismatch between occupation and schooling: a prevalence measure, recent trends, and demographic analysis. *Demography, 21*(2) 235-257.

21 Dr. Sullivan is currently serving as President of the University of Virginia.

22 Sullivan, T. A. (1978). *Marginal workers, marginal jobs: The underutilization of American workers*. Austin, TX: University of Texas Press, p. 9.

23 *Id.* at p. 10.

24 Hirschman, C. (1980). Book review of Sullivan's *Marginal Workers Marginal Jobs* in *American Journal of Sociology, 86*(1), 208-210. Retrieved from: http://www.press.uchicago.edu/ucp/journals/journal/ajs.html

25 Sullivan, (1978), Ibid. at p. 4.

26 Brown, G. & Pintaldi, F. (2006). A multidimensional approach to the measurement of underemployment. Statistical Journal of the United Nations, ECE 23, 43-56.

27 Verhaest, D., & Omey, E. (2006). Measuring the incidence of over- and undereducation. *Quality and Quantity, 40*, 783-803.

28 *Id.*

29 Khan, L. J., & Morrow, P. C. (1991). Objective and subjective underemployment relationships to job satisfaction. *Journal of Business Research, 22*(3), 211-218.

30 Johnson, W. R., Morrow, P. C., & Johnson, G. J. (2002). An evaluation of a perceived overqualification scale across work settings. *The Journal of Psychology, 136*, 425-441.

31 Bonnal, M., Lira, C., & Addy, S. (2009). Underemployment and local employment dynamics: New evidence. *The Review of Regional Studies, 39*(3), 317-335. Retrieved from: http://journal.srsa.org/ojs/index.php/RRS/article/view/202/157

32 Rubb, S. (2006). Educational mismatches and earnings: Extensions of occupational mobility theory and evidence of human capital depreciation. *Education Economics, 14*(2), 135-154.

33 Ponthiére, G. (2008). Can underemployment persist in an expanding economy? Clues from a non-Walrasian OLG model with endogenous longevity. *Economic Change and Restructuring, 41*(2) 97-124 at p. 120.

34 Livingstone, D. W. (1999). *The education-jobs gap: Underemployment or economic democracy*. Toronto, Ontario: Garamond Press.

35 *Id*. at p. 133.

36 Leuven, E. & Oosterbeek, H. (2011). Overeducation and mismatch in the labor market. Institute for the Study of Labor Discussion Paper No. 5523. Retrieved from: http://ftp.iza.org/dp5523.pdf

37 Sicherman, N. (1991). "Overeducation" in the labor market. *Journal of Labor Economics, 9*(2), 101-122.

38 Heckman, J. J. (1994, Spring). Is job training oversold? *Public Interest, 115*, 91-115. Retrieved from: http://www.nationalaffairs.com/public_interest/detail/is-job-training-oversold

39 Chevalier, A. (2003). Measuring overeducation. *Economica, 70*(279), 509-531.

40 Halaby, C. N. (1994). Overeducation and skill mismatch. *Sociology of Education, 67*(January), 47-59.

41 Rubb, S. (2006). *Supra.*

42 Clogg, C. C., Eliason, S. R., & Wahl, R. J. (1990). Labor-market experiences and labor force outcomes. *American Journal of Sociology, 95*(6), 1536-1576 at p. 1564.

43 Brynin, M. (2002). Overqualification in employment. *Work, Employment & Society, 16*(4), 637-654; also Whitaker, S., & Zenker, M. (2011, July 12). Are underemployed graduates displacing non-graduates? *Economic Trends*, 21-23. Retrieved from: https://www.clevelandfed.org/newsroom-and-events/publications/economic-trends/2011-economic-trends/et-20110712-are-underemployed-graduates-displacing-nongraduates.aspx

44 Feldman, D., Leana, C., & Bolino, M. (2002). Underemployment and relative depravation among re-employed executives. *Journal of Occupation & Organizational Psychology, 75*(4), 453-471.

45 McGuiness, S. & Wooden, M. (2009). Overskilling, job insecurity, and career mobility. *Industrial Relations, 48*(2), 265-286 at p. 282.

46 Cable, D., & Edwards, J. (2004). Complementary and supplementary fit: A theoretical and empirical integration. *Journal of Applied Psychology, 89*, 875-884.

47 Kristof-Brown, A. L., Zimmerman, R., & Johnson, E. C. (2005). Consequences of individual's fit at work: A meta-analysis of person-job, person-organization, person-group, and person-supervisor fit. *Personnel Psychology, 49*, 1-49.

48 Center on Budget and Policy Priorities. (2013). Chart book: The legacy of the Great Recession (updated June 7, 2013). Retrieved from: http://www.cbpp.org/cms/index.cfm?fa=view&id=3252

49 *Id.*

50 Greenstone, M. & Looney, A. (2013, Sept 12). The lasting effects of the Great Recession: Six million missing workers and a new economic normal. Brookings Institution, The Hamilton Project. Retrieved from: http://www.brookings.edu/blogs/jobs/posts/2013/09/12-jobs-gap-greenstone-looney; also Krugman, P. (2010, August 1). Defining prosperity down. *The New York Times.* Retrieved from: http://www.nytimes.com/2010/08/02/opinion/02krugman.html

51 McLaughlin, J., Trubskyy, M., & Sum, A. (2011, June). Underemployment problems experienced by workers dislocated from their jobs between 2007 and 2009. Center for Labor Market Studies. Retrieved from: http://scholar.google.com/scholar?cluster=13337971676986556741&hl=en&as_s dt=0,35

52 Abel, J. R., Deitz, R., & Su, Y. (2014). Are recent college graduates finding good jobs? *Current Issues in Economics and Finance 20*(1), 1-8. Retrieved from http://www.newyorkfed.org/research/current_issues/

53 *Id.* at p. 7.

54 Ishwar Khatiwada and Joseph McLaughlin.

55 Sum, A., & Khatiwada, I. (2010). Underemployment problems in U.S. labor markets in 2009: Predicting the probabilities of underemployment for key age, gender, race-ethnic, nativity, educational attainment, and occupational subgroups of U.S. workers. Center for Labor Market Studies, Paper 27. Retrieved from: http://webcache.googleusercontent.com/search?q=cache:http://www.northeast ern.edu/clms/wp- content/uploads/Underemployment_Problems_February_2010_Paper.pdf

56 Sum, A., & Khatiwada, I. (2010). Labor underutilization problems of U.S. workers across household income groups at the end of the Great Recession: A truly Great Depression among the nation's low-income workers amidst full employment among the most affluent. Center for Labor Market Studies, Paper 26 at p. 2. Retrieved from: https://www.researchgate.net/publication/48802944_Labor_underutilization_pr oblems_of_US_workers_across_household_income_groups_at_the_end_of_the_ Great_Recession_A_truly_great_depression_among_the_nation's_low_income_ workers_amidst_full_employment_amo

57 Sum, A., & McLaughlin, J. (2011). Who has benefited from the post-great recession recovery? A new look at the growth performance of jobs, wages, corporate profits, and stock price indices during the first two years of recovery. Center for Labor Market Studies, Paper 33. Retrieved from: http://webcache.googleusercontent.com/search?q=cache:http://www.northeast ern.edu/clms/wp-content/uploads/Who-Had-Benefitted-from-the-Post.pdf

58 *Id.* at p. 5.

59 Friedland, D. S., & Price, R. H. (2003). Underemployment: Consequences for the health and well-being of workers. *American Journal of Community Psychology, 32*(1/2), 33-45.

60 Lewchuk, W., Clarke, M., & de Wolff, A. (2008). Working without commitments: Precarious employment and health. *Work, Employment, & Society, 22*(3), 387-406.

61 Dooley, D., & Prause, J. (1998). Underemployment and alcohol misuse in the National Longitudinal Survey of Youth. *Journal of Studies on Alcohol, 59*(6), 669-680

62 Pocock, B. (2003). *The work/life collision: What work is doing to Australians and what to do about it.* Sydney, Australia: Federation Press.

63 Nabi, G. R. (2003). Graduate employment and underemployment: Opportunity for skill use and career experiences amongst recent business graduates. *Education and Training, 45*(7), 371-382.

64 Maynard, D. C., Joseph, T. D., & Maynard, A. M. (2006). Underemployment, job attitudes, and turnover intentions. *Journal of Organizational Behavior, 27*(4), 509-536.

65 Leana, C. R., & Feldman, D. C. (1995). Finding new jobs after a plant closing: Antecedents and outcomes of the occurrence and quality of reemployment. *Human Relations, 48*(12), 1381-1401.

66 Johnson, W. R., Morrow, P. C., & Johnson, G. J. (2002). An evaluation of a perceived overqualification scale across work settings. *The Journal of Psychology, 136*, 425-441.

67 Feldman, D. C. (1996). The nature and consequences of underemployment. *Journal of Management, 22*(3), 385-407.

68 Feldman, D. C., & Turnley, W. H. (2004). Contingent employment in academic careers: Relative deprivation among adjunct faculty. *Journal of Vocational Behavior, 64*(2), 284-307.

69 Broman, C. L., Hamilton, V. L., & Hoffman, W. S. (1990). Unemployment and its effects on families: Evidence from a plant closing study. *American Journal of Community Psychology, 18*(5), 643-659.

70 Bittman, M., England, P., Folbre, N., Sayer, L, & Matheson, G. (2003). When does gender trump money? Bargaining and time in household work. *The American Journal of Sociology, 109*(1), 186-214.

71 Borgen, W. A., Amundson, N. E., & Harder, H. G. (1998). The experience of underemployment. *Journal of Employment Counseling, 25*(4), 149-159.

72 Bausman, K., & Goe, W. R. (2004). An examination of the link between employment volatility and the spatial distribution of property crime rates. *American Journal of Economics and Sociology, 63*(3), 665-695.

73 Herring, C., & Jones-Johnson, G. J. (1990). Political responses to underemployment among African Americans. *National Political Science Review, 2*, 92-109.

74 Mendes, E. (2011, June 29). Underemployment tougher on highly educated Americans. Gallup, Inc. Retrieved from: http://www.gallup.com/poll/148301/underemployment-tougher-highly-educated-americans.aspx

75 Vaisey, S. (2006). Education and its discontents: Overqualification in America, 1972-2002. *Social Forces, 85*(2), 835-864. This study measured overeducation using GED values from the Dictionary of Occupational Titles and data from the General Social Survey (GSS) from 1972 to 2002.

76 *Id*. at p. 856.

77 *Id*. at p. 836.

78 Kluegel, J. R., & Smith, E. R. (1986). *Beliefs about inequality: America's views of what is and what ought to be*. New York, NY: Aldine De Gruyter.

79 Starks, B. (2003). The new economy and the American dream: Examining the effect of work conditions on beliefs about economic opportunity. *Sociological Quarterly, 44*(2), 205-225.

Chapter Three
The Skills Shortage "Crisis" and the Paradigm Clash of Ideologies

ECONOMISTS HAVE PROPOSED a number of theories and models to explain underemployment, and some of these will be examined further in Chapter 4. This chapter analyzes two apparently competing ideological foundations for the explanations of underemployment. Based on the results of this study, both of these theories have merit, but, as with all theoretical models, they only explain a portion of observed reality. The problem in the United States is that the human capital theorists have dominated policy agendas intended to address un- and underemployment.

The two theories that comprised the analytical frameworks of this study are human capital theory and deskilling theory, which is alternatively known as labor process theory, or labor degradation theory. The first part of this chapter looks at the historical origins of both theories. Human capital theory is founded upon principles first described by Adam Smith in *The Wealth of Nations*. Alternatively, deskilling theory is founded upon the concept of worker alienation as described by Karl Marx. Although Adam Smith and Karl Marx are considered to be ideological opposites (the capitalism vs communism dichotomy), they were actually quite similar in a number of ways. Both Smith and Marx were descriptive economists with keen observation and narrative skills. As such, they examined economic phenomenon in the context of larger social and cultural structures rather than the narrow quantitative descriptions that characterize most economics research today.

Notwithstanding their methodological similarities, Smith and Marx described two very different historical periods. In the case of Smith, the nation-state was the ascendant economic unit of analysis, as feudal fiefdoms consolidated power under a single ruler and attempted to expand their empires. As such, Smith's work described the operation of mercantile systems, of agricultural systems, systems of political economy, and how the "sovereign or commonwealth" managed its revenues and expenses. Indeed Smith noted that the wealth of the American colonies was due in large part to the fact that they paid nothing for their own defense, having "hitherto been defended almost entirely at the expence of the mother country."[1] In the case of Marx, the ascendant economic unit of analysis was the modern corporation. The large and ever-increasing aggregations of private capital, as well as the effect of corporate production on the work and way of life of everyday people, could not have been foreseen by Smith, only some 100 years earlier.

Although most people focus on their differences, both Smith and Marx expressed humanitarian, and even moral, concerns about their observations. Both of them recognized that economies were more than about quantitative production, but should encompass the well-being of everyday people. Just as Smith would likely be aghast at the dog-eat-dog, everyone-for-himself social Darwinism that is justified by his writings, so too would Marx be aghast at the top-down, command-and-control economy that characterized the former Soviet Union. While the society of today is nothing like the societies described by either Smith or Marx, many of their fundamental observations continue to have explanatory value, even if many of the details are no longer relevant or applicable. The same holds true for the more modern theories based on these historical frameworks: Neither human capital theory nor deskilling theory can fully explain the modern job market, but both can contribute to our understanding of it.

Human capital theorists propose that economic growth is proportional to investments in skills, education and training of the relevant population. There is considerable empirical evidence to support this proposition. At the individual level, workers who have more skills, education and training generally earn more. At the national level, those nations who make more substantial investments in educating their citizens generally have higher GDP. The more humane tenets of human capital theory also go beyond just the dollars and return-on-investment data, but also suggest that individuals and economies do better when other human needs are met as well. These recommendations include the provision of employee health care and wellness programs, and in some cases even such amenities as on-site gyms and day care.

The alternate, or "contrarian" deskilling theory is almost never discussed outside academia in the United States. Deskilling theory is referred to in academic literature alternatively as "labor process theory" or the "degradation of work." This theory came about in the early days of industrialization, when production shifted from skilled craftsmen to corporate factories. In order to maintain control over the workers, production was broken down into discrete tasks, such that no worker, or group of workers, would have sufficient knowledge to produce the whole. These jobs were also deliberately minimized for the practical purposes of increasing efficiency and reducing labor costs. The main contribution of modern deskilling theory is that it requires workforce development policies to consider the quality of jobs as much as it currently focuses on the quality of workers.

In the case of professional workers, their skills and education give them more options in the job market, which generally keeps their pay above that of less-skilled workers, even when they are underemployed. As this study found, there also seems to be a limit to how much professional-level job tasks can be broken down and rationalized. That is, health care professionals, engineers, attorneys, accountants, and teachers still need to exercise a certain degree of independent judgment in order to do their work. However, what this study suggests is that labor degradation occurs in professional occupations not by reduction of the individual tasks (i.e., industrial-style deskilling), but by organizational structures and processes. These restructurings are sometimes referred to in popular language as "bureaucratization" or by economists as "rationalization." Thus, modern work processes that are not motivated solely by profit maximization can create negative job effects in public and non-profit organizations as well as private corporations.

The rest of this chapter looks at the origins and developments of human capital theory and deskilling theory. It examines their strengths (that is, those points where they actually describe reality) and their weaknesses, as well as their relevance to the understanding of underemployment and overeducation. The last section looks at how rationalizing processes have effected both political/public and economic life, and how this has impacted how work is now organized in various professions.

Origins of Human Capital Theory

The essence of human capital theory is that economic prosperity depends on both physical resources and "human capital," that is, the aggregate skills and education level of the relevant population. Adam Smith was an early social-economic analyst who articulated a connection between the development of skills and both individual and national prosperity. The foundation of this "improvement in the productive powers of labour" was a direct result of increasing specialization of occupations, or the "division of labour."[2] Smith is also known for articulating the law of supply and demand, particularly as it applies to prices, wages, and profits, with greater demand increasing the price of goods and labor, and oversupply of goods and labor decreasing their price.

Smith's analysis divided the wealth of society into four broad categories of capital stock: (1) labor produce for immediate consumption (self-provisioning), (2) property that produces income, (3) improvements in land, and (4) "the acquired and useful abilities of all the inhabitants or members of the society."[3] Smith acknowledged that "the acquisition of such talents…always costs a real expence" of fixed capital,[4] implying that both individuals and society at large had to make trade-offs between immediate needs and future prosperity. In Smith's worldview, there was a substantive difference between productive labor, which resulted in some tangible good or "vendible commodity" and unproductive labor, which was represented by the state.[5]

Smith also made a similar distinction between "useful" knowledge that enhanced productivity and knowledge that served other purposes. Smith suggested that a certain minimum level of universal knowledge was essential for national prosperity, but additional "inputs" of education and training did not necessarily result in corresponding benefits. Smith supported a publicly financed system of education for the "common people" to learn the essential elements of reading, writing, and accounting.[6] He also noted that, the "discipline of colleges and universities is…not for the benefit of the students, but for the interests…[and] ease of the masters,"[7] and universities were slow to adopt improvements in knowledge.[8] Thus, a proportion of educational resources served the interests of elites, but did not necessarily devolve to benefit the public at large. Even in 1776, Smith alluded to the possibility of overeducation—a concept that was two centuries away from recognition.

Notwithstanding his extolment of labor specialization, Smith criticized "the exclusive privilege of incorporated trades" which operated to restrain competition and protect the tradesman's wages and/or profits.[9] However, even in instances where "common" education was poorly taught, both the individual and the public were better off than not having been educated at all.[10] In Smith's analysis, there was a base level of universal education that was necessary for society to prosper (and even justified public expenditures therefore), but forms of higher education beyond this minimum served to either restrain competition (specialized trade apprenticeships) or maintain social privileges (universities).

Although the origin of modern, post-industrial human capital theory is frequently attributed to Theodore Schultz,[11] its broader, analytical framework was developed by the Chicago School economist Gary Becker. Early educational studies found a positive correlation between length of time spent in school and earnings, as well as an inverse relationship between skill level (both formal and informal) and unemployment rates. This new theory—that investment in people paid off in national prosperity—ushered in the golden age of American education, where the public treasury made huge commitments to education in the form of investments in schools, teacher training, and student subsidization.

This golden age of American education also coincided with a period of American global economic and political supremacy. Thus, there is substantial empirical evidence supporting the basic premise of human capital theory. Moreover, human capital theory upended the traditional economic notion of scarcity, in that knowledge, unlike physical capital, was almost infinitely expandable, self-generating, and able to be transmitted and shared with others. Public investments in education also served to promote the promises of democracy and egalitarianism, as the doors to higher education (with concomitant better jobs and professional occupations) were now open to students from middle and working class families.

When Becker wrote the first edition of *Human Capital* in 1964, there was increasing interest by economists in the economics of education, particularly the importance of education in promoting economic growth. Becker's intention was to develop an explanatory model for investments in education based on a calculated rate of return similar to that applied to investments in physical capital. Becker acknowledged the concerns of others that the economics-based terminology could be misconstrued as equating human beings with inanimate "inputs," as well as potential connections with capitalist exploitation of workers. However, Becker's model provided an explanatory framework for a number of previously unexplained phenomena, but most especially for consistent observations of a positive correlation between educational attainment and wages and inverse correlation between education and unemployment.

Becker divided human productive activity into the production of non-market commodities (self-provisioning), the production of human capital (investments in education and training), and the production of earnings. He then derived a series of equations to describe shifts in the allocation between consumption, investment, and earning over a typical lifespan. These statistical models were then applied to census data from demographic cohorts in 1939 and 1949. Just as with physical capital, individuals make decisions about educational investments based on expected rates of return. Thus, people are more likely to make educational and training investments early in their working lives, due to both lower opportunity costs (in the form of foregone current earnings) and longer period to amortize the costs of investment. Focusing primarily on the rates of return for college-educated white males, Becker calculated a private rate of return (ROI) of between 10% and 12%. This ROI for a college degree compared favorably with similar returns on manufacturing capital in small firms, an investment that Becker deemed to be similar in risk and liquidity.[12]

Becker's model demonstrated a great degree of variability in rates of return, both between and among demographic groups, or cohorts. Although gains from a college education were near universal, they varied by sex, race, urban or rural residence, or whether or not the individual completed college. Cohort variation was attributed to a combination of variation in costs, variation in returns, the correlation between returns and costs, and correlations between returns in different periods.[13] Variations *within* demographic groups were correlated with "ability," which Becker defined as a combination of IQ score, high school class rank, and father's educational attainment/occupation. Variations *between* demographic groups appeared to be more dependent on social factors, which also was explained by Becker's model. Returns on college completion were not significantly lower for non-whites and females in spite of discrimination because they tended to attend "cheaper" local colleges. So, although discrimination (and for women, less attachment to the labor force) resulted in lower wages, the investment and opportunity costs for non-whites and women also tended to be lower.

Becker's model also provided explanation for how education dynamics contribute to growing income inequality and the perpetuation of social privilege. Individuals with greater ability will be more likely to invest in education because they receive higher returns. The same is true for white males (who are not subject to market wage discrimination) when compared to non-whites or females. Individuals from less privileged families generally need more time to accumulate physical capitals to invest in education, thus decreasing the recoupment period of higher wages and lowering the rate of return.

Becker's model thus explains how education can operate to increase aggregate wealth while at the same time aggravating existing socio-economic inequalities. Becker suggested that his model contained arguments both "for" and "against" compulsory public educational requirements. While universal public education can serve to reduce inequality by lowering supply elasticities, it does so at the cost of reducing efficiencies by penalizing "abler" persons with higher marginal educational costs. That is, there is a trade-off when society provides everyone an "equal" opportunity to obtain an education which result in reduction of educational opportunities for more talented students.[14]

Although Becker's analysis focused primarily on private rates of return, he attempted to derive some measure for gains in "social productivity."[15] That is, more education—and more broad-based education—results in not just a wealthier society, but also a better one. Becker admitted that the absence of direct measures for external effects (e.g., cultural advance and democratic governance) necessitated the use of indirect and less reliable measures, and Becker suggested that future research be directed to developing better methodologies.[16] However, Becker's calculations produced a range of social ROI between 13% and 25%, which Becker estimated was likely to be conservative.[17]

Like most models of neoclassical economics, Becker's model makes a number of presumptions about behavior. Primarily, Becker's model presumes an informed and rational investor. The hypothetical "rational investor" is also presumed to make decisions on the basis of accurate information. Moreover, this rational investor ideally has some understanding of Becker's carefully crafted equations, as well as the means to collect appropriate data. These calculations are made even more difficult by the uncertainties associated with prediction of lifespans, long-term occupational and market projections, and even accurate assessment of someone's own abilities.

To Becker's credit, he broadened the discussion about traditional economic concerns with wages, costs, and marginal product to include considerations of the availability of accurate labor market information, information about the "political or social system,"[18] the effects of investments in worker physical and emotional health, and worker "morale, motivation, and aspirations."[19] In essence, Becker's model could potentially be corrupted by behavioral motivators such as unrealistic American Dream ideology (the promise of upward mobility) and deliberately distorted labor market information.

Becker's human capital theory has been widely accepted because it provides a logical model that explains a number of empirically observable phenomena, and integrates both theoretical and empirical analysis. As a former member of the U.S. Dept. of Labor commission on labor quality, Becker aligns with the skills shortage proponents that advocate for policy objectives designed to "improve the quality of workers in the United States."[20] Becker dismisses overeducation as a temporary phenomenon, and cites continuing increases in the monetary gains to education that keep college enrollments going up in spite of increasing costs.[21] Human capital theory thus represents a form of supply side economics with respect to education. It proposes that increasing the aggregate level of education operates to increase the demand for educated workers; i.e., the supply will produce adequate demand to absorb it.

Development of Human Capital Theory

Like early studies of overeducation that focused on the question of whether workers were realizing returns to educational investments, early studies of human capital theory focused on testing Becker's proposition that increasing educational levels were correlated with increasing wages. Early studies of overeducation in the context of human capital theory also emphasized calculation of the return on educational investment by examining wage differentials. The majority of these studies found some positive correlation between education and wages as well as lower levels of unemployment However, this wage premium was reduced for workers that were inappropriately "matched" to the job. That is, most studies found that persons who had so-called surplus schooling with respect to their current employment earned more than their appropriately educated (i.e., "matched") occupational peers, but less than others with the same level of education who occupied education-appropriate jobs (i.e., their educational peers).[22] Thus, workers with more education do indeed earn more than those with less, but it does not necessarily offset investments in education. This is especially so for workers who cannot (or do not) find work that requires the level of education that they have paid for.

Other studies attempted to examine the more complex construct of occupational mismatch and its effect on wages and education ROI. A Dutch study by Herman Van De Werfhorst[23] suggests that the "matching" process begins when students select a course of study. This selection is based on preferences, and students may even choose courses of study that have high "cultural status" but lower incomes (such as journalism, teaching, and social science). In essence, Van De Werfhorst suggests that students sometimes choose academic majors (and subsequent professions) knowing that such choices could lower their educational ROI, but have other personal reasons for doing so. Consistent with most other studies, Van De Werfhorst found a positive correlation between increased educational level and higher wages, although there was no wage gain for educational attainment in "mismatched" occupations. Van De Werfhorst's regression models show that wages are determined by a complex combination of educational level, type of job, and "match" between educational resources and occupation. The study also alluded to the dynamics of career choice, although it did not explore this in depth.

Firm-Specific vs. General Human Capital

Later studies expanded the concept of human capital beyond a one-time measure of a worker's educational attainment to include a combination of formal education, on-the-job training, generally acquired skills, and specific skills gained or developed through experience on the job. These post-educational skills are developed as a function of learning and performing job duties as well as training provided by the employer. Because even academic research tends to be oriented toward corporate interests, the focus here became how to design on-the-job training programs that delivered the most returns to the employer and minimized the ability of the worker-trainee to avail himself of the benefits elsewhere.

Becker himself did not fail to recognize that the development of human capital involved allocation of costs and benefits between workers and firms. Specifically, Becker developed a formula by which employers could make decisions about on-the-job training by calculating their returns on job training costs. In this analysis, Becker distinguished between firm-specific training and general training. So-called "firm specific" training increased human capital in a manner that was particularized to a firm's specific market. Firm-specific training made the worker more valuable to the firm, but the worker could not realize a wage gain by taking this specialized knowledge elsewhere. Conversely, general training increased the worker's nonspecific human capital, which is more easily traded in competitive labor markets. The argument is that specialized (or firm-specific) training thus benefits both employer and worker because it provides disincentives to the employer to fire a trained employee and disincentives to the worker to look for employment elsewhere.

Becker made a number of suggestions for employers to maximize benefits from their training dollars. For example, employers could use semi-contractual arrangements such as pension plans with incomplete vesting provisions as a form of insurance against "quits" by trained employees.[24] Becker also suggests that the benefits of specific training have larger payoffs to employers with monopsony power, implying that a hyper-competitive business environment would operate as a disincentive to on-the-job training. Becker's expanded analysis also included transactional costs (recruitment costs for employers and job search costs for employees) as a form of human capital, because they assisted the parties with maximizing their other investments.

The human capital issue for corporations is obviously about cost versus benefits. That is, how much and what kind of "investments" are going to generate the highest returns. A group of academics[25] examined the role of human capital in organizational competitive advantage. This study conducted a meta-analysis of 66 prior studies to determine why the results and findings were mixed. That is, some of these prior studies found a positive correlation between firm human capital and performance and others did not. Two concepts that were explored in this study were phenomena the authors term imperfect strategic factor markets and appropriability. The authors also explored potential variations between cross-sectional versus longitudinal studies (what they termed a "path-dependency" analysis). Their hypothesis was that increases in performance generally follow, but are not concurrent with, investments in human capital, so measuring both at the same time will give inaccurate results.

The imperfect strategic markets analysis revisited the work of Becker in proposing that firm-specific human capital is better for the firm than more general human capital. As employee knowledge "becomes idiosyncratic to solving problems...specific to the firm's unique competitive context," this knowledge is less transferable, and thus it becomes "difficult for employees to demand compensation that is commensurate with their full value to the firm."[26] Conversely, workers with high value "general" capital can move among the highest bidding competitors until their cost is roughly equal to their added value to the firm. Not surprisingly here, firm-specific human capital produced greater performance gains, with the authors recommending that managers "develop a long-tenured workforce whose skills are tied to the firm's unique context."[27] The authors also suggest that a cynical interpretation is that practices designed to limit employee mobility can also operate to "place a cap on wages."[28]

The appropriability analysis proposes that "powerful stakeholders" such as highly skilled employees or their managers could "extract above-market prices for their contributions to the organization."[29] With so many current studies demonstrating a growing gap between productivity and wages, this would hardly seem to be a problem worthy of academic effort, except perhaps in the case of highly paid executives. This appropriation by "overpaid" employees appeared to reduce performance measures based on "highly aggregated constructs" such as return on assets or return on sales (i.e., profitability), but not if such measures were based on "operational performance measures [that] capture specific value chain activities within the firm, but not the firm globally."[30] That is, whether high value human capital delivers increased benefits to the firm or not depends on how output is measured. Data from this study also suggested that correlation between human capital and firm performance is bolstered when human capital is distributed across multiple levels of hierarchy and not simply limited to top management or core employees.

This study thus acknowledges that "knowledge embedded within people is ultimately the only source of competitive advantage,"[31] while at the same time lamenting the "potentially negative effect of general human capital"[32] in the form of imperfect strategic factor markets and appropriability. In essence, human capital is only "good" for firms when they can realize a profit, but not when workers can get paid what they're worth. Other studies found that workplace training can indeed be profitable for employers. One study found that a 10% increase in training produced a 3% increase in labor productivity but only a 1.5% gain in wages.[33] However, even these studies note the possibility that trained workers can be "poachable" by competitors, and recommend steep wage-tenure profiles to discourage mobility, as well as "institutionally driven wage compression."[34]

At least one study examined the longitudinal development of human capital from the standpoint of worker mobility.[35] Specifically, this study analyzed the relationships between occupational mobility, work experience, and overeducation. In this study, work experience unrelated to education was under-rewarded (in terms of wage gains) for overeducated workers. The author suggests that either employers are reluctant to invest in on-the-job training of overeducated workers because they view them as transient, or there is an actual depreciation of human capital in overeducated workers from non-use of their skills.

This bias was also compounded by age effects. While younger workers' gains in job experience had a positive effect on wage growth and a negative effect on occupational mobility, the experience of older workers led to greater job mobility along with wage stagnation.

The development of human capital (and particularly firm-specific human capital) is a long-term investment. Many human capital researchers warn that in a hypercompetitive environment, few firms will be able to attain long-term advantages. Moreover, a number of other factors now operate to reduce incentives to offer on-the-job training. The most obvious is a culture of über-efficiency and downsizing, which regards workers as fungible and disposable "inputs." Many firms have adopted organizational structures comprised of a core and a periphery. Core workers are viewed as investments, and tend to enjoy predictable schedules and wages, benefits such as health insurance and matching retirement, and internal opportunities for training and advancement. Conversely, peripheral workers are viewed as costs, generally work part-time and unpredictable hours, earn lower wages, and receive no employee benefits or opportunities for training and advancement. In an economy characterized by wage compression, it is often cheaper for a firm to "poach" skilled workers from other employers rather than develop them from within. An alternative strategy is to lobby policy-makers to provide job training at state expense, thus externalizing training costs onto taxpayers.

Criticisms of the Human Capital Theory Model

Although the majority of studies (particularly those that are economics-based) as well as empirical evidence support the fundamental premise of human capital theory—that increasing education, training and skills results in benefits for both individuals and society—it is not without its critics. Criticism of human capital has tended to fall into six major themes. The first is that education is used as a screening, or form of shorthand that signals a level of productive ability to employers, without the necessity of conducting a more thorough person-job suitability match.[36]   The screening hypothesis connects with credentialism theory, which proposes that educational degrees are "culturally based stratifying entry barriers to occupations and organizations."[37]   Indeed, it is not only the degree, but from which institution it was conferred (private elite school, state flagship university, or publicly funded community college) that determines career trajectory as much as the degree itself. A second criticism is that data reliability and methodological issues result in exaggerated rates of return to education.[38] A third criticism is that the focus on direct economic benefits ignores indirect or externalized benefits to society, in essence, under-estimating the benefits of education.[39] A fourth criticism is that the link between education and earnings presumes a corresponding link between earnings and productivity,[40] an analogy to Adam Smith's "unproductive" knowledge.

The focus of this study was on the fifth and sixth criticisms of human capital theory. The fifth criticism is not so much a criticism of human capital theory itself, but a criticism of the narrow neoclassical economic presumptions that underlie it, namely that all economic growth is automatically socially beneficial and utility maximization is the primary motivator of human behavior. The sixth criticism is that human capital theory ignores the social, political and institutional context in which careers are chosen, value is ascribed, productivity is defined, and rewards are allocated.[41]   According to the French sociologist Pierre Bourdieu, the value of symbolic forms of capital (cultural, social, and human) is arbitrarily determined by elites, which is then used as a basis for exclusivity.[42] That is, a white male with a degree from Harvard will be ascribed a higher "value" in the job market than, for example, an Asian female with an identical degree in an identical subject matter (and possibly higher IQ and more developed work ethic) from State U.

While human capital theory provides a logical framework from which to advocate for the advancement of individual and collective knowledge, it is limited by the foundational concepts of neoclassical economics. This model is based on the concept of *homo economicus,* or the belief that all human motivation is based on utility maximization. Utility maximization is accomplished through the satisfaction of preferences, which are presumed as a given and remain stable across persons, cultures, and time.[43] This framework also presumes that unfettered free markets are the natural condition of human kind, both self-regulating and self-correcting. The operation of free markets and utility maximization, i.e., optimization of the individual's pursuit of his own self-interest, inexorably leads to economic growth, which economists view as synonymous with individual wellbeing and collective welfare, or the outcome of Adam Smith's "invisible hand."[44]

The neoclassical economic view of preferences presumes that these are a given, and this consumer sovereignty is what directs the operation of markets. When markets are permitted to operate unrestricted, individual utility maximization leads toward an optimum state, in which no one can be made better off without others being made worse off. Moreover, it is presumed that choices and preferences are influenced by accurate information about relevant markets that has not been manipulated to serve ulterior agendas. In the neoclassical economic model, educationis a choice—an expression of a preference in the marketplace—by individuals who are motivated solely to increase either their wealth or their social status. According to this model, an individual's position in the social hierarchy is determined by his willingness to "invest," either in physical or educational resources. In the educational free market, schools compete to offer students lower costs, more choices, or better connections to post-graduate employment.

When individuals pursue higher education, they generally do so with the expectation that such pursuit will result in self-betterment, either financially, socially or both. However, even most classical economists recognize what they term the "individual-collective problem." This is frequently presented as the Prisoner's Dilemma, or the choice between cooperation or defection. In these situations, if everyone makes the decision that is most rational from an individual perspective, the group as a whole is worse off. The existence of overeducation illustrates the individual-collective problem: When an individual earns a credential, she/he improves her/his own employment and career prospects, but when large numbers of persons earn the same credentials, it dilutes the value of all of them by creating an oversupply.

While economic studies focus on human capital and objective measurement of skills, sociological studies examine the related phenomenon of social capital and cultural capital. The concept of cultural capital, i.e., that consumer preference is a function of social class, was developed by the French sociologist Pierre Bourdieu, who also argued that the value of knowledge (human capital) is arbitrarily determined by dominant elites, and the educational establishment is ordered to reflect those values.[45] Others examined what is termed social capital, defined as a network of social contacts. This social capital provides access to "embedded resources" that enhance status attainment, and the amount of social capital possessed by an individual is contingent on initial position in the social hierarchy.[46] Moreover, these social networks are often more effective in job search success than the skills and training associated with human capital.[47]

Although the human capital theory model was able to describe the occupational attainment of white males, some studies found that dual labor market and Marxist theories better described occupational outcomes for women and other disadvantaged persons, whose wages and job market status did not reflect either their educational attainment or their social contributions.[48] However, the most forceful criticism

88

of human capital theory is that it serves as an apologetic for the status quo by "ultimately attribut[ing] social or personal ills either to the shortcoming of individuals or the unavoidable technical requisites of production."[49] By reducing the complexity of labor, which is "not a commodity, but an active agent" in its own right, to "a market mediated matching of technically defined skills with technically defined production requirements,"[50] the class struggle has been resolved because now every worker is also a capitalist.[51] In summary, human capital theory fails to account for the mutually reinforcing influence of status cultures on preferences, the influence of social networks and status on occupational outcomes, and the reproduction of social hierarchies.

Human Capital Theory and Overeducation

Human capital theory and overeducation studies arose and developed over the same general time period, yet they seem to be mutually contradictory. The promise of human capital theory was that it offered a simplified method of determining whether society was overinvesting or underinvesting in education by comparing educational rates of return with rates of return on physical capital. Yet, the policy agenda appears to be driven by continuous exhortations to increase educational levels without reference to comparative rates of return because the educated almost always do better with respect to higher wages and lower unemployment rates. Moreover, human capital theory presumes that workers are paid in accordance with their marginal product, which is a direct function of their accumulated human capital (skills, training, and education) and that so-called "overeducation" is only a manifestation of a short-term disequilibrium. The human capital theory counterargument to overeducation is that measures of overeducation do not take into account every aspect of human productivity, *aka* the "omitted variable bias,"[52] and that the fundamental framework only needs to be broadened to accommodate the variety of descriptors for job characteristics and worker skills.[53]

Seamus McGuiness is a research professor at the Economic and Social Research Institute, a Research Fellow at the international Institute of Labour Studies, and Associate Professor at the National Institute for Labour Studies at Flinders University in Australia. McGuiness, who has himself conducted a number of studies on skill mismatch (both over- and under-education) conducted a meta-analysis of studies that measured wage effects of overeducation between 1981 and 2003.[54] One purpose of this study was to analyze the measurement controversies within the context of the human capital theory framework. McGuiness found that overeducation appeared to be relatively stable over time (neither increasing nor decreasing), but there was stronger evidence that overeducation represented an economic reality rather than a statistical artifact. In speculating about the reasons for academics (particularly economists) to persist in their beliefs about the infallibility of the human capital theory model, McGuiness states, "The unwillingness of many researchers to accept the notion [that overeducation is real] is perhaps due to the fact that to do so raises some very serious questions with respect to the validity of some of the assumptions and predictions associated with the conventional (neoclassical) view of the labour market."[55]

Origins of Deskilling Theory

The socialist economist Karl Marx[56] was the first to analyze the division of labor into ever more specialized functions and its connection with the expropriation of human capital for purposes of profit. While Adam Smith described a process (he used the making of pins as an example) where workers developed a higher and more productive level of skill by performing a narrower range of functions, Marx described a process where work was reduced to simplistic functions to service industrial machinery. The Marxian separation of the worker from control over the work and centralized control of knowledge by management served to create a low-paid and insecure industrial reserve army as a means to reduce labor costs.

Adam Smith's "productive" division of labor involved the division of occupations among craftsmen, but not division of labor within the craft. For example, a sailing ship was built by (in modern terms) a "team" comprised of ironworkers, carpenters, and cloth-makers, each with his own area of craft expertise. As industrialism took root, the primary objective was finding a means to control the various tradesmen in the pursuit of collective production. This was accomplished initially by centralization (gathering all workers in one location as opposed to allowing them to work from home) and the enforcement of regular hours of work. The ultimate form of industrial centralization was the company town, with its "total economic, spiritual, moral, and physical domination buttressed by the legal and police constraints of a servile administration of justice…"[57]

As capital expands into newly created industries, these newly created industries then themselves become "necessary" for economic functioning. Because these industries are now necessary for economic growth, they can ask for (and usually receive) government subsidization. The historical examples of this phenomenon in the United States are railroads, electricity generation and delivery, telecommunications, and now IT. As industries mature and competition increases, commodities are cheapened, and in order to compete, the capitalist needs to increase the productivity of labor, the scale of production, or both. Although the rise of new industries creates many new capitalists, they are eventually cannibalized by larger capitalists, resulting in an "increase in the minimum amount of individual capital necessary to carry on a business under its normal conditions."[58] This increasing need for ever larger amounts of capital resulted in creation of the banking and financial industries, which now themselves have become "too big to fail" and subject to government bailout.

In this manner, the general law of capital accumulation requires both the production of reserve armies of labor as well as increasing firm size. Borrowing the concept of commodification from

91

the previous era of mercantilism, early industrial capitalists realized they could cheapen labor by reducing crafts into discrete component activities, which reduced the need to pay for workers with the skills and knowledge to execute the entire process. The need for increasing firm size operates to decrease opportunity for smaller competitors to enter the market and increases the need for worker control. Marx's law in essence states that the drive to accumulate capital creates massive wealth at one end of the socio-economic continuum and extreme poverty and deprivation at the other. That is, it creates the paradox of poverty in the midst of plenty.

An industrial-friendly version of the division of labor was proposed by Frederick Winslow Taylor, who sold his *Principles of Scientific Management*[59] on the premise of economic efficiency and increased labor productivity. Marx did not live to see the adoption of scientific management, nor its extension to office work by William Henry Leffingwell's *Scientific Office Management.*[60] Although Taylor and Marx are regarded as ideological opposites, both described workplaces designed around the disaggregation of complex tasks into discrete functions, the separation of executive (decision-making) and conceptual functions from production (or service delivery) functions, and the fungibility of workers. Initially, scientific management was viewed as a strategy for industrial mass production of goods that was not suitable for the provision of professional services.

In 1974, Harry Braverman's *Labor and Monopoly Capital* revisited Marx's theories in the context of modern post-industrial society. Although Braverman's analysis has come to be termed "deskilling theory," Braverman himself never used the term, but instead referred to the "degradation of work." Deskilling theory is challenged by the same types of methodological issues as overeducation, namely, how to define what "skill" is and how to measure its changes over time. For example, most people today know how to use computers, various software programs, and other technical devices that were virtually unknown to their grandparents' generation.

Unlike their grandparents, most people today also do not know how to saddle or shoe a horse, or even the rudimentary basics of care for simple livestock such as chickens. Thus, social and technological change—even that which is unrelated to the workplace—*ipso facto* creates simultaneous gains and losses of certain skills within society.

At the time of Braverman's publication, it was countered by critics who argued that the incorporation of more sophisticated science and technology into the work process actually raised the aggregate level of worker skills. However, Braverman's argument was that the relevant question is not whether the average technical content of work was trending upward, but whether the labor process is becoming polarized. In answer to this question, Braverman cites substantial evidence that the expansion of jobs during the 1960s was primarily in positions that had relatively low control over labor processes alongside a much smaller number of positions with high levels of relative autonomy. Braverman describes this polarization, where the majority of low-skilled, tightly constrained jobs exist alongside a smaller number of high-skilled, highly paid jobs in the context of Marx's general law of capital accumulation. In order to create the self-perpetuating accumulation of capital necessary to support capitalist economies, it is necessary to generate a surplus of labor, or what Marx terms an "industrial reserve army."

In an industry's early phase of capital accumulation, demand for labor, particularly skilled labor, is highest. This creates a short-term illusion that there is a trend of upskilling and rising wages. Although new production technologies and emerging industries may result in a temporary shortage of labor (and rising wages), older industries are designed to evolve toward maximizing the ratio of constant capital (machinery) to variable capital (labor), and so there is a continuous process of making workers redundant. This reserve army of cast-off workers creates pressure on active employed workers to work longer hours and/or accept lower wages. Skilled workers are "progressively replaced...by less skilled, mature labour-power by

93

immature, male by female, that of adults by that of young persons or children."[61]

An example of this today in the United States is the high tech industry. It is growing, but also experiences bouts of boom and bust. While un- and underemployed tech workers either take retail jobs or work in part-time and contract tech positions, the tech industry is hounding Congress to liberalize the H1-B visa program, purportedly to increase the supply of cheaper foreign tech labor. "The working population therefore produces both the accumulation of capital and the means by which it is itself made relatively superfluous, and it does this to an extent which is always increasing."[62]

Marxist theories about the deconstruction of craft have generally been discredited in developed capitalist democracies. Although this is largely ideological, some of it is based on the premise that jobs in a modern "knowledge economy" require higher level skills and thus are not susceptible to Taylorist-style deconstruction. Early critics of Marx's theories tended to hold the clerical profession out as "evidence" that his "proletarianization" thesis was false, or at least was inapplicable to higher status white collar occupations. Marxist theory did not explain the existence of clerks who, although they performed a number of routine functions such as filing and typing, also served as managers and advisers to business owners, especially in the smaller enterprises that were more common in the late 19th century.

Braverman counters this argument by describing the process of massification, differentiation, and deskilling of the majority of office jobs in the early half of the 20th century in great detail. Braverman documents the process by which the occupation of "clerk," which was once considered to be a profession, was expanded and split into a hierarchy of managers (the top), administrators (the middle) and clerks (the bottom). Moreover, Braverman does not simply blame technological developments for the deconstruction of skill, but instead describes how technology is used to enhance and accelerate labor processes that have already been predetermined by capitalist design. Therefore, while the mechanical typewriter increased the productivity of individual clerks, the development of the typing pool removed the need for higher-level clerks to type.

This process was different and more complex than the Taylorist form of deskilling by reduction of existing jobs into discrete, repetitive, and simple tasks. However, both resulted in "the progressive elimination of thought from the work...reducing mental labor to a repetitious performance of the same small set of functions" and resulting loss of relative status and pay for the majority of clerical workers.[63] According to Braverman, the distinction between blue collar and white-collar work is an artificial construct, because either form of labor can be expropriated: "The distinction between commodities in the form of goods and commodities in the form of services is important only to the economist or statistician, not to the capitalist."[64]

As industries are able to increase output with fewer workers, newly redundant workers became the new laboring masses that provided lower wage labor for new industries. As manufacturing jobs were replaced by machines, the surplus labor moved into office work. As office work itself became deskilled and rationalized, its surplus labor moved into service and retail jobs. Braverman bolsters this analysis with historical documentation of stagnating or declining employment in occupations with high wages (manufacturing) which produce surplus labor for newly created office jobs; followed by stagnating or declining employment in office jobs that produce surplus labor for even lower-paid service and retail jobs. Braverman's analysis thus explains today's observable phenomena of the destruction (or outsourcing) of high-wage manufacturing jobs, while the majority of employment growth is in the low-wage service sector. Under capitalism, un- and underemployment (i.e., the reserve army of labor) are not economic aberrations, but a necessary requirement to maintain its mode of production.[65]

Braverman further argues that management had to develop creative methods of using elaborate work rules and credentialism to further divide workers and centralize control. Moreover, the deskilling process itself continually evolves, as each "crisis of control"[66] and an increasingly educated workforce requires the application of more sophisticated managerial techniques. In addition to the division of labor, control was imposed in the form of work speed-ups and production quotas. The irony is that the modern worker had to be both faster and better at discrete technical skills yet remain ignorant of the overall process

The deskilling of work has affected the larger society beyond the organization of labor processes and the world of work. Braverman describes how general deskilling (even in non-work activities) has made the majority more dependent on wage labor to provide for necessities. He documents how the typical working class family in the late 1800s purchased over 1,000 pounds of flour annually and hardly any bread, while the majority of flour today is purchased by commercial bakeries because working class families buy bread rather than make it themselves. A combination of urbanization, marketing, and the destruction of traditional community ties renders the working class more dependent on wage labor and market relationships rather than on themselves or each other. Women, who formerly served the system by working outside of it to feed today's worker and breed tomorrow's, are now increasingly part of the reserve army of low-wage labor as men are. The labor that is now required to supplant family provisioning activities once performed by homemakers can now itself be expropriated.

Labor is only "productive" when it is serving the accumulation of capital. Thus, household and self-provisioning activities are "unproductive" in that they result in no surplus value (and are not available for expropriation), nor are these activities accounted for in measures of national economic progress. Productivity thus has nothing to do with the utility (or actual value to individuals and society) of the labor performed, or even the form that labor takes. The irony of "unproductive" labor is that, although it has declined outside of capitalism's reach, it has increased within it.[67]

As expropriated labor surplus becomes ever more immense and concentrated, all of it cannot be put to productive use (i.e., the enlargement of capital), but it is put to nonproductive uses that nevertheless serve capital in other ways. Thus, new "industries" are created based on advertising, marketing, credit, speculation, and other financial activities that are not associated with either the production of goods or the provision of services. Economists term such activities "rent seeking," or an attempt to receive an economic gain without providing a corresponding social benefit. Thus, in some respects rent seeking mirrors the expropriation of labor surplus, but it is generally associated with lobbying for government taxing, spending, and regulatory favors rather than "productive" business-related or entrepreneurial activity.

Deskilling and the New Middle Class

Because capitalist relationships are inherently adversarial, a certain number of persons must be employed to monitor the work of the laboring masses, which creates the need for a hierarchy of managers, each keeping watch over the activities of those below it. Such necessities also created the occupations of accounting and auditing, whose purported "professions of honesty" were designed to offset "the dishonesty [which is] presumed of all corporations."[68] These occupations of management overseers and technical specialists (accountants, attorneys, investment bankers, lobbyists) who are not engaged in capital accumulation, but nonetheless are in service to it, occupy what Braverman terms the "middle layers" of employment.

This middle level of employment enjoys a favored position in the capitalist hierarchy due to its higher-level, specialized skills, training, and education, and Braverman estimates that these individuals occupy between 15 to 20 percent of total employment. Even this group is subdivided and hierarchically organized based on its relationship to the power and wealth that commands it from above, although its members (carefully screened) are occasionally permitted entry into those higher echelons of power. However, unlike the small farmers, tradesmen, shopkeepers and professionals that previously made up the "middle class" (neither capital nor labor), the new middle class "possesses no economic or occupational in-dependence...possesses no access to the labor process or the means of production outside that [of] employment [by capital], and must renew its labors for capital incessantly in order to subsist."[69] Thus, notwithstanding their relatively privileged position and higher wages, this new middle class, "Feeling the insecurities of their role as sellers of labor power...they begin...to know those symptoms of dissociation which are popularly called 'alienation'...which the working class has lived with for so long that they have become part of its second nature."[70]

Just as early critics of Marx proposed that the existence of white-collar occupations disproved his theories, modern management apologists claim that Taylorism is an anachronism that has since been replaced by more enlightened theories of management, which were developed to accommodate a more sophisticated work force. Braverman criticizes what he terms the "faddish" management theories that were popular during the 1950s and 1960s. According to Braverman, these theories purported to facilitate greater worker participation, but were in reality a "a gracious liberality in allowing workers to adjust a machine, replace a light bulb, move from one fractional job to another, and to have the illusion of making decisions by choosing among fixed and limited alternatives designed by management which deliberately leaves insignificant matters open to choice."[71]

Braverman was not the only one to observe the duplicity of ostensibly humane new management theories. Joan Ciulla documents the evolution of management theory in America,[72] which arose as a response to labor strife in the early 1900s and increasing government regulation following World War II. Ciulla cites the work of C. Wright Mills, who lamented the passing of the golden age of work, an era of small family farms, independent tradesmen, and shopkeepers, when work was integrated into daily life, gave people roots in their communities, and connected them to society.[73] According to Mills, the modern white-collar worker was in some ways worse off than the blue-collar worker, whose job may have been physically more demanding, but whose time was his own at the end of the day. In Mills' analysis, the white-collar worker sells not only his time and energy, but his very personality, rendering him politically apathetic, rootless and disconnected, always in a hurry but not knowing where he is going.[74]

Ciulla then picks up where Braverman left off in analyzing management fads that arose during the 1970s and 1980s, and the resulting explosion in spending on consultants and training programs. Buzzwords like employee empowerment and work engagement along with redesigned processes such as Total Quality Management and teamwork seemed to suggest that job design was evolving from Taylorist reductionism to more holistic use of worker skills. However, Ciulla notes that most of these newer, seemingly more humane models were thinly disguised attempts to get more out of workers by inculcating them into corporate culture.[75] Ciulla also notes that, notwithstanding all the evidence that giving workers more information and voice into decisions that affect work improves productivity, managers are "constantly amazed by this [which] tells us something about the respect they have…for employees."[76]

Criticisms of Deskilling Theory and Braverman's Legacy

Subsequent studies that examined Braverman's theory tended to fall into three categories. The first group challenged Braverman's theory on the basis of increased complexity of modern jobs and requirement of higher-order skills in order to perform them. Braverman's critics contend he was overly preoccupied with social class and the details of Taylor's scientific management. A second group attempted to expand Braverman's theory by examining workers' subjective experiences of resistance and consent, as well as including gendered and racial divisions of work and workers. A third group emerged, which came to be termed post-structuralism.[77] This group attempted to develop models that accommodated the empirical reality of concurrent deskilling, upskilling, and reskilling in a wide variety of occupations. While this third group did a better job of capturing the complexity of modern work, it tended to lose the critical social analysis of Braverman's original theory. Notwithstanding the differences among the three groups, some researchers[78] found the emergence of a consensus around certain themes. Skill is comprised of both the internalized capacities of individual workers as well as task-specific activities associated with job design, division of labor, technology, and control. Skill is also a socially constructed phenomenon, which is subject to Bourdieu-like status sorting.

Doug Fraser, who is among the post-structuralists, attempted to construct more accurate models to measure skill—and skill changes over time—from data collected by the Household Income and Labor Dynamics in Australia (HILDA), a panel survey similar to the U.S. Census initiated in 2001. Fraser intended to derive a measure of skill that distinguished it from confounding factors such as educational prerequisites and social prestige, as well as a measure that would capture the dynamism of skill changes, rather than treating it as a fixed quantity. Fraser states that the motivation for his studies was the paradox of "dominant policy obsessions" with workforce skills while the evidence suggested that "skill was getting less valued, less utilized, and less developed in the average Australian workplace as time went by."[79]

Fraser first makes note of the HILDA's data deficiencies with respect to skill-relevant variables. Fraser's goal was to design a way to measure skill as it is actually exercised on the job rather than a measure of unrealized potential productivity (i.e., overeducation). Fraser developed a combined measure of substantive complexity (the level, scope, and integration of mental, manipulative, and interpersonal tasks), autonomy/control (discretion and ability to control the content, manner, and speed at which tasks are performed), and skill-intensity (the degree to which a job "stretches" the skill base of the jobholder).[80] In essence, the national labor database was not even accurately measuring the skills actually used on the job, let alone whether or not a particular worker was "matched." A secondary goal was to suggest explanations for the paradox of increasing knowledge content of jobs (substantive complexity) alongside decreasing job quality (autonomy/control).

Looking only at the skill content of jobs, the application of Fraser's model found a deskilling trend between 2001 and 2004, followed by a slight upskilling trend between 2004 and 2008, although "scarcely any of the year-on-year variation reaches the 95% level of statistical significance."[81] Fraser then disaggregated the results by occupation and industry and found a number of discrepancies. As a general rule, correlations between skill-intensity and autonomy/control move together, and were twice as high in the private sector as in the government sector. The strongest negative discrepancies between skill-intensity and autonomy/control were in the public sector, particularly in the education, health care and protective services occupations. This appears to indicate classic "bureaucratization," in which the job-holder is required to have higher level skills and training, but then must conform to the organization's rules and red tape.

Fraser suggests four explanatory scenarios that are consistent with his findings, but also states that "the data suggest no reason to prefer" any one scenario over another. For example, "that skill usage becomes more efficient as the market for skilled labor tightens" could possibly explain the upskilling trend between 2004 and 2008. High levels of learning and skill development could also be the result of rapid change and worker turnover, as learning is typically associated with new hires regardless of job skill requirements. Moreover, the "rise and fall" of skill trends was consistent with prior decades, which were subject to the same kinds of socio-economic trends usually associated with large-scale skill change: globalization, managerialism, longer periods of schooling, transition to a post-manufacturing economy, and "the relentless rollback of industrial democracy."[82] That is, there were no corresponding data to compare earlier periods, and Fraser acknowledges that no conclusions about long-term trends can be deduced from his analysis.

Fraser concludes with two primary recommendations. First, there is a need for more occupation and/or industry specific studies that examine the gap between skill requirements and decision-making latitude, particularly with respect to control over the timing and sequence of tasks, and its effect on productivity. This more particularized data is necessary to determine how much of the problem is due to "specific characteristics of the work" and how much to "system failures."[83] The second recommendation is the necessity to collect longitudinal data to track individuals and cohorts over time. However, like many other researchers who lament the quality of labor market data even at the national level, Fraser questions whether such data will be available over the long term, "*in a fiscal climate unsympathetic to such investments in evidence* [emphasis added].[84]

Braverman's critics also included some Marxists and progressives. This line of criticism proposes that when job tasks are subdivided, it increases the level of social skill required among the workers. As capitalist firms expand to include national and international markets, the workers themselves must broaden their own skills to operate across different cultures. This "good" side of corporate production serves to facilitate the development of cooperative skills workers can then use to challenge their own subjugation.

Paul Adler, a Professor of Management and Organization at the Marshall School of Business, is one such critic. Adler does not maintain the romantic view of the pre-industrial worker, but rather describes individuals who are conditioned by social conformity and constrained by social status. Although these romanticized "sole proprietors" have near complete control over their work, to a large degree it is lonely and monotonous. Adler further proposes that the concept of autonomy itself represents a "nostalgic regret" for a past era characterized by self-sufficient individualism and parochial craft monopolies.[85]

The pursuit of competitive advantage thus makes capitalists involuntary promoters of socialization, as firms are forced to expand into ever larger and broader markets. Consequently, while there is incentive to deskill technical tasks, the mandate for constant growth operates to develop social skills among the workers. That is, bureaucracies can be both enabling and coercive,[86] and social interdependence can take on either coercive or collaborative forms. In Adler's view, even work that is technically "deskilled" can provide avenues for personal growth. Rather than focusing solely on the deskilled and alienating features of work, Adler proposes what he terms a "paleo-Marxist" dialectic, which views workers as simultaneously creative members of collective organizational society and "disposable, variable-cost, budget item[s] under another's control."[87] Adler adds a note of hope by suggesting that the "progressive aspects of capitalist development"[88] could extend this socialization process to the "institutional superstructure of culture, politics, and law."[89]

Peter Sawchuk is a Professor at the University of Toronto and Director of the Centre for Social Economy, Learning, and Work. Sawchuk also views work as a complex co-existence of mutually contradictory relationships, and suggests that skill be examined along a dialectic similar to previously identified workplace dialectics of conflict/cooperation, control/resistance, bureaucracy/creativity, and engagement/alienation.[90] Sawchuk proposes what he terms the "use-value" theory, that is, workers acquire skills that have utility to them and meet the workers' various needs (material, psychological and cultural). These "use-value" skills may or may not also comprise "exchange-value" skills, which are those skills that the worker trades for income in the labor market. Use-value skills are continually produced and become a subjective component of the worker. Conversely, exchange-value skills (commodified skills) exist as objective tasks to be performed outside of the worker, and are more easily defined, measured, and evaluated for someone else's purpose.

Thus, workers are continually acquiring skills, even those that cannot be expropriated by the employer. Indeed, skills may be developed that are antithetical to the employer, such as worker organization, resistance, and advocacy designed to advance workers' interests. In this manner, Sawchuk's use-value theory could account for increased aggregate worker skills, credentials and education (as well as underemployment that exists simultaneously with employer demand for more worker training.

While Braverman's theories focused primarily on the redesign of jobs and restructuring of occupations to facilitate capital accumulation, he did have a few observations about the relationships between skill, education, and jobs. Perhaps the biggest unanswered question in Braverman's theory is that if the majority of jobs require fewer skills, then what is driving the demand for more education? Braverman suggests that the expansion of mass education serves capital in a number of ways unrelated to the development of skills. It removes large numbers of young people from the job market, which serves to keep unemployment within acceptable bounds; it replaces the socialization function that used to be provided by family, community, and church; and it creates profitable markets for support and subsidiary industries (e.g. privatization). Braverman further asserts that the "purposelessness, futility, and empty forms" of the educational system and resulting "antagonism" between students and schools duplicates the social structures of capitalism.[91] Moreover, Braverman suggests that the educational requirements for jobs are subject to "deliberate confusion" in order to permit a form of status sorting by employers, and thus tend to be inflated.[92]

Whether one uses the term "deskilling," "labor degradation," or "labor process theory," subsequent research has shown that concepts such as the separation of decision and execution, hierarchical class structure, and the division of labor processes are complex and multidimensional. Braverman's critics may indeed have a valid argument that his analysis is too simplistic to accommodate modern workplace realities. However, the larger issues addressed by Braverman continue to plague modern work: worker disempowerment through loss of worker ownership of productive capital, disconnection of the worker from decisions involved in work processes (loss of autonomy), lack of worker input into institutional governance (loss of agency), destruction of avenues to upward mobility, and alienation from the work.

Loss of ownership has perhaps been the most significant change in the American middle class of all occupations, as sectors that were once dominated by independent businesses—drugstores, grocers, barbershops, and even veterinary practices—have mostly been replaced by corporate chains.[93] A common feature of both Taylorized job design and occupational restructuring is the wholesale reduction of pathways to upward mobility. Once the craft and apprenticeship systems had been destroyed, the next objective was "habituation" of the worker to the capitalist mode of production, which Braverman describes thusly:

> *"The apparent acclimatization of the worker to new modes of production grows out of the destruction of all other ways of living...the weaving of the net of modern capitalist life that finally makes all other modes of living impossible. But beneath this apparent habituation, the hostility of workers to the degenerated forms of work which are forced upon them continues...[and] renews itself in new generations, expresses itself in the unbounded cynicism and revulsion which large numbers of workers feel about their work."[94]*

The human outcome of Braverman's foundational theory is echoed in more recent popular accounts of modern workplaces: Ciulla's *The Working Life: The Promise and Betrayal of Modern Work* (2000); Shulman's *The Betrayal of Work* (2003); and Ehrenreich's *Bait and Switch: The Futile Pursuit of the American Dream* (2005). For many Americans, including those who work hard, follow the rules, and even make substantial personal investments in their own betterment, work is not working. Vicki Smith, Chair of the Department of Sociology at the University of California, Davis, conducted a review of the development of Braverman's theory over two decades.[95] Smith traces how Braverman's work has conceptually transformed various topics related to workers' interests and identifies continuing problems that confront scholars of labor process theory. Notwithstanding continuing debates, Smith concludes that *Labor and Monopoly Capital* has "become a canonical text for those studying the transformation of work in monopoly capitalism and postindustrial society,"[96] and that, "[its] core insights continue to constitute a flourishing and much needed critical paradigm for analyzing work in the late twentieth century." [97]

<u>Rationalization</u>

During the American Progressive Era (generally defined as 1890s through the 1920s), there was widespread demand for political reform, specifically the elimination of corruption. Max Weber was a German political economist that wrote extensively on the benefits of bureaucratization in the administration of the modern state. Modern public administration is characterized by a rigid division of labor among fixed and official jurisdictional areas. Decisions are governed by rules, laws and regulations rather than fallible (and possibly corrupt) human judgment. The "pure type" of bureaucratic official was appointed rather than elected, and chosen on the basis of particularized training or expertise.[98] This system of formalized rules administered by a professionalized workforce was intended to thwart the nepotism, cronyism and favoritism that had characterized political decisions and appointments under the old political "spoils system." Rationalization is justified because it requires that decisions (and hence, outcomes) are neutral and meritocratic.

As both corporations and the administrative state increased in size, formal rationality became the idealized institutional structure for both public and private bureaucracies, modern law, and the capitalist economy. Weber viewed formal rationality as characterized by efficiency, predictability, quantifiability (or calculability) and the replacement of fallible human judgment (or more expensive human labor) with technology. Later in his career, Weber recognized that a focus on efficiency and quantifiability could operate to emphasize quantity over quality. He also came to recognize that there was a downside to replacing human judgment with the dictates of rules, regulations and institutional structures. Although Weber has been quoted as saying "The future belongs to bureaucratization" as well as "Bureaucratic administration means fundamentally domination through knowledge," in his later years be began to express reservations about the spread of bureaucracy. As people are increasingly trapped into rationalized workplaces, they either become slaves to the system or they rebel in the form of passive-aggressive sabotage. In essence, what was designed to be a highly rational system becomes irrational and dysfunctional.

With respect to the modern workplace, sociologist and professor George Ritzer has created the term "McDonaldization" to describe the effects of rationalization on society. Ritzer uses the analogy of the fast food industry to illustrate how rationalizing influences have infected society at all levels.[99] Thus, there is now not only "junk food," there is "junk food journalism" and "overproduction of routine scholarship." Ritzer goes on to describe the "deskilling" of jobs from fast food workers to supermarket checkers to telemarketers who must follow rigidly timed scripts and KinderCare instructors who teach from a uniform, pre-determined curriculum.

However, while the "rationality" of McDonalds produces huge profits for its owners, it is not necessarily "efficient." Not only are McDonald's meals nutritionally deficient, the operation produces huge amounts of non-biodegradable waste. It may not even be efficient for a family to gather everyone, drive somewhere else, and wait in line to pick up dinner when they may well be able to prepare something faster (and nutritionally better) at home. Moreover, there is a qualitative, unmeasured loss from the destruction of the communal family meal.

With an emphasis on quantity over quality, Ritzer cites a growing concern among a number of social critics about the decline of quality in life generally. Ritzer further criticizes rationalized systems for being dehumanizing. People (i.e. customers or citizens) are now "processed" rather than served. Just as Weber predicted, rationalized systems have come to dominate an ever greater part of our society, and they have reached a point where they have become irrational and even destructive. As Weber warned of the "iron cage of bureaucracy" that increasingly bound humans to the point where they could no longer escape, Ritzer describes the "iron cage of McDonaldization." Ritzer warns that a system of interlocking rationalized systems that comes under the control of an increasingly smaller number of persons has ominous implications for authoritarianism and even totalitarianism. In other words, more and more of us will be subject to technocratic systems that harness our skills, energy, and even our lives in service to an impersonal organization that does not serve us in return.

<u>Deskilling of Professional Work</u>

Professionals have traditionally been accorded a high degree of deference in society. This deference was earned, however, in that professionals generally have to pass through a number of stringent assessments to insure that they have a minimal amount of expertise and professional ethics. Professionals have historically been associated with a high level of education and specialized skills, and they enjoy a distinctive occupational culture. Because of their specialized knowledge, professionals are entrusted with a high degree of autonomy, both in dealing with their clients' affairs as well as in self-regulation.

In the past, it was practically assumed that professionals were relatively immune from the separation of work and worker with resulting alienation as described by Marx. Because professional occupations required, by definition, the exercise of independent judgment and critical thinking, their work could not be subjected to the Taylorist "one best way" applicable to lower order mass production. However, there is increasing evidence that forms of labor degradation have crept into professional jobs and organizational structures—a perfect storm of confluence between the degradation of jobs and rationalizing work processes.

Engineers, whose employment tends to be more closely associated with industrial production models, have been experiencing underutilization of skills for decades, and this underutilization has been found to be correlated with restrictions imposed by industrial dictates of efficiency (profits) and the division of labor.[100] The structure of the medical profession is increasingly dominated by Health Maintenance Organizations (HMOs), where headquartered financial analysts and not physicians make decisions about patient care. Law firms are increasingly focused on profitability and marketing rather than improvement in the delivery of legal services, and nearly 50% of law firm managing partners believe that the outsourcing of legal work has become a "permanent trend."[101] Additionally, adoption of New Public Management (NPM) practices in public agencies (on the premise that government should operate "more like a business") has resulted in policy alienation among the professionals charged with implementation.[102]

Deskilling can be created by occupational growth and evolution as much as by the deliberate application of Taylorist job redesign strategies. In a manner similar to Braverman, Thomas Diprete, Giddings Professor of Sociology and co-Director of the Center for the Study of Wealth and Inequality at Columbia University in New York describes the process by which the nineteenth century occupation of "clerk" was both simultaneously professionalized and deprofessionalized.[103] The nineteenth century "clerk" was almost always a male and had responsibilities ranging from copying and filing, to keeping accounts, to assisting the business owner (or public official) with the management of various tasks. Beyond some basic reading, writing, and mathematical ability, the clerk gained higher-level skills primarily through the job itself.

As private organizations and public agencies grew in both size and complexity, the "clerk" profession began to bifurcate into managerial positions with higher level responsibilities (still occupied primarily by higher status males) and lower level administrative functions, primarily occupied by females or lower status males. In this manner, the clerical hierarchy was "stretched"[104] into a proliferation of sub-occupations, which included the birth of the accounting profession. The clerical occupations increased in heterogeneity at the same time they encountered a growing "culture of professionalism,"[105] which now required outside credentials, rather than on-the-job experience, to occupy higher-level functions. The clerical "profession" underwent a form of status redefinition, as its functions were redefined into administrative, managerial, and routine tasks, with the term "clerk" being dropped from all but the most routine functions in revised job classification descriptions.

Thus, the clerical occupation was not so much "deskilled" by operation of Taylorist restructuring as it was expanded and then bifurcated into new high-skilled and low-skilled occupations. What this phenomenon did, however, was remove a route to managerial positions through learning on the job and working one's way up. Diprete concludes by suggesting that a similar analysis of concurrent upgrading and downgrading could be conducted on engineering and other professions.

At least one study suggests that the nature of employer demand itself operates as a form of deskilling. In the face of a saturated market for academic jobs, academic sociologists conducted a survey of 65 non-academic employers who had advertised for Ph.D. level applied sociologists.[106] The survey indicated that these non-academic employers were looking for candidates with general expertise in research methods and statistics, but were typically not concerned with specific skills or knowledge in sociology *per se*. One employer commented, "When one steps out of the academic setting, it is imperative to realize that a bureaucracy has established procedures…that must be followed. Anyone who joins our organization must become part of that company for the benefit of all. Individuality is not productive in a large organization."[107]

The sociologists that were hired in these environments were assigned to a wide variety of tasks that were primarily technical and administrative, with very few of them engaged in conducting seminars, training sessions, or basic research. The researchers (who were themselves sociologists) also comment on the employers' lack

111

of regard for substantive sociological knowledge and complete absence of acknowledgement that sociology is an intellectual discipline with its own norms and objectives. The researchers express concern not only that non-academic employment will operate to deskill and deprofessionalize those who must, by necessity, take those jobs, but also that the continuing unfavorable labor market will pressure graduate sociology programs to tailor instruction to meet the "narrow political and social outlooks" of non-academic employers.[108]

Summary and Conclusion

While Marxist/Taylorist-style deconstruction of specific work tasks may not be possible with professional occupations, the increasing size and bureaucratization of organizations has permitted new ways of organizing work processes. These processes appear to have dehumanizing features, and thus have implications for the once-personal relationships between professionals and their clientele. Perhaps the biggest loss to professionals has been autonomy and power. There is evidence that incursions have been made to professional discretion: teachers are instructed what and how to teach; doctors may be limited by corporate dictates as to what services are available to their patients; IT engineers and web developers are subjected to "just in time" hourly work schedules and struggle to make ends meet while keeping up with the latest certification requirements. It has become more difficult for professionals of all occupations to compete as solo enterprises against huge national and global corporate chains. As the dictates of rationalization encompass ever more segments of society, professionals can find themselves also caught in its iron cage. Perhaps the greatest social damage comes from the breaching of the social contract. We play by the rules, invest years of our lives and thousands of dollars to better ourselves, develop our talents, and "market" ourselves to the world, only to find that we are regarded as nothing more than an expendable cost item on some corporate bottom line.

Notes

1 Smith, A. (1776). *The Wealth of Nations*. Cannan, E. (Ed. 1904). New York, NY: Bantam Dell/random House (2003 Edition) at p. 727.

2 *Id.* at p. 9.

3 *Id.* at p. 358.

4 *Id.* at p. 358.

5"The sovereign, for example, with all of the officers both of justice and war who serve under him, the whole army and navy, are unproductive labourers. They are the servants of the public, and are maintained by a part of the annual produce of the industry of other people. Their service, how honorable, how useful, or how necessary soever, produces nothing for which an equal quantity of service can afterwards be procured." Id. at p. 423).

6 *Id.* at p. 990.

7 *Id.* at p. 969.

8 *Id.* at p. 977.

9 *Id.* at p. 164.

10 *Id.* at p. 970.

11 Schultz, T. W. (1971*). Investment in human capital*. New York, NY: The Free Press.

12 Becker, G. (1964/1993). *Human capital: A theoretical and empirical analysis, with special reference to education, 3rd Ed*. Chicago, IL: University of Chicago Press at p. 206.

13 *Id.* at p. 199.

14 *Id.* at p. 140-141.

15 *Id.* at p. 208.

16 *Id.* at p. 249.

17 *Id.* at p. 211.

18 *Id.* at p. 53.

19 *Id.* at p. 57.

20 *Id.* at p. 18.

21 *Id.* at pp. 17-18.

22 Rubb, S. (2003). Overeducation in the labor market: A comment and re-analysis of a meta-analysis. *Economics of Education Review, 22,* 621-629.

23 Van De Werfhorst, H.G. (2002). Fields of study, acquired skills and the wage benefit from a matching job. *Acta Sociologica, 45*(4), 287-303.

24 Becker, G. (1964/1993). *Supra* at p. 48.

25 Crook, T. R., Combs, J. G., Todd, S. Y., Woehr, D. J., & Ketchen, D. J. (2011). Does human capital matter? A meta-analysis of the relationship between human capital and firm performance. *Journal of Applied Psychology, 96*(3), 443-456.

26 *Id.* at 445.

27 *Id.* at p. 450.

28 *Id.* at p. 452.

29 *Id.* at 445.

30 *Id.* at p. 446.

31 *Id.* at p. 443.

32 *Id.* at p. 444.

33 Barron, J. M., Black, D. A., & Loewenstein, M. A. (1989). Job matching and on-the-job-training. *Journal of Labor Economics, 7*(1), 1-19. Retrieved from: http://www.press.uchicago.edu/ucp/journals/journal/jole.html

34 Blöndal, S., Field, S., & Girouard, N. (2002). Investment in human capital through post-compulsory education and training: Selected efficiency and equity aspects. OECD Economics Department Working Papers, No. 333. OECD Publishing at p. 37.

35 Rubb, S. (2006). Educational mismatches and earnings: Extensions of occupational mobility theory and evidence of human capital depreciation. *Education Economics, 14*(2), 135-154.

36 Winkler, D. R. (1987). Screening models and education. In G. Psacharopoulos (Ed.), *Economics of Education, Research and Studies*. Oxford, England: Pergamon Press.

37 Brown, D. K. (2001). The social sources of educational credentialism: Status cultures, labor markets, and organizations. *Sociology of Education, 74*(4), 19-34 at pp. 19-20.

38 Bennell, P. (1996). Using and abusing rates of return: A critique of the World Bank's 1995 education sector review. *International Journal of Educational Development, 16*(3), 235-248.

39 Woodhall, M. (2001). Human capital: Educational aspects. In N. J. Smelser & P. B. Baltes (Eds.), *International Encyclopedia of the Social and Behavioral Sciences, 10*. Oxford, England: Elsevier.

40 Little, A. W. (1984). Education, earnings and productivity—the eternal triangle. In J. C. P. Oxenham (Ed.), *Education versus Qualifications: A Study of Relationships Between Education, Selection for Employment and the Productivity of Labor*. London, England: George, Allen & Unwin.

41 Little, A. W. (2003). Motivating learning and the development of human capital. Compare: *A Journal of Comparative Education, 33*(4), 437-452.

42 Bourdieu, P. (1984). *Distinction: A social critique of the judgment of taste*. London, England: Routledge and Kegan Paul.

43 Gilead, T. (2012). Education and the logic of economic progress. *Journal of Philosophy of Education*, 46(1), 113-131.

44 Smith, A. (1776). *Supra* at p. 572.

45 Bourdieu, P. (1990). Artistic taste and cultural capital. In J. Alexander and S. Sedman (Eds.), *Culture and Society: Contemporary Debates* (pp. 205-215). Cambridge, England: Cambridge University Press.

46 Lin, N. (1999). Social networks and status attainment. *American Review of Sociology, 25*(1), 467-487.

47 Zippay, A. (2001). The role of social capital in reclaiming human capital: A longitudinal study of occupational mobility among displaced steelworkers. *Journal of Sociology and Social Welfare, 28*(4), 99-119. Retrieved from: http://wmich.edu/socialwork/journal

48 Kay, F. M., & Hagan,J. (1995). The persistent glass ceiling: Gendered inequalities in the earnings of lawyers. *British Journal of Sociology, 46*(2), 279-310; also Osmond, M. W. (1984). If attitudes were income, women would thrive: Comment on Acock and Edwards. *Journal of Marriage and Family, 46*(1), 243-246.

49 Bowles, S., & Gintis, H. (1975). The problem with human capital theory—a Marxian critique. *American Economic Review, 65*(2), 74-82 at p. 82. Retrieved from https://www.aeaweb.org/aer/index.php

50 *Id.* at p. 77.

51 *Id.* at p. 74.

52 Leuven, E., & Oosterbeek, H. (2011). Overeducation and mismatch in the labor market. Institute for the Study of Labor Discussion Paper No. 5523 at p. 39. Retrieved from: http://ftp.iza.org/dp5523.pdf

53 Sloane, P. (2003). Much ado about nothing? What does the overeducation literature really tell us. In Buchel, de Grip & Mertens (Eds.), *Overeducation in Europe*, pp. 11-49. Cheltenham, England: Edward Elgar.

54 McGuiness, S. (2006). Overeducation in the labor market. *Journal of Economic Surveys*, 20(3), 387-418.

55 *Id.* at p. 388.

56 Marx, K. (1867). *Capital, Vol. 1.* Vintage Books Edition, 1977. New York, NY: Random House, Inc.

57 Braverman, H. (1974). *Labor and monopoly capital: The degradation of work in the twentieth century* (1998 Edition). New York, NY: Monthly Review Press at p. 46.

58 Marx, K. (1867). *Supra* at p. 777.

59 Taylor, F. W. (1911). *The principles of scientific management*. New York, NY: Harper & Brothers.

60 Leffingwell, W. H. (1917). *Scientific office management*. New York, NY: A. W. Shaw Co.

61 Marx, K. (1867). *Supra* at p. 788.

62 *Id*. at p. 783.

63 Braverman, H. (1974). *Supra* at p. 220.

64 *Id*. at p. 250.

65 *Id*. at p. 267.

66 Edwards, R. (1979). *Contested terrain: The transformation of the workplace in the twentieth century*. New York, NY: Basic Books.

67 Braverman, H. (1974). *Supra* at p. 287.

68 *Id*. at p. 210.

69 *Id*. at p. 279.

70 *Id*. at p. 282.

71 *Id*. at p. 27.

72 Ciulla, J. B. (2000). *The working life: The promise and betrayal of modern work*. New York, NY: Times Books/Random House, Inc.

73 *Id*. at p. 109.

74 Mills, C. W. (1951). *White collar: The American middle class*. New York, NY: Oxford University Press at p. xvii.

75 Ciulla, J. (2000). *Supra* at p. 108.

76 *Id.* at p. 141.

77 Knights, D. (1990). Subjectivity, power, and the labor process. In D. Knights and H. Willmott (Eds.), *Labor process theory*, pp. 197-335. London, England: Macmillan.

78 Warhurst, C., Grugulis, I., & Keep, E. (Eds). (2004). *The skills that matter*. London, England: Palgrave Macmillan.

79 Fraser, D. (2010a). Deskilling revisited: New evidence on the skill trajectory of the Australian economy 2001-2007. Paper delivered to the International Labour Process Conference, Rutgers, N.J., March 15, 2010 at p. 12. Retrieved from: http://papers.ssrn.com/sol3/papers/cfm?abstract_id=1804618 .

80 Fraser, D. (2010b). Deskilling: A new discourse and some evidence. The *Economic and Labour Relations Review, 21*(2), 51-74.

81 Fraser, D. (2010a) *Supra* at p. 8.

82 *Id.* at p.13.

83 Fraser, D. (2010b). *Supra* at p. 69.

84 *Id.* at p. 68.

85 Adler, P. (2007). The future of critical management studies: A paleo-Marxist critique of labour process theory. *Organization Studies 28*(9), 1313-1345 at p. 1319.

86 *Id.* at p. 1336. "a contradictory unity"

87 *Id.* at p. 1330.

88 *Id.* at p. 1339.

89 *Id.* at p. 1326.

90 Sawchuck, P.H. (2006). 'Use-value' and the re-thinking of skills, learning and the labor process. *Journal of Industrial Relations, 48*(5), 593-617.

91 Braverman, H. (1974). *Supra* at p. 305.

92 *Id.* at p. 232.

93 Brook, D. (2007). *The trap: Selling out just to stay afloat in winner-take-all America*. New York, NY: Henry Holt & Co., LLC.

94 Braverman, H. (1974). *Supra* at p. 104.

95 Smith, V. (1994). Braverman's legacy: The labor process tradition at 20. *Work and Occupations, 21*(4), 403-421.

96 *Id.* at p. 404.

97 *Id.* at p. 416.

98 Weber, M. (1946). *Bureaucracy*. In Shafritz, J., Hyde, A., & Parkes, S. (Eds.) Classics of Public Administration (2004), pp.50-55.

99 Ritzer, G. (1993). *The McDonaldization of society*. Thousand Oaks, CA: SAGE Publications, Inc.

100 Ritti, R. R. (1970). Underemployment of engineers. *Industrial Relations 9*(4), 437-452.

101 Friedmann, R. (2012, January). The impact of legal process outsourcing you might not have noticed. American Bar Association, Law Practice Today. Retrieved from:
http://www.americanbar.org/content/dam/aba/publications/law_practice_today/the-impact-of-legal-process-outsourcing-you-might-not-have-noticed.authcheckdam.pdf

102 Tummers, L., Beckkers, V., & Steijn, B. (2009). Policy alienation and public professionals. *Public Management Review, 11*(5), 685-706.

103 Diprete, T. A. (1988). The upgrading and downgrading of occupations: Status redefinition vs. deskilling as alternative theories of change. *Social Forces, 66*(3), 725-746.

104 *Id.* at p. 732.

105 *Id.* at p. 729.

106 Lyson, T. A., & Squires, G. D. (1984). The promise and perils of applied sociology: A survey of non-academic employers. *Sociological Inquiry, 54*(1), 1-15.

107 *Id.* at p. 10.

108 *Id.* at p. 11.

Chapter Four
Political Agendas and Alternative Economic Models

ON THE OPPOSITE SIDE of the overeducation debate is the argument that the United States is actually experiencing a skills shortage because workers are untrained and unprepared for the high-skilled, high-tech jobs in the new "knowledge economy." Major federal programs such as the Job Training Partnership Act (1982) and the Workforce Investment Act (1998) are based on the premise that training workers and/or upgrading job skills will lead to lower unemployment as well as decrease overall wage inequality. Bolstering this premise are futurist authors touting the brave new "information age," in which jobs will increasingly require higher-level analytical skills as opposed to brute strength or high-speed monotonous routines.[1] Politicians at all levels of government have taken up the crusade for more worker training. In 2010, President Obama compared the skills shortage crisis to "our generation's Sputnik moment" and warned that America was in danger of falling behind.[2] In Texas, former Lt. Governor Dewhurst lamented that, "Businesses…are complaining to me almost daily about the lack of a trained workforce here in Texas" and alleges that Texas is not producing enough engineering, math, science, nursing graduates— and even not enough teachers.[3]

What is the Real Evidence of Skills Shortages?
Skills shortage proponents trace the foundation of their argument to a 1983 report issued by President Reagan's National Commission on Excellence in Education called *A Nation at Risk: The Imperative for Educational Reform*. The oft-quoted opening paragraphs appeal to the jingoist competitiveness and anxiety that characterized the Cold War era:

> *Our Nation is at risk. Our once unchallenged preeminence in commerce, industry, science, and technological innovation is being overtaken by competitors throughout the world. This report is concerned with only one of the many causes and dimensions of the problem, but it is the one that undergirds American prosperity, security, and civility. We report to the American people that while we can take justifiable pride in what our schools and colleges have historically accomplished and contributed to the United States and the well-being of its people, the educational foundations of our society are presently being eroded by a rising tide of mediocrity that threatens our very future as a Nation and a people. What was unimaginable a generation ago has begun to occur—others are matching and surpassing our educational attainments.*

> *If an unfriendly foreign power had attempted to impose on America the mediocre educational performance that exists today, we might well have viewed it as an act of war....We have, in effect, been committing an act of unthinking, unilateral educational disarmament.*[4]

The basis of this argument is that the U.S. is falling behind either because it has not been investing in education to the same extent as its global competitors, or it has not been demanding sufficient accountability for its education dollars. The 1983 report instigated calls for political action directed at educational reform, which to some extent continues today.

More recent claims about skills shortages are often based on employer surveys,[5] or propounded by organizations representing employer interests such as the National Association of Manufacturers.[6] The skills shortage alarmists advocate policies that range from increasing or enhancing the instruction of STEM (science, technology, engineering, and math) subjects,[7] to publicly funded job

122

training, to liberalizing immigration laws, particularly the granting of H1-B visas. Many of these studies have legitimate purposes, that is, they are not intended as ammunition for lobby campaigns designed to reduce the cost of labor and/or disempower the tech workforce. Some of these studies are designed to provide tools that permit corporations to identify, predict, and fill their internal talent gaps.[8] Other studies have focused on the demand side, which is created by the increasing complexity of managing outsourced and interconnected intergovernmental services in the public sector,[9] and the increased managerial complexity resulting from globalization and regulation in the private sector.[10]

ManpowerGroup is a global corporate conglomerate with five discrete subsidiaries that operate in 80 countries. ManpowerGroup provides workforce consulting, recruitment, assessment, training, outsourcing, and career management and development to primarily corporate clients. Beginning in 2006, ManpowerGroup conducted annual "talent shortage" surveys of approximately 10,000 hiring managers located on the American continents (ten countries, including the United States, Canada, and Mexico). The first survey was in 2006—just prior to the Great Recession—and 70% of employers reported difficulty filling jobs due to lack of available talent. This number dropped to 62% in 2007, then fell again to 31% in 2008 (at the height of the Great Recession), and has since fluctuated between 34% and 41% from 2009 to 2013.[11]

The ManpowerGroup surveys attempted to identify more precisely the skills that employers regarded as lacking in the workforce. According to the data for 2013, 33% of employers allege the problem is due to a lack of technical, or "hard" skills, another 31% allege the problem is due to a lack of applicants, and a somewhat smaller number (24%) cite lack of experience. Among employers reporting a shortage of "hard" skills, the study cites this as being some combination of professional certifications and skilled trades experience, although the report does not break this down further. The next-most-frequently-cited explanations are lack of workplace competencies (so-called "soft" skills) at 16%, and workers "looking for more pay than is offered" at 11%.[12] In the American surveys, the occupations with the top five skills shortages (in descending order) are technicians, sales representatives, engineers, skilled trades workers, and production operators.[13]

A survey of some 50,000 employers in the Chicago area who hire recent college graduates also found that many employers consider job candidates, including those who were recent college graduates, deficient on some parameter.[14] Although nearly 70% of employers felt that colleges were doing a good or excellent job in preparing students for employment, almost a third (31%) gave colleges a fair or poor rating. The main complaints of surveyed employers were that job candidates lacked more general workplace skills rather than more specific technical skills. The skills that employers alleged to be lacking were written and oral communication skills, adaptability, the ability to manage multiple priorities, decision-making, and problem solving skills

Skills shortage reports[15] that examine actual labor market data outside of employer surveys usually involve small samples of discrete occupations or industries that require highly specialized, technical knowledge.[16] One skills shortage "analysis" was a combined review of three separate studies.[17] The first study was the Third International Mathematics and Science Study conducted by the International Association for the Evaluation of Education Achievement, which found various grade levels of American students finishing last or near last on measures of math and science achievement. The other two studies were employer surveys conducted by the Information Technology Association of America (ITAA) and the U.S. Department of Commerce. Although the ITAA and Department of Commerce studies were criticized by the GAO on a number of analytical and methodological grounds, these reports nonetheless generated the introduction of remedial legislation in the U.S. House and Senate.[18]

A common argument that is raised by employers is that, notwithstanding that there are more degree-holders in the workforce, the drive to produce more graduates has cheapened credentials and produced a lower quality cohort of graduates. In the UK, there was a deliberate national policy to expand university education in the 1990s, which doubled the number of individuals with university education. Researchers at the Royal Holloway University of London attempted to compare the "quality" of these new graduates by comparing various skill levels between the underemployed and "matched" employees. [19] The new graduates were classified as "matched," apparently overeducated, or genuinely overeducated. A primary finding of this study was that there was "no evidence that post-expansion graduates are of substandard quality."[20] The next analysis was to determine the amount of wage penalty experienced by the new cohort of overeducated graduates. Although the number of post-expansion graduates had doubled, the wage penalty for overeducation remained relatively stable. When controlled for measurable skill differentials, this wage penalty ranged from 5% (for apparently overeducated jobholders) to 18% (for genuinely overeducated jobholders).

The authors suggested that what seemed to make a greater difference between the wages of overeducated workers and matched workers was not academic skills (i.e., written, spoken, foreign language, numeracy, basic computer, advanced IT, research, and creativity skills), but a lack of skills connected with "unobserved characteristics" favored by employers (i.e., nonacademic skills such as entrepreneurial, management, and leadership skills). However, only one-third of this wage penalty could be attributed to differences in both observed and unobserved skills, with the remaining two-thirds attributable to "idiosyncratic job characteristics as well as time varying unobservable characteristics."[21] Although these characteristics are neither described nor defined, the authors make oblique reference to such behaviors as motivation, punctuality, and "presentation."[22] In essence, the expanded universities were fulfilling their obligation as far maintaining academic quality was concerned, but these were not necessarily the skills desired by employers.

At least one academic[23] believes that employers are to blame for creating what appears to be a skills shortage because they are either demanding too much by way of specifically defined skills, refusing to pay market-clearing wages (i.e., paying too little), or failing to make even minimal investments in worker training. Professor Peter Cappelli has coined the terms "purple squirrel" and "pink unicorn" to describe the elusive, hypothetical perfect job candidate.[24] Even in specialized sub-fields of engineering, where there is some evidence that a real skills shortage may exist, at least one former electronics engineer echoes Cappelli's suggestion that employers are being over-prescriptive, unrealistic, and not effectively utilizing recruitment agencies.[25] Dwyer asks the rhetorical question, "How—if there's a shortage—can engineers be bought so cheaply?"[26] Others state the problem more bluntly: Policymakers should spend less time concerning themselves over purported skills deficiencies in the workforce because, "the lack of decent jobs is the obvious basic problem."[27]

Michael Handel, a sociologist at the University of Wisconsin, explored the question of whether workplace skills demands were outpacing worker skills supply by separately analyzing worker skills and job requirements.[28] Worker cognitive skills were measured using a combination of IQ tests, U.S. Dept. of Education National Assessment of Educational Progress and the National Adult Literacy Surveys. Not surprisingly, the unemployed (retirees, immigrants) and working poor did exhibit below average scores. However, scores were generally stable across most demographics, with skills scores for younger workers slightly higher and the "race gap" narrowing.[29] Assuming that worker skills were basically stable, a skills gap would be created only if job skill requirements were increasing.

Handel then measured job skills using the *Dictionary of Occupational Titles* and the National Employers Survey, although noting that, "the absence of a standardized, up-to-date method of collecting information on the actual skill content of jobs is a significant obstacle..."[30]   Using various methodologies from the research of others, Handel found that job skill requirements were rising, but no more rapidly than in the past. He also found that employers generally gave greater weight to non-cognitive factors such as work effort, motivation, and attitude than to actual skills. Moreover, "the skills...for which [workers] are rewarded are partly a function of the jobs employers offer, rather than the intrinsic capacities of individuals acting as a kind of hard constraint."[31]

Handel's conclusion is that the cause of low or stagnating wages is more likely due to structural factors in the operation of labor markets rather than aggregate shortages of worker skills,[32] and blaming the workers for a skills deficit "diverts attention from the role of free-market government policies and management's shortcomings..."[33] Handel alludes to the possibility that the worker skills shortage crisis has been manufactured, as it "generates a form of moral panic...that is disproportionate to what is warranted by a sober assessment of the evidence."[34] He also discounts the popular proposed policy solutions of increased worker education and training programs: "Raising everyone's absolute cognitive skills and work readiness will not increase wages and decrease inequality if wages are determined by the structure of jobs and one's relative position in the worker queue."[35]

Gordon Lafer, Associate Professor at the University of Oregon Labor Education and Research Center, exhaustively researched both the legislative history and performance statistics of the Job Training Partnership Act (JTPA).[36] The JTPA was a product of the Reagan administration, and it replaced the public employment programs of the former Comprehensive Employment and Training Administration (CETA) with a system of job training programs run by outsourced (i.e., privatized) providers. The theory was that by getting government out of job training (and job creation), privatized training would produce the necessary skills for jobs in the private sector and (by operation of the free market) create jobs. Lafer's review of every reputable study of JTPA finds that it has failed to deliver on its promises with respect to the creation of jobs and the reduction of poverty and inequality. At best, job training mainly served to give participants a more favorable position in the job queue. Moreover, because incentives revolved around placement numbers and not job quality, the system was characterized by deliberate selection of the most highly skilled candidates (so-called "creaming"). Even in those instances where participants did improve skill levels, this did not result in significant increases to wages or job security. Lafer attributes this to a flawed fundamental assumption that the private sector job market is working as it should, notwithstanding the lack of any evidence connecting unemployment and poverty with so-called "skills mismatches."

Lafer then proceeds to deconstruct the political motivations behind programs such as JTPA (and its successor Workforce Investment Act). Notwithstanding the programs' unsuccessful record, job training rhetoric continues to be promoted and the programs continue to be funded. So what is driving support for what is essentially a failed policy? Lafer suggests that such programs serve to "allow…lawmakers of both parties to survive the politics of recession by placating the poor without alienating the mighty,"[37] and divert attention away from the real problem by "focus[ing] instead on the failures of individual workers."[38] In a more cynical, yet salient remark, Lafer delves further into the motivations of groups like the Chamber of Commerce and the National Association of Manufacturers for supporting programs such as JTPA as they are currently operated: "The fact that employers prefer to hire workers who are cheap, desperate, and uneducated rather than secure, knowledgeable, and well-paid, suggests that the 'soft skills' they look for in job applicants have more to do with subordination than with team-building."[39]

Economic Models to Explain Overeducation

The benefit of economic models is that they can help us understand a complex reality. Their disadvantage is that they fail to capture the whole of reality, and a focus on one model can blind analysts to empirical problems. Human capital theory can possibly explain wage inequality, but it does not explain underemployment. Deskilling theory appears to provide a logical explanation for un- and underemployment, but it fails to account for increasing demand for education in conjunction with increasing costs and decreasing rates of return. Therefore, is it possible that other economic models might offer a better explanation of overeducation/underemployment, particularly underemployment of degreed professionals? The rest of this chapter examines possible explanations provided by traditional (i.e., neoclassical) theories of supply and demand, credentialism, bifurcated labor markets, winner-take-all markets, job competition and assignment models.

Traditional Supply and Demand

Is there a simple supply-and-demand explanation for overeducation? That is, are there simply too many people with advanced degrees such that the job market is not able to absorb them? Under a traditional economic model, aggregate overqualification would tend to explain wage stagnation better than the skills deficit arguments. Combined with status theory, increased demand for education is created when individuals value the status of education more than return-on-investment. Demand for education can also be created by state policy decisions that require the broadening of educational opportunity as a strategy for balancing social equity. Either of these scenarios could explain increases in educational costs that outpace both "natural" demand and inflation.

Economists tend to be enamored of the concept of equilibrium. In classical economics, the equilibrium price of something is represented by the point where the supply and demand curves intersect. This hypothetical state in which all supply is consumed and all demand is satisfied is also known as the "market clearing" price. The theoretical inevitability of market clearing was challenged during the Great Depression because it could not explain persistent high rates of unemployment. The problem with labor markets is how one determines what is considered "supply" and what is considered "demand." Jobs are traditionally regarded as the "demand" side, which economists generally define as the aggregate number of dollars chasing a particular good or service. Workers and their skills are usually regarded as the "supply" side, although workers can also represent a source of "demand" for jobs—either certain types of jobs, certain wage rates, or other factors of job quality. When there are more workers than jobs, this constitutes both an over-supply of labor (Marx's reserve army) and an under-supply of jobs, which operates to lower wages.

The supply-demand mismatch is further complicated when skills are factored into the equation. Thus, it is possible that there can be a state where there are more workers than jobs (driving average wages down), but employer demand for particular skills can drive wages up in certain "markets." This scenario could explain bifurcated labor markets. In some cases, these markets can be skill or credential-based, i.e., higher paid jobs that require college degrees and lower-paid jobs that do not. Bifurcation can also be industry or occupation-based, as in the example of STEM jobs paying more than jobs involving fine arts or social work.

However, such simplistic analysis does not explain wage differentials within the same occupation. For example, an attorney who works in a large global law firm is paid a substantially higher salary than an attorney working for a state or local government, notwithstanding near identical credentials, job tenure/experience, and

130

possibly similar sized (in terms of number employees) employers. It also does not explain employer demand to increase the number of H-1B visas while at the same time they are laying off workers who have the very skills they allege are in short supply.

The economic concept of oversupply (or overproduction) was first discussed by Marx[40] in the context of industrial production of goods. Marx predicted that the inevitable crisis of capitalism would result from the production of too much material wealth without corresponding real economic value. Production of ever larger quantities permits what is called economies of scale, in which the price per unit falls as the number of units produced increases. Cheaper per-unit costs of production generates production of quantities much greater than can be absorbed by natural demand. As the price of overproduced goods falls, they cannot be sold for a profit, and so their price is further reduced. As constrained producers reduce their labor costs in order to accommodate falling prices, even more constrained workers are unable to buy the reduced-price goods, thus creating the paradox of poverty in the midst of plenty.

Another line of reasoning proposes that job skill mismatches can also arise due to structural labor market inefficiencies and lack of market transparency. Even so-called "free market" economists generally believe that there are certain conditions that must be met for these markets to operate the way they are intended. First, there should be a sufficiently large number of buyers and sellers such that no one of them (or small group of them) can artificially distort the "natural" market. The second condition is that barriers of entry and exit into markets are low. In the realities of today, new and start-up businesses require significant investments of time, money and technical know-how. Moreover, consistent with Braverman's theory, even new businesses require a certain level of scale economies in order to compete, and thus require ever larger (i.e., out of reach for more potential entrepreneurs) initial infusions of capital. The third requirement is that the flow of information regarding prices and quality of goods and services is both trustworthy and accessible to everyone in the market. Proponents of this line of reasoning believe that if the "system" provided better information about job markets, better matching mediators between workers and jobs, and better support systems for job seekers (i.e., relocation assistance), incidents of both underemployment and skills shortage complaints would be greatly reduced.

Malcolm Brynin, a Professor and researcher at the University of Essex (UK) Institute for Social and Economic Research, attempted to find causal explanations for overeducation in the context of traditional supply and demand analysis. In this study,[41] Brynin combined measures for both credentials and status, perhaps attempting to determine if there was some sort of "status" premium desired by credential–seekers unrelated to economic returns. The main component of Brynin's study was a longitudinal measure of first and second job status across two worker cohorts, acknowledging that most workers have low status jobs starting out. As expected, second jobs had higher status measures than first jobs for both cohorts, but the later cohort started out at even lower status jobs than the earlier cohort, and was subject to declining social status in second jobs as well.

Brynin suggests that his data tends to refute theories that overqualified individuals move into more appropriate occupational levels as they advance in their careers. Additionally, the premium afforded by overqualification appeared to be declining over time. Brynin concluded that he could not support a theoretical explanation for overqualification other than excess supply.[42] However, the bottom line of Brynin's findings are that as more people are bettering themselves through education, the jobs as a whole are declining in both status and pay. Just as Braverman argues that commodification can apply to services as well as physical goods, overproduction can apply to educated workers in the same manner.

Laura Servage, a Professor at the University of Alberta, describes a similar phenomenon with the production of "professional doctorate" degrees.[43]   For example, as doctoral students have increasing difficulty finding employment in the academic job market, degree-conferring institutions are tailoring their offerings to produce graduates with more interdisciplinary and applied research skills for employment in non-academic industries. While acknowledging that doctoral education should be designed to fulfill societal needs and not be constrained to narrow academic pursuits, Servage expresses concern that the proposed reforms will induce academia to "align itself with the work of post-industrial capitalism, rather than maintain the intellectual autonomy necessary to examine and critique it."[44]

What studies like Servage's suggest is that "knowledge" in the broad sense of comprehensive understanding, problem-solving, and critical thinking is not the same as more mundane "skills" around which most job descriptions are based. Moreover, neither the credentialism theory model nor the human capital theory model accounts for the paradox of a persistent statistical link between educational attainment and income in conjunction with the phenomenon of credential inflation. What most of the neo-liberal and economics-based theories lack is any accounting for the effects of social capital and educational and labor market positioning, i.e., status issues.   They also fail to account for the socio-ideological environment that determines what skills are "valued" and will be rewarded in the marketplace. As C. Wright Mills describes it, "In such an atmosphere, intellectual activity that does not have relevance to established money and power is not likely to be highly valued."[45]

The perversion of the education-jobs paradox is that workers acquire more schooling not when urged by employer demand, but return to school when employer demand is at its lowest. One academic study found that enrollment in community colleges rose 4% among adults for each 1% rise in the unemployment rate.[46] Another study examined the relationship between recessions and total college enrollment over four decades (1970-2010), and found that during and one to two years following recessions, college enrollment increased about 3.7 times more than the average annual enrollment increase between recessions. [47] A third study suggests that mass credentialing systems supported by an "educational welfare state" serve to alleviate un- and underemployment by temporarily removing workers from the labor market and ensuring political stability. [48]

Credentialism

Credentialism represents the opposite side of the skills shortage coin. Credentialism is defined as an over-emphasis on formal academic credentials when making hiring or promotional decisions. While the skills shortage argument proposes that the educational process is not delivering "value" in terms of worker skills, credentialism proposes that ever-higher levels of formal education are required (but not necessary) to perform what are essentially the same jobs. Credentialism has also been associated with status sorting, a form of signaling shorthand to employers that the individual has not only some basic level of skills, but can perform in an environment of institutional dictate and accepts the legitimacy of social and institutional hierarchies.[49]

There are some reasons that could explain why credentialism is on the rise. The economic explanation is that increasing aggregate educational levels operates as the sociological equivalent of inflation, with ever-higher levels of formal schooling required for jobs that traditionally did not require it. In a weak job market, where there are literally hundreds of applicants for each advertised open position, employers are able to demand higher levels of formal credentialing. There is also some evidence that employers may view education as a proxy for other desired traits such as intelligence, trainability, or self-discipline. "Employers…prefer more highly educated employees, if it were not for their higher wages or their higher likelihood of resigning from less challenging jobs."[50] There is also the practical task of screening a large number of applicants, which can be expedited through a simple upgrade of job requirements. From a workforce development policy perspective, credentialism pushes those without formal education further down the job queue, and as these individuals are increasingly unable to find jobs, there is increasing public pressure to create job-training programs. The result is a feedback loop in which workers are motivated to continually upgrade their training and credentials solely to insure that they do not lose ground in the competition for jobs.

Employer responses to the 2012 *Chronicle of Higher Education*/American Public Media survey suggest that credentialism is alive and well:

Most entry-level positions require a BA; It [BA] is absolutely required for entry into the workforce.

A Bachelor's is needed to get in the door. It's the new HS diploma.

...most think of a BA today as the equivalent what was thought of years ago as a High School Degree.

It seems that for a lot of the higher paying jobs you will still need graduate level education. A standard undergrad degree just doesn't cut it in some fields anymore.

A Bachelor's degree is the lowest degree possible to succeed. In reality, a Masters is preferable.

Everyone has a Bachelor's. They come a dime a dozen, if not more than that. A Master's is the beginning degrees/experiences that cause a person to stand out now.

Some employer statements directly address the phenomenon of credential inflation:

... the value of a Bachelor's degree has declined since there are so many prospective employees with graduate degrees looking for jobs and willing to accept a position and salary that would have been filled by someone with a Bachelor's degree a few years ago.

A degree may get you the job but not more money than the original salary guidelines.

These same employers also prefer a five-year combined Bachelor's and Master's degree over the traditional four-year Bachelors. However, only about a third of them (31%) would absolutely insist on a Bachelor's degree, with approximately another third (34%) stating they would waive the degree for "a particularly outstanding candidate," while the final third (36%) admitted they "look for candidates with the right fit regardless of degree." Indeed, experience outweighed academic credentials in hiring priorities, even when results were broken down by level of hiring authority and type of industry.[51]

Some survey comments also suggested that employers viewed a college degree as a proxy for other skills: "…it prepares individuals for the workforce by teaching them responsibility, strong work ethic, writing, and computer skills;" "A person with a degree is more likely to show maturity and motivation;" "Proves a student has 'staying power.'" Survey results thus lend evidence to theories that employers value educational credentials, even if they are not absolutely necessary to perform the specific job functions.[52]

Bifurcated Labor Markets

The bifurcation of labor has its origins in the beginning of industrialization, even prior to Taylorism and scientific management. The motivation for bifurcation was proposed by Charles Babbage (1791-1871), an English mathematician from an elite, wealthy family who is credited with the invention of the earliest computing device. Babbage's *On the Economy of Machinery and Manufactures*[53] proposed that it was wasteful and inefficient to pay someone a manager's salary to engage in lower level activities, thus the better practice was to delegate all lower level activities to lower paid workers so that the manager's time could be spent on higher level activities (and justified his higher wage). Braverman suggests that Babbage's logic, rather than Taylorist job redesign, was the motivation that transformed the traditional clerical profession from general office workers to higher-paid managers, mid-level administrators, and the masses of lower-paid "clerical" personnel, and it continues to transform work today.[54]

In more modern times, labor economists began to take note of a documented disappearance of jobs in the middle range of incomes beginning in the 1980s—an observable loss of the kind of jobs which traditionally supported the American middle class.[55] So-called "segmented market theory" had appeared earlier, but it was promulgated by a small group of radical political economists that developed a line of research outside of the economics mainstream. Segmented, or dual market theory, proposes that the labor market is divided into a primary sector of high-wage jobs, stable employment, and substantial returns to investments in human capital, and a secondary market of low wage, insecure jobs with low rates of return to human capital.

However, some economists found that, when tested against empirical data, the dual labor market model outperformed an equally complex single labor market model, and also performed well against an absolute standard.[56] These studies found that wage differentials were highly correlated across various industries and occupations and "cannot be attributed to temporary disequilibria."[57] In this model, un- and underemployment are created through two mechanisms. First, primary jobs are rationed, and workers may rationally choose to be unemployed while awaiting a place in the primary sectors. Secondly, workers in the secondary sector suffer considerable frictional unemployment as the "market" adjusts to continual shifts in the level and distribution of demand (the so-called "flexible" work force).

By the 1990s, most economists recognized the reality of some form of dual labor markets, or the bifurcation of jobs into "good" higher paying, full time jobs with benefits, and "bad" low-paying, part-time jobs without benefits.[58]   Structurally, this has been represented by corporate outsourcing, or the division of work functions into "core" (regular, full-time employees) and "periphery" (the outsourced, contingent employees). While this bifurcation has resulted in wage growth in higher paying occupations, the aggregate effect of a loss of the majority of jobs in the middle has been lower growth in real average wages.[59] Evidence that wage dispersion occurs within as well as across occupational groups supports this hypothesis. Thus, those workers who are stuck in the secondary labor markets, regardless of their level of skill or education, do not (or cannot) realize gains from investments in education or their own productivity. Or, in the words of Livingstone, "The knowledge society is alive and well...[T]he knowledge economy...is still illusory."[60]

Bifurcated labor market theory also provides an explanatory framework for income inequalities, or what economists term "wage dispersion." This phenomenon explains how wages could be stagnant at the same time employment was growing. One study found that while employment growth was highest for upper and lower earnings groups, middle earners experienced the greatest wage losses from the recession of the early 1990s.[61] These studies also suggested that the causes of wage dispersion were more complex than a simple replacement of manufacturing jobs with "service" jobs. For example, the broad "service" sector contained executives and professionals, whose incomes were rising sharply, and operators, fabricators, administrative, sales, and retail workers whose incomes were also rising, but to a much lesser degree. Thus, although there was some growth in high-wage jobs, the greater growth in low-wage jobs— along with the destruction of middle-wage jobs—resulted in the paradox of relatively stagnant wages in the aggregate, in spite of considerable growth in overall employment.

A study by the Economic Policy Institute[62] confirmed that the "typical worker" has been experiencing overall wage stagnation between 1989 and 2010, although high school graduates (without college degrees) and the public sector were more negatively affected. Post-Great Recession studies[63] again found a shift toward both high paying and low paying occupations with losses in the middle, but the mean real average wage decline could be specifically attributed to growth of employment in lower paying occupations (food service, health care support, and personal care service) that outweighed the growth in high paying occupations (management, computer, technical, mathematical, and healthcare practitioner). An alternate explanation for the development of a two-tiered job market is corporate demand for a "flexible" workforce. Such a workforce is comprised of a dichotomy of low-wage jobs with intermittent and unpredictable just-in-time work schedules, and professional salaried jobs that require workers to be electronically tethered to work 24 hours a day to accommodate a globalized economy, creating the paradox of both involuntary part-time and "overwork."[64] Increasing public recognition of a bifurcated labor market also encouraged social change advocates to urge public support for more young adults to attend college or the provision of alternative training programs as a solution to income inequality.[65]

Sociologists have recently regained an interest in income stagnation and wage inequality, which they had ceded for decades to labor economists. Sociology by definition concerns itself with how social structures impact individual behavior and outcomes, yet its recent contributions to wage theory tend to focus on gender and racial wage gaps or poverty, that is, on how positions in the earnings distribution are allocated rather than on how the system itself is structured.

Martina Morris and Bruce Western, sociologists at Pennsylvania State University and Princeton University respectively, conducted a meta-analytical review of the literature in an attempt to encourage sociologists to develop an alternative framework for the study of stratification and inequality. They found that income polarization was not only occurring between demographic groups (women and racial minorities) but within groups as well, with full-time employed white men, "traditionally the most privileged and secure group" also experiencing wage stagnation and polarization.[66] Their review suggested that demographic factors such as the entry of the Baby Boom cohort, large numbers of women, and an influx of both legal and illegal immigrants into the labor force did not significantly depress overall wages.

Morris and Western then turn to an analysis of macroeconomic and institutional factors. They found that deindustrialization, or the loss of manufacturing jobs with concomitant replacement by "service" jobs, seems to be a good explanation for the "good jobs/bad jobs" dichotomy, but, as earlier studies also suggested, it could not explain the wage inequality found within the sectors. Morris and Western then analyzed the effect of the apparent abandonment of the practice by large companies of creating internal labor markets. Rather than compete for labor in the external market, large firms in the past created internal markets by means of lifetime employment, firm specific on-the-job training, pathways to upward mobility, and relative job security. Competitive pressures have nearly eliminated these internal job markets, as large firms began a wave of downsizing in the late 1980s, and formerly "secure" jobs were replaced (if at all) by part time and contingent jobs. Morris and Western state that, "technology may have played a role in growing inequality but not in a skill-based way," and suggest that firm-level changes present a key area for future research.[67]

Morris and Western then examined globalization in the context of trade and capital flows. Capital flows have received little attention even though they theoretically suggest an effect on inequality, but the overall magnitude of foreign investment is very small. Trends in trade also superficially support inequality effects of globalization, but the authors cite studies that find its effects are concentrated in manufacturing and thus represent a small share of total employment. The only phenomena that Morris and Western found to have had a fairly consistent causal role in wage inequality were a decade-long freeze in the legal minimum wage (resulting in a dramatic decline in the real earnings of those at the bottom) and a decline in unionization (accounting for 20% of the overall rise in male wage inequality). Ironically, a number of studies find increasing wage inequality even among union members.

The bifurcated labor market model explains how demand for higher level skills can co-exist with underemployment and also explains wage inequality. It is consistent with Braverman's criteria that the issue of relevance is not the level of technology or even the type of work, but whether or not the work process is resulting in the polarization of skill and wages. It also is apparent that these phenomena cannot be examined apart from institutional, political, and global trends. However, regardless of discipline (economics or sociology) or analytical framework (human capital theory, labor degradation theory, or dual labor market model), nearly every study seems to suggest that while the majority of working Americans are losing ground, professional employees are gaining both in terms of absolute and relative wages. So, if professionals are underemployed, it cannot be explained by economic models examined thus far.

Winner-Take-All Markets
Extreme forms of wage polarization can create what economists term winner-take-all markets, in which a relatively few at the top receive excess rewards disproportionate to their marginal product while everyone else receives disproportionately less. The

141

typical example used to illustrate this phenomenon is the astronomical salaries of sports and entertainment celebrities when compared to the majority of low-paid artists and minor league athletes. In such markets, it is the relative ranking that determines reward and not traditional productivity. Winner-take-all markets create massive inefficiencies when some markets attract too many competitors while others are underserved (an analogy to Marx's poverty in the midst of oversupply). For example, in the late 1980s and early 1990s, the media touted astronomical salaries of some business executives and some lawyers, resulting in a massive influx of students into M.B.A. and law programs. There are arguments that this skewed a more "natural" operation of occupational choice and drew talent away from more socially necessary STEM and teaching occupations.

One of the best comprehensive discussions about winner-take-all markets is Robert Frank and Philip Cook's 1995 *The Winner Take All Society.* Frank and Cook provide detailed, real-life examples that demonstrate how barely perceptible "quality" margins can be magnified into huge gains. One example is what they term "production cloning," which has been particularly prevalent in the entertainment industry. Because the "best" performers are now able to distribute their work on mass, national markets, this crowds out potential local markets for those talented, but slightly less stellar performers.

Other processes involve early capture of markets, one of which Frank and Cook term "lock-in through learning or investment,"[68] and what others have termed "path dependency." Early market capture is also facilitated by more traditional economic operations such as economies of scale and globalized distribution networks. These self-reinforcing feedback mechanisms permit those who capture an early advantage, no matter how slight, to continue leveraging early advantages to create compounding advantages. These processes crowd out competitors from the market by making it more difficult for everyone else to find and secure a profitable position.

A more problematic concern is what exactly constitutes "talent" or "quality." Frank and Cook further discuss how behaviors and attitudes such as habit formation, acquired tastes, and positional anxieties are affected by winner-take-all environments. That is, as a few become successful, they tend to set the standards that are desired by everyone else, which further increases their own market dominance. Additionally, as purchasing power itself becomes more concentrated, this creates what Frank and Cook term "deep pocket" winner-take-all markets. They cite the example of wealthy individuals who spare no expense in the purchase of everything from corporate tax attorneys and lobbyists to artwork and restaurant meals. Market research itself becomes more narrowly focused on gratifying the desires of ever fewer people with huge fortunes while the needs of the majority are neglected.

Frank and Cook make the argument that winner-take-all markets are economically inefficient. Since most people tend to overestimate their odds of success,[69] winner-take-all markets attract too many contestants, and society's total income would be higher if all of the "losers" in these markets chose other occupations instead. In winner-take-all markets, people are incentivized to engage in socially unproductive activities and even wasteful "positional arms races"[70] because the potential for gain is so great. Investment and consumption patterns are developed with no thought toward the long term. The talents and abilities of the "losers"—talents which could serve to address the complex problems of modern society—are wasted.

However, Frank and Cook suggest that economic inefficiency is not the worst threat from winner-take-all markets. There is an overall degradation of society, as people have to compete even harder for fewer rewards. The constant scramble for every minute advantage results in both wasteful investment and overwork, destroying families and friendships. Moral imperatives that once served to limit rampant greed are shattered. Society glorifies the meteoric rise along with instant fame and success, rather than genuine social merit or consistent, predictable quality which must be developed over time. The quality of culture itself becomes degraded, because as markets influence culture, culture itself shapes preferences. Frank and Cook cite the increasing amount of violence in popular entertainment, notwithstanding public complaints against it. Frank and Cook argue that this phenomenon has even "increasingly impoverished political debate," leading to "an increasingly ill-informed and ill-tempered electorate."[71] Others have also lamented how the winner-take-all phenomenon has affected the organizational landscape of American politics, creating a kind of self-perpetuating feedback loop that continues to favor the fortunes of the rich and impoverishes everyone else.[72]

One of the weaknesses of human capital theory in explaining underemployment is that it focuses almost solely on the attributes of the worker and ignores the attributes of both the individual job and the aggregate job market. Economists who subscribe to human capital theory suggest that income dispersion occurs because somehow the best performers have gotten better with respect to everyone else. In Frank and Cook's contrarian view, skill distribution among people has not so much changed as the transformation of markets. A person with a certain level of human capital will realize its full value only if they are in a position that provides adequate opportunity to do so. Thus, early advantages take on an urgent necessity. Elite academic institutions have become gatekeepers to the avenues of privilege, and failure to be accepted into one of these institutions can foreclose certain opportunities forever. Even after a student graduates from school, the job market is subject to the same kind of self-reinforcement and amplification of early advantage that create winner-take-all markets, which becomes particularly acute in a job market where upward mobility is constrained by hierarchy. As Frank and Cook conclude, it is the distribution of opportunities and not the distribution of talent that makes the greater difference in personal outcomes.

Job Competition and Assignment Models

Because no single economic model could adequately explain overeducation and underemployment in non-recessionary economies, academic economists continued to work on the problem. Greg Duncan of the University of Michigan Survey Research Center and Saul Hoffman, a professor of economics at the University of Delaware, developed an alternative to the human capital theory model to explain overeducation, which they termed the job competition model.[73] In this model, wages (i.e., marginal product) are pre-determined by the job and not by the worker. This model takes the extreme view that wages are solely determined by employers (who create the job requirements) and the aggregate skill level of workers is irrelevant. In the job competition model, an individual's wages are determined by the worker's relative position among job seekers and not some absolute skill level.

While the job competition model accounts for the phenomenon of overeducation (and the acquiring of education as a defensive necessity), it predicts a zero rate of return to surplus education because wages are predetermined by job requirements. Job competition theory therefore does not account for the observed fact that increasing education does indeed produce a wage premium, even if this premium represents a lower (and decreasing) rate of return to education. Thus, while the job competition model fills a significant gap in human capital theory, it does so at the cost of creating a conflicting model that ignores significant empirical evidence.

Michael Sattinger, a professor of economics at the University at Albany, has developed a model that provides a plausible explanation for overeducation while at the same time accommodates human capital theory. Sattinger's model describes the job market as a group of N dogs presented with a batch of *n* bones delivered by a dump truck.[74] Assuming that each dog can only receive one bone and that the bones can be assigned a value, equilibrium is established when every dog has a bone that is not desired by any other dog that could

145

take it away, and each dog prefers its own bone to any bone it could take away from another dog. In this so-called "assignment" model then, the value of any dog's bone is a function of both the assortment of bones available and the individual dog's ability to compete for them.

Analogized to the job market, an individual's wages are thus a function of both the jobs that are available and the individual's ability to compete in the market. That is, the assignment models seem to describe the actual reality of labor markets, especially those where there are more dogs than bones. In such conditions, dogs lowest in the hierarchy will receive no bone at all and the rest of the dogs will accept less than desirable bones—or bones that are lower in quality than the dog would receive if there had been enough bones to go around. Sattinger argues that assignment models explain why the distribution of abilities does not conform to the distribution of earnings because it emphasizes the roles of both choice and demand in the valuation of particular abilities, as well as the "extent to which the economy exaggerates or moderates those differences."[75]

Other researchers[76] found the assignment model to be most consistent with observed data in that the wage return to surplus education was greater than zero (defying the prediction of job competition theory), but overeducated individuals were nonetheless subject to a wage penalty (not accounted for by human capital theory). However, like the human capital theory model and other models based on neoclassical economics, assignment models also presume that choices are motivated by utility maximization and there is a universal consensus on "value."

Summary and Conclusion

Consistent with academic findings, the US Bureau of Labor Statistics predicts the greatest job growth in low wage jobs, some growth will occur in high wage jobs, and the greatest loss of jobs will be in the middle.[77] This is also consistent with a bifurcated market, which has been created by the dictates of profit and efficiency. In order to compete for the decreasing number of "good" jobs, the continuous accumulation of credentials becomes a defensive necessity. Because there are many more workers with credentials than "good" jobs, the excess is cast off into the "bad job" market, where they indeed may have a competitive advantage, but not much of a future.

In such a system, the efficiency gains are captured by the owners of capital, which further enlarges not just their wealth, but their ability to dictate the terms of labor market structures. When the owners of capital can dictate which skills will be valued, this eventually translates into educational offerings, as schools are naturally motivated to insure that their graduates can secure decent employment. However, educational credentials are not pursued for the noble purposes of serving the world or even of making the highest and best use of one's natural skills and abilities. Credentials are pursued (and designed) solely for their value in the labor market, that is, their ability to serve the accumulation of capital for others. Education itself is constructed to serve the system by producing obedient "workers" rather than citizens who have been trained to think critically and could possibly challenge it.

While the owners of capital expropriate the gains of the system they have created, the inefficiencies are externalized onto individual workers, taxpayers, and society as a whole. Taxpayers are becoming increasingly aware that state-provided income support payments are not, for the most part, going to some mythical welfare queen, but providing subsistence to people with jobs. As workers experience more frequent and longer periods of un- and under-employment, they are unable to plan for a future, including perhaps providing education for their own children. Many will be unable to retire, creating friction with younger generations who are looking to move into their jobs. Workers frustrated by their inability to build a decent life begin to view "the other" (men vs. women, Whites vs. Blacks, natives vs.

immigrants, young vs. old) as depriving them of opportunity. Sattinger's model of desperate junkyard dogs fighting over scraps in a situation where they have no power is the model that probably rings the truest. But the real tragedy is that human talent—talent that could be put to use to solve some of our seemingly intractable social problems—is going to waste.

Notes

1 Naisbitt, J., & Aburdine, P. (2000). Megatrends 2000. London, England: Pan Books.

2 https://www.whitehouse.gov/blog/2010/12/06/president-obama-north-carolina-our-generation-s-sputnik-moment-now

3 Merchant, N. (2012, December 7). Dewhurst says state needs more job-ready graduates. *Austin-American Statesman*, p. A12. Ironically, Texas had laid off 25,000 public school workers in 2012, 10,718 who were teachers, due to state budget shortfalls. Mellon, E. (2012, March 16). *Houston Chronicle*. Retrieved from http://www.chron.com/news/houston-texas/article/School-districts-statewide-cut-25-000-positions-3413929.php

4 National Commission on Excellence in Education. (1983). A Nation at Risk: The Imperative for Educational Reform. Report retrieved from: http://www.scribd.com/doc/49151492/A-Nation-at-Risk

5 Chronicle of Higher Education/American Public Media. (2012, December). The role of higher education in career development: Employer perceptions. Retrieved from: http://chronicle.com/items/biz/pdf/Employers%20Survey.pdf

6 National Association of Manufacturers. (2013, January). Skills gap holding back U.S. economic growth. Washington, DC: National Association of Manufacturers. Retrieved from: http://www.nam.org/Newsroom/Press-Releases/2013/01/The-NAM-Announces-Formation-of-New-Immigration-Coalition-to-Boost-STEM-Education/

7 Lenton, D. (2010). Analysis: Looming skills gap threatens economy. *Engineering and Technology 5*(10), 10.

8 Ruse, D. H., & Jansen, K.E. (2008). Using human capital planning to predict future talent needs. *CUPA-HR Journal, 59*(1), 28-33; also Heffes, E. M., & Marshall, J. (2007). Most company programs seen as inadequate. *Financial Executive, 23*(4), 10. Retrieved from: http://www.highbeam.com/doc/1G1-163868658.html

9 Galagan, P. (2009-2010). Bridging the skills gap, Part I. *Public Manager, 38*(4), 61-67. Retrieved from: http://www.astd.org/Publications/Magazines/The-Public-Manager.

10 Thomson, J. C. (2009, December). Closing the accounting talent gap. *The CPA Journal*, 13-14. Retrieved from: http://www.nysscpa.org/cpajournal/toc2009.htm

11 ManpowerGroup. (2013). 2013 Talent Shortage Survey Research Results at p. 13. Retrieved from: http://www.manpowergroup.com/wps/wcm/connect/587d2b45-c47a-4647-a7c1-e7a74f68fb85/2013_Talent_Shortage_Survey_Results_US_high+res.pdf?MOD=AJPERES

12 *Id.* at p. 16.

13 *Id.* at p. 15.

14 Chronicle of Higher Education/American Public Media. (2012). Ibid.

15 Acton, R. (2008, April). Pharmaceutical engineers: Your country needs you! TCE: *The Chemical Engineer*, 802, 46-47; Yongbeom, K., Hsu, J., & Stern, M. (2006). An update on the IS/IT skills gap. Journal of Information Systems Education, 17(4), 395-402; TCE: *The Chemical Engineer*. (2007, November 6). Engineering to face 15% "people deficit," 797; Goldstein, R. (2005). The intelligence skills gap: Building the right workforce to meet our nation's security needs. *Public Manager*, 2005, 34(3), 49-52; Mander, K.C. (2001). The decline and fall of the American programmer? Communications of the ACM, 44(7), 43-44.

16 Although these reports are based primarily on industry-sponsored surveys or other anecdotal data, their findings and conclusions are frequently reported in the mainstream media and incorporated into political speeches and policy agendas.

17 Dietz, F. (1998). Teaching the technology workforce. https://www.asme.org/about-asme/news-media/newsletters

18 *Id.*

19 Chevalier A., & Lindley, J. (2007, August). Overeducation and the skills of UK graduates. Centre for the Economics of Education, London School of Economics. Discussion Paper 79.

20 *Id.* at p. 11.

21 *Id.* at p. 11.

22 *Id.* at p. 17.

23 Cappelli, P. (2011, October 24). Why companies aren't getting the employees they need. *Wall Street Journal Reports*. Retrieved from http://online.wsj.com/article/SB10001424052970204422404576596630897409182.html

24 Beach, G. J. (2013, June 15). "Skills gap" fault can be laid at foot of education. *Austin American-Statesman*, p. A14.

25 Dwyer, J. (2007). Take your pick. *IET Engineering Management, 17*(1), 34-37.

26 *Id.* at p. 34.

27 De Witte, M. & Steijn, B. (2000). Automation, job content, and underemployment. *Work, Employment & Society, 14*(2), 245-264 at p. 261.

28 Handel, M. J. (2003*). Skills mismatch in the labor market. Annual Review of Sociology, 29*(1), 135-165.
 Retrieved from: http://www.annualreviews.org/journal/soc

29 *Id.* at p. 146.

30 *Id.* at p. 135.

31 *Id.* at p. 147.

32 *Id.* at p. 159. "...the absence of better-paid employment partly reflects structural shifts in the kinds of jobs the economy generates rather than the intrinsic limits of potential workers."

33 *Id.* at p. 139.

34 *Id.* at p. 139.

35 *Id.* at p. 160.

36 Lafer, Gordon. (2002). *The job training charade.* Ithaca, NY: Cornell University Press.

37 *Id.* at p. 189.

38 *Id.* at 157.

39 *Id.* at 72.

40 Marx, K. (1844). Economic and philosophical manuscripts. In Marx-Engels *Gesamtuasgabe, Vol. 3.* Berlin, Germany: Marx-Engels Institute (Pub. 1932).

41 Brynin, M. (2002). Overqualification in employment. *Work, Employment & Society, 16*(4), 637-654.

42 *Id.* at p. 650.

43 Servage, L. (2009). Alternative and professional doctoral programs: What is driving the demand? *Studies in Higher Education, 34*(7), 765-779.

44 *Id.* at p. 768.

45 Mills, C.W. (1951). *White collar: The American middle class.* New York, NY: Oxford University Press at p. 156.

46 Betts, J. R. & McFarland, L. L. (1995). Safe port in a storm: The impact of labor market conditions on community college enrollments. *Journal of Human Resources*, 30(4), 741-765.

151

47 Kantrowitz, M. (2010, August 16). Countercyclicality of college enrollment trends. Retrieved from http://www.finaid.org/educators/20100816countercyclicality.pdf

48 Brown, D. K. (2001). The social sources of educational credentialism: Status cultures, labor markets, and organizations. *Sociology of Education, 74*(4), 19-34 at p. 29.

49 *Id.*

50 Van De Werfhorst, H. G. (2002). Fields of study, acquired skills and the wage benefit from a matching job. *Acta Sociologica 45*(4), 287-303.

51 Chronicle of Higher Education/American Public Media. (2012, December). The role of higher education in career development: Employer perceptions. Retrieved from: http://chronicle.com/items/biz/pdf/Employers%20Survey.pdf

52 *Id.*

53 Babbage, C. (1835). *On the economy of machinery and manufactures (4th Ed.).* London, England: Charles Knight.

54 Braverman, H. (1974). *Labor and monopoly capital: The degradation of work in the twentieth century* (1998 Edition). New York, NY: Monthly Review Press.

55 Myles, J. (1988, October). The changing wage distribution of jobs, 1981-1986. *The Labour Force* (Statistics Canada, 71-001), 85-129.

56 Dickens, W. T. & Lang, K. (1988). The re-emergence of the segmented labor market theory. *American Economic Review, 78*(2), 129-134. Retrieved from: https://www.aeaweb.org/aer/index.php

57 *Id.* at p. 131.

58 Morris, M. & Western, B. (1999). Inequality in earnings at the close of the twentieth century. *Annual Review of Sociology, 25*(1), 623-657; also Kalleberg, A. L., Reskin, B., & Hudson, K. (2000). Bad jobs in America: Standard and nonstandard employment relations and job quality in the United States. *American Sociological Review, 65*(4), 256-278. Retrieved from: http://asr.sagepub.com

59 Keller, R. (2009). How shifting occupational composition has affected the real average wage. *Monthly Labor Review, 132*(6), 26-38. Retrieved from: http://www.bls.gov/opub/mlr/2009/06/art2full.pdf

60 Livingstone, D. W. (1999). *The education jobs gap: Underemployment or economic democracy.* Toronto, Ontario: Garamond Press at p. 163.

61 Ilg, R. E., & Haugen, S. E. (2000). Earnings and employment trends in the 1990s. *Monthly Labor Review, 123*(3), 21-33. Retrieved from: http://www.bls.gov/opub/mlr/2000/03/art2full.pdf

62 Mishel, L. & Shierholz, H. (2011, March 15). The sad but true story of wages in America. Economic Policy Institute. Retrieved from: http://www.epi.org/publication/the_sad_but_true_story_of_wages_in_america/

63 Keller, R. (2009). *Supra.*

64 Rasmus, J. (2006) *The war at home: The corporate offensive from Ronald Reagan to George W. Bush.* San Ramon, CA: Kylos Productions, LLC.; also Lambert, S. (2012, Sept. 19). When flexibility hurts. *The New York Times.* Retrieved from: http://www.nytimes.com/2012/09/20/opinion/low-paid-women-want-predictable-hours-and-steady-pay.html?ref=opinion&_r+1

65 Autor, D. (2011). The polarization of job opportunities in the U.S. labor market: Implications for employment and earnings. *Community Investments, 23*(2), 11-16. Retrieved from: http://www.frbsf.org/community-development/files/CI_IncomeInequality_Autor.pdf

66 Morris, M. & Western, B. (1999). Inequality in earnings at the close of the twentieth century. *Annual Review of Sociology, 25*(1), 623-657 at p. 623.

67 *Id.* at p. 642.

68 Frank, R. H. & Cook, P. J. (1995). *The winner-take-all society.* New York, NY: Free Press at p. 34.

69 Adam Smith, in *The Wealth of Nations* (1776) noted, "The over-weening conceit which the greater part of men have of their own abilities...[and] the absurd presumption in their own good fortune."

70 Frank & Cook. (1995). *Supra* at p. 15.

71 *Id.* at p. 203. As I cite this sentence, the 2016 U.S. Presidential election provides ample evidence of its truth.

72 Hacker, J. S. & Pierson, P. (2010). Winner-take-all-politics: Public policy, political organization, and the precipitous rise of top incomes in the United States. *Politics & Society, 38*(2), 152-204. Retrieved from: http://pas.sagepub.com/content/38/2/152.short

73 Duncan, J. & Hoffman, S. (1981). The incidence and wage effects of overeducation. *Economics of Education Review, 1*(1), 75-86.

74 Sattinger, M. (1993). Assignment models of the distribution of earnings. *Journal of Economic Literature, 31*(2), 831-880. Retrieved from: https://www.aeaweb.org/journals/jel/issues

75 *Id.* at p. 875.

76 McGuiness, S. (2006). Overeducation in the labour market. *Journal of Economic Surveys, 20*(3), 387-418.

77 For a list of the top 15 occupations projected between 2014 and 2024 see: http://data.bls.gov/cgi-bin/print.pl/news.release/ecopro.t06.htm. Eight of these occupations require no formal educational credentials and another three require only a high school diploma or some (non-degree) secondary education. The majority of these occupations pay near or less than the federal poverty level for a family of four. Only four occupations require a Bachelor's degree: registered nurses (#2), general and operations managers (#9), accountants and auditors (#11), and software developers (#14). The largest declines are projected to be in manufacturing, information, and the federal government. http://www.bls.gov/news.release/ecopro.t03.htm

Chapter Five
Professional Underemployment: Findings from the Study

Study Background, Purpose, Design and Objectives

<u>The Nature of Professional Work</u>

CREDENTIALED PROFESSIONALS REPRESENT THE APEX of the workforceskills continuum. The attainment of these credentials represents a huge personal and financial investment. In modern labor markets, the first rung of professional attainment begins with a minimum of a four-year Bachelor's degree. Many also have a Master's Degree or Doctorate (Ph.D.), which requires an additional one to six years of post-graduate schooling. A law degree (J.D.) represents a minimum three-year post-graduate commitment, and a medical degree (M.D.) usually requires at least an additional four years, sometimes more, depending on specialization and medical residency requirements. In the case of many professions (medicine, law, nursing, teaching, and engineering), the degree is not sufficient by itself to gain entry into the profession, as each state imposes additional credentialing requirements (usually in the form of an examination and/or personal background check) before granting a license to practice. On top of the time commitment is enormous costs in terms of tuition, licensing exam preparation, and opportunity costs from delay of entry into the labor market.

The popular media is replete with stories about the skyrocketing cost of higher education and astronomical levels of student educational debt. In addition to costs borne by individual students, the public as a whole also funds their education to varying degrees, in the form of subsidized loans, grants, scholarships, and taxes used to support public colleges and universities. Thus, when a person is unable to utilize professional training, it represents a form of lost human capital both to the individual and to society.

Professional occupations are traditionally associated with a high degree of personal autonomy, high intrinsic job satisfaction, and relative occupational security. Even when a professional is terminated from employment at one organization, the individual's skills are (hypothetically) in sufficient demand that he or she should have relatively little difficulty securing comparable employment elsewhere. Braverman and even later proponents of labor degradation theory had a tendency to assume (at least such can be inferred from their writings) that professionals were generally immune from the forces of rationalization that affected most other occupations. One reason is that their occupations simply required a higher level of independent judgment that could not be reduced to Taylorist formulas (this was obviously before the day of algorithmic supercomputing). A second reason is that many professionals have the option of opening their own practices or otherwise finding ways to offer their services on a consulting basis, which to some degree frees them from the tyranny of organizational dependence. A third reason is that professional societies serve as gatekeepers that, under the guise of protecting "quality" actually operate to limit the competition.

The public sometimes views professional organizations with skepticism, believing that their sole purpose is to preserve monopoly and protect their own. Indeed, public hostility to professional societies goes as far back as Adam Smith's complaints about craft guild monopolies, particularly those in old Europe. However, these organizations also serve purposes that are publicly beneficial. Professionals who belong to these organizations (medical, state bar, scientific, educational, or public interest nonprofits) are required to meet both minimal and aspirational standards—standards that apply to both technical competence and ethical behavior.

Where industrial and corporate organizations are structured hierarchically for the sole purpose of profit, professional organizations are structured as a collegiate group of equals for the purpose of betterment of the profession and the individuals comprising it. Moreover, many professional organizations require the individual to take a professional oath of membership, pledging to maintain professional values and norms against the less noble demands of world and self. In this respect, professionals answer to higher dictates than the production of profit, and are less likely to be motivated by Taylorist incentives such as monetary bonuses for increased quantitative production. Indeed, some research suggests that professional training by its very nature predisposes the individual to "unhappiness and rebellion when faced with the administrative process as it exists in most organizations."[1]

Sources of Professional Alienation

Marx was the first to describe the phenomenon of alienation in the context of work, which he described as separation of the worker from both the production process and ownership of the work product.[2] Later sociological studies describe alienation as a process by which a person becomes estranged from himself by first becoming separated from physical objects, then separated from people, and finally separated from ideas.[3] Most contemporary studies on workplace alienation were conducted in the 1960s and 1970s and were primarily focused on manufacturing and blue-collar employment.[4] There is limited contemporary research on alienation in organizational studies, which has tended to take the form of studies on job dissatisfaction, job commitment, and organizational identification. In an effort to develop an updated construct for the measurement of work alienation, some researchers have discovered some of the same issues that arise with the measurement of overeducation, namely wide variability in how it is measured and how narrowly or broadly it is defined.[5]

Notwithstanding the lack of consensus on measurement and definition of alienation, there are a few consistent themes. With respect to job design, factors found to be associated with alienation are powerlessness/control, which has been described as a lack of control over immediate work processes and conditions, an inability to influence general managerial policies, and an expectancy that an individual's behavior has no impact on outcomes;[6] and meaninglessness/purpose, which is defined as an inability to connect one's work with the larger purpose of the organization or society.[7] Organizational factors that have been found to be associated with alienation are formalized and/or centralized rule-bound bureaucratic hierarchies that interfere with individual autonomy in day-to-day decisions.[8] Professionals, who tend to identify with their work more so than blue-collar workers who view work solely as a means to subsistence, also tend to become alienated if they are not provided creative opportunities to utilize their particularized knowledge.[9]

Moreover, professionals are more likely to be susceptible to alienation emerging from work-role conflicts.[10] One source of this conflict is when organizational demands (e.g., for increased production, output, and efficiency) conflict with professional norms for service, quality, precision, safety, or integrity. Another source of this conflict arises when organizational demands interfere with the professional's relationship with clients. This can occur when the cost dictates of an HMO require a physician to compromise patient care, or when a law firm requires an attorney to compromise a duty of zealous representation (because a client is not deemed sufficiently profitable) or forego representation of a client whose case is politically incorrect (i.e., unacceptable to the firm's owners or traditional clientele).

Current Trends in Professional Occupations

Although this study did not analyze every labor market phenomena that could potentially impact professional underemployment, it supports some major trends that have been documented by both academics and the mainstream media. The STEM (science, technology, engineering, and math) professions have been most affected by globalization, both with respect to outsourcing of jobs and importation of immigrant workers. In medicine and health care, the primary occupational restructuring has been the development of HMOs, which divest decisions about patient care from physicians and other providers on the basis of cost savings (the Taylorist division of conceptual and productive functions). The most significant change to the traditional legal profession has been the adoption of the billable hour, rendering even high-paid attorneys more like blue-collar workers who trade time for dollars. Academia has been subject to the most obvious example of the bifurcated labor market, with a decrease in the total number of tenured faculty, a small increase in the number of "celebrity" faculty with astronomical salaries, and a large increase in the number of non-tenured, lower-paid, contingent adjunct faculty. Professions that once were considered to represent a higher calling, along with associated status and occupational security, now appear to be riddled with working class discontents. Nearly unheard of and practically unthinkable only 20 years ago, today there is talk of unionization among engineers,[11] physicians,[12] and attorneys.[13]

Rationale for Methodology

A challenge in adopting academic work for popular consumption is providing sufficient detail and context about the "how" and the "why" of a study without bogging down in technical minutiae that would likely bore most readers. One also hopes to provide enough of a foundation to convince skeptics that the study was conducted in a rigorous and unbiased manner. With this in mind, I will describe in lay terms how and why this study was constructed as it was without reference to supporting academic literature.

The first part of the study collected quantitative data in the form of surveys that were administered online. From this quantitative data, profiles were constructed of the "typical" respondent (based primarily on specific occupation and type of school) in order to select persons to participate in interviews. The interview material was then analyzed for themes—both those that appeared in the quantitative data and those that emerged from the qualitative data. The final round of analysis cross-corroborated the findings from both sources to identify points of convergence and divergence. The purpose of using both statistics and stories to describe professional underemployment was to use the strength of one type of data to offset the weaknesses of the other. That is, quantitative data gives you a better picture of the population as a whole, but it can miss crucial detail. Conversely, qualitative data provides rich descriptive detail, but is not generalizable to the population as a whole. The final cross-corroborative analysis served as a form of triangulation, which especially reinforced the findings that were consistent.

Data Collection and Initial Analysis

The quality and trustworthiness of any study begins with the quality and trustworthiness of data. However, there is no such thing as "perfect" data, and this is even more so in the context of the limited resources of a doctoral dissertation. For a researcher operating in an environment of constrained resources, the most productive way to deal with less than perfect data is to recognize its inherent deficiencies and accommodate them to the extent possible during the analysis and interpretation phase.

In this study, the initial objective was to collect quantitative surveys from a broad occupational, geographic, and demographic sample of professionals. Survey respondents were screened for 28 specifically defined occupations in the STEM, health care, legal and academic occupations located in the United States (i.e., national in scope). A total of 596 "qualified" online surveys were completed between late March and late May, 2014. There were two primary sources of survey respondents. The first was through a paid survey panel provider, which generated 499 completed surveys. Survey panels are selected through proprietary algorithms, so other than the requested parameters of panelists having a Bachelor's degree or higher, as the researcher I did not know how these panelists were otherwise selected. The online survey itself was set up to automatically disqualify respondents who did not complete a Bachelor's degree or belong to one of the broad occupational categories of STEM (twelve specifically defined occupations or "other STEM"), health care (six specifically defined occupations or "other health care"); law (five specifically defined occupations or "other legal") and academia (five specifically defined occupations or "other academic").

The remaining 102 surveys were collected through the cooperation of various professional organizations, who made the survey link available to their members either via a web page or email invitations. The first group to be contacted about a web page link was the unemployment insurance or workforce development agencies in each of the 48 continental United States. Although a number of these agencies expressed interest in this study, the bottom line for most of them was that state regulations would not permit the agencies to display Internet links from "unaffiliated" sources. Other groups that were contacted about sponsorship were nine national engineering and IT organizations, twenty-six nursing and health care professional organizations, sixteen organizations for teachers and other academics, and all major national and state bar associations. The vast majority of these organizations did not respond. A few of them responded that they were unable to sponsor the survey for various reasons. In the end, the following organizations agreed to make the surveys available to their members: the American Engineering Association (STEM), the Washington Alliance of Technology Workers (STEM), the American Public Health Association (Health Care), the Mississippi State Bar (Law), and the Kansas Bar Association (Law). Overall, information from 596 individual qualified respondents was used in the analysis.

Upon completion of the quantitative analyses, statistical profiles were generated to determine representatives of each occupational group who were underemployed, in addition to identification of respondents chosen to address unreliable career information and labor degradation issues. Although nearly a third of respondents (32.1%) initially agreed to participate in a follow-up interview, many of these individuals were not underemployed or otherwise did not satisfy the parameters of the statistical profiles. Moreover, some three months had elapsed since the earliest surveys were complete, and the interviews were conducted during the prime summer vacation period (July, 2014).

Because of these logistics, there was a significantly decreased response rate in the interviews. Twenty-one invitations to interviews were issued, and five respondents agreed to participate. The interviews explored career motivators and satisfactions, career decision resources, unreliable job market information, professional dissatisfactions, the microeconomics of individual occupations, and labor degradation issues in greater depth and detail. In addition to the interviews, qualitative data was obtained from the unique "other" responses to survey questions.

The benefit of obtaining all survey respondents through third-party intermediaries is that there was no way for me, as the researcher, to consciously or unconsciously, "cherry pick" respondents or influence their responses by verbal or non-verbal cues. The down side of obtaining responses in this matter is that there was no way to gauge the attention of respondents or clear up potential misunderstandings or ambiguities. In the case of the state bar associations, these respondents were from a more limited geographic area than the other professionals. As with all studies using voluntary respondents, there is likely to be a certain degree of self-selection bias. The first level of potential bias is that persons who participate in anonymous surveys differ in some manner from the general population. The second level of potential bias was that all respondents were members of either an

162

online survey panel or a professional organization, which would tend to exclude "lone wolves" and non-joiners, who may indeed have even higher levels of underemployment due to lack of professional networks and other social capital. The third level of bias occurs through subject matter interest. In this case, doctoral dissertation students are typically required to disclose the subject matter of surveys by university Institutional Review Boards. Additionally, my own proclivity is to err on the side of disclosure, fully informing participants about what to expect in terms of subject matter and purpose. Consequently, survey participants in this study are likely to have some reason for interest in underemployment and occupational satisfaction issues. Thus, the underemployment rate among the survey sample should be interpreted conservatively, as it is likely to be higher than among the professional population as a whole.

Quantitative Analysis and Findings

Who is Underemployed?

The initial analysis was run on 596 surveys. Most of these surveys were complete (587), while the remainder (9) were mostly complete, lacking only respondent's demographic data. The occupational breakdown of the sample was STEM (44.8%), health care (15.8%), law (15.8%) and academia (23.7%). Respondents were first asked whether they had been underemployed at any time during their careers. That is, the intention was to determine probabilities that individuals in certain occupations would experience underemployment over their careers rather than determine a cross-sectional underemployment rate for a discrete time period.

Moreover, underemployment was defined conservatively, in order to avoid the ambiguities and construct validity issues identified in the literature, particularly the so-called omitted variable bias (skills differential). Respondents were to affirmatively consider themselves underemployed *only if,* upon attainment of their highest educational degree, they experienced (1) involuntary unemployment, (2)

163

involuntary part-time employment, (3) involuntary contingent employment (temporary or contract work), and (4) any employment in which the job description did not expressly require the respondent's highest educational credential or occupational license. For the sample as a whole, six in ten professionals (60.0%) experienced underemployment at some point over their professional careers.

The respondents were geographically dispersed across the continental United States, residing in 46 of the 50 states plus the District of Columbia. Seventy-nine respondents declined to provide their state of residence. Most of the respondents resided in California (45), New York (37), Mississippi (35), Florida (28), Illinois (27), Pennsylvania (24), Michigan (22), and Ohio (20). This was one of the benefits of obtaining the surveys through a nationwide survey as opposed to locally, in that one avoids the possible anomalies associated with local labor markets (e.g., recent mass layoffs, closing of a military base, meteorological/geophysical disruption, or other events that could skew the data). In addition to educational credentials, survey respondents made additional investments in human capital by obtaining a required state professional license (58.7%) and membership in a professional organization (42.11%).

The initial expectation was that some degree of underemployment would be found in all occupations, but it would be higher in legal and academic occupations and lower in STEM and health care occupations. These expectations were based not so much on the academic literature, but on media stories about the difficulties of recent law school graduates and adjunct faculty in higher education. Conversely, media stories tend to emphasize a skills shortage with respect to STEM and health care careers. Notwithstanding some commentators statements that the "tech industry's persistent claims of worker shortage may be phony,"[14] I was willing to give the skills shortage alarmists the benefit of the doubt in that there might be some possibility of skills shortages in certain technical fields. The overall underemployment rate for the sample as a whole was 60.0%.

Surprisingly, the STEM and health care professionals had the highest rates of underemployment. In descending order, underemployment rates among the occupational categories were: health care (63.8%), STEM (60.3%), academia (60.0%), and law (55.3%).

One possible explanation is that the surveys picked up respondents who were in obscure occupations for which there might be a limited labor market, thus creating higher levels of underemployment. However, the most common occupations in the STEM sample were information technology (IT) professionals (27.4%) and engineers (18.6%), the very professions most likely to be the focus of skills shortage alarmists. Likewise for health care: the primary occupations here were nurses (39.0%) and "other health care" (31.6%). Another curiosity is that the STEM and health care samples were the most occupationally diverse. The majority of the academia sample was comprised of K-12 teachers (53.2%), and legal professionals were for the most part (74.5%) attorneys. One possible explanation for the lowest underemployment rate among attorneys is that, if they are unable to secure traditional employment, they have the option of opening their own law practice. Indeed, two of the interviewees were recent law graduates who had actually done so, following a futile search for regular legal jobs.

Another quantitative analysis was performed to test so-called status-sorting theories. Status sorting is associated with what most people think of as "discrimination." That is, women, racial and ethnic minorities, and graduates of lower "status" educational institutions receive lower returns in the labor market (i.e., they receive lower pay and are more likely to be un- and under-employed) given the same type and level of credential. These tests are based on a statistic called a chi square test for independence, denoted as χ^2. This measurement summarizes the association between two variables, in which a significance (ρ) value has a maximum value of 1 when the variables are perfectly related and a minimum value of zero when the variables have no relationship between them. Larger values of χ^2 are evidence against the null hypothesis (H₀), because the observed counts are far from what would expected if H₀ were true. It is presumed that the majority of readers are not statisticians, but a few of you may want to "know the numbers," so the statistical results are reproduced in the notes.[15] The following paragraphs summarize the results in lay terms and simple percentages.

The sample as a whole was comprised of a majority of women (59.2%) and Whites (73.9%). The breakdown of gender (by percent of women) by occupational category was: STEM (52.6%), health care (72.3%), law (54.4%), and academia (77.5%). A series of two-way contingency analyses was performed which tested underemployment against gender, race, and school status (the status-sorting tests), as well as age and highest academic degree. With respect to demographics, women (61.0%) were more likely to be underemployed than men (58.5%), with a moderate to strong relationship between gender and underemployment.

Racially, the majority of respondents were White (73.9%), followed by Blacks (9.1%), Asians (8.8%), and Hispanics (4.1%), with 4.1% belonging to a variety of other races or declining to answer. While there was also a moderately strong relationship between underemployment and race, this appears to be primarily due to the anomalies of low-N racial minorities, with American Indian and Alaskan Natives ($N = 3$) having an underemployment rate of 100% and Native Hawaiian/Pacific Islanders ($N = 2$) and "Some Other Race" ($N = 1$) having an underemployment rate of zero. Among the remaining five racial groups, the results were not as widely divergent: Asians had the lowest rate of underemployment (57.7%), followed by Whites (59.7%), Black/African Americans (61.1%), Hispanic/Latinos (62.5%), and two or more races (63.6%). Thus, there is some tangential support to gender and race-based status-sorting theories, but these are not conclusive.

School status was determined by the type of institution from which respondents received their highest educational credential. In descending order, institutional status was defined as: (1) private, elite college or university, (2) state flagship university, (3) small private college, and (4) second-tier state college. With respect to school status, there is a moderate to high relationship with underemployment. Not surprisingly, graduates of second-tier state colleges had the highest rate of underemployment at 67.9%. However, graduates of private elite colleges had the next highest rate (61.4%), followed by state flagship universities (58.2%) and small private colleges (58.0%), suggesting that even degrees from prestigious and expensive institutions do not inoculate against underemployment.

The next analysis attempted to determine if post-graduate degrees operated to reduce the incidence of underemployment. The degree breakdown in the survey sample was Bachelors (53.7%), Masters (26.7%), Doctorate/Ph.D. (5.5%), M.D. (1.5%), J.D. (12.1%) and "other post-graduate" (0.5%). Higher-level degrees for most professionals appear to offer a modicum of protection against underemployment, with Ph.Ds. experiencing lower underemployment (51.5%) than Masters (59.8%), who fared better than Bachelors (60.5%). However, other types of post-graduate professional degrees did not provide lower underemployment rates, with M.D.s suffering underemployment at 88.9%[16], J.D.'s underemployed at 58.3%, and other post-graduates underemployed at 66.7%. In this test, the results suggested a fairly high relationship between these variables.

Time Effects of Underemployment

There are mainstream economists and workforce development professionals who do not (or prefer not to) acknowledge that degree underemployment/overeducation is a persistent structural problem, but rather explain such results as either due to deficiencies in the job candidate (the "omitted variable" economists) or a sluggish labor market caused by economic recession that eventually resolves through the economic cycle. It was anticipated that the survey sample might be skewed toward newly degreed or young professionals who were experiencing underemployment because they lacked relevant job experience. In order to control for this, survey respondents were asked the length of time (in years) since they had earned their highest degree.

Additionally, respondents were asked to identify their age group. Respondents' age ranges were fairly representative of the US working population: 20-30 (24.5%), 30-40 (26.7%), 40-50 (16.6%), 50-60 (19.5%) and over 60 (12.2%). There was a moderate to strong relationship between underemployment and age. The surprise here is that the age group with the highest underemployment rate (66.3%) was the 40-50 group, which is generally believed to represent the "peak" years of earning and professional development. Younger professionals (age 20-30) had the next highest underemployment rate at 62.1%. The remainder of the age group breakdowns is age 30-40 (59.5%), age 50-60 (56.5%) and over 60 (54.2%). The data suggest that older, more experienced professionals are less likely to be underemployed. Alternatively, the results could indicate that structural underemployment is increasing over time and will statistically have a greater impact on newer workers entering the profession.

Survey respondents were asked to indicate the length of time they had possessed their highest academic degree. These responses are summarized in Figure 1. As the graphical data shows, many respondents in all occupational categories had earned their professional degrees in the past one to ten years. The largest number of respondents in all occupational categories except health care had practiced in their profession over 20 years. Law (30.9%) and academic (28.7%) professionals had their professional degrees the longest. Of those respondents who had their degrees less than one year, the largest number was health care professionals (7.7%) and academics (6.3%). In summary, survey respondents were not over-represented by new graduates looking for their first professional job.

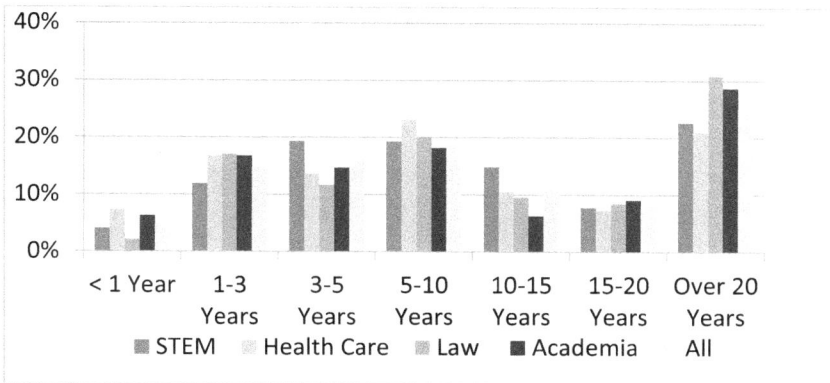

Figure 1: How Long Respondents had their Professional Degrees.

Underemployment, BLS Metrics, and Recession

Another question was designed to address the relationship between underemployment and recession. A U.S. Bureau of Labor Statistics (BLS) graph illustrates a definite pattern of spiking levels of unemployment following officially designated economic recessions, which then falls and levels off.[17] If underemployment (which is not measured) follows the same pattern as unemployment; i.e., both are the result of a weak labor market, one would expect underemployment to follow the same pattern. The surveys in this study were conducted in the spring of 2014, nearly five years after the official end of the Great Recession. However, because the surveys were conducted during what could be appropriately characterized as a "post-Great Recession" economy, it was necessary to design the study to account for time variation in underemployment rates.

Thus, survey respondents were not asked a single "point in time" question as to whether they were currently underemployed, but to recount periods of underemployment over the span of their professional careers, indicated in two-year increments. The purpose of this particular form of data was twofold. First, was to determine if there was some correlation with recessions, particularly the "dot com" recession of 2000-2001 and the Great Recession of 2007-2009. The

169

second was to compare underemployment rates with BLS unemployment measures averaged over the corresponding time period. Capturing this phenomenon over the long term of entire careers avoids anomalies associated with current economic conditions, individual employers (layoffs and downsizing), fluctuations in local labor markets, or temporary personal situations. These results are summarized in Figure 2.

As the figure indicates, underemployment among the survey respondents was not greatly affected by the 2001 recession, but there was a marked rise of underemployment among all occupational categories beginning in 2008, peaking between 2010 and 2012, but continuing to remain high through 2014. Thus, the data supports a correlation between underemployment and recession. It also supports the findings of other analyses that suggest the Great Recession may have been different from prior recessions, either a cause or an effect of more fundamental and permanent economic changes.

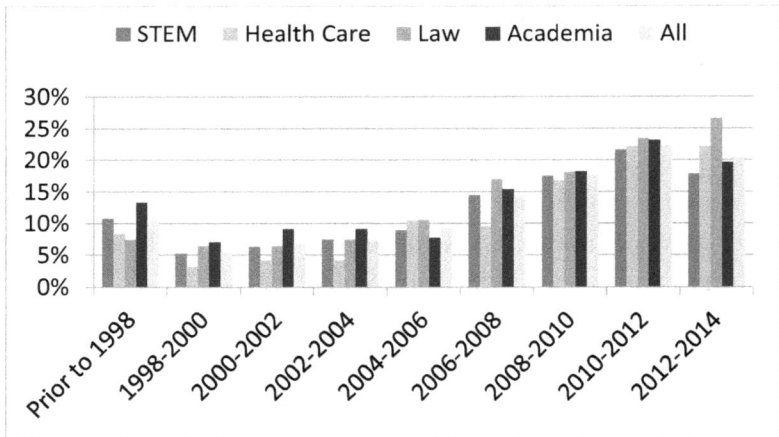

Figure 2. Professional Underemployment by Time Period

The next part of this time-based analysis compared survey underemployment rates against official BLS measures of labor under-utilization (U-3 through U-6) to determine if there is a connection between professional underemployment and labor market conditions (as opposed to overall economic conditions generally). This part of the test was also intended to determine the degree to which BLS measures are failing to capture labor disutility not amounting to officially-defined unemployment. It is obvious from Figure 3 that BLS measures are not capturing professional underemployment, even at the U-6 level.

These results concur with those of other researchers in that Census surveys and BLS metrics need to be expanded to include questions and measures for credential and skills underutilization. From a purely economics viewpoint, this represents a tremendous waste (of educational and training resources) and inefficiency in the form of unproductive human capital. It also represents a challenge from a public policy perspective—there is a tremendous amount of skill and talent that could be directed toward the fulfillment of unmet social needs given the appropriate infrastructure to do so.

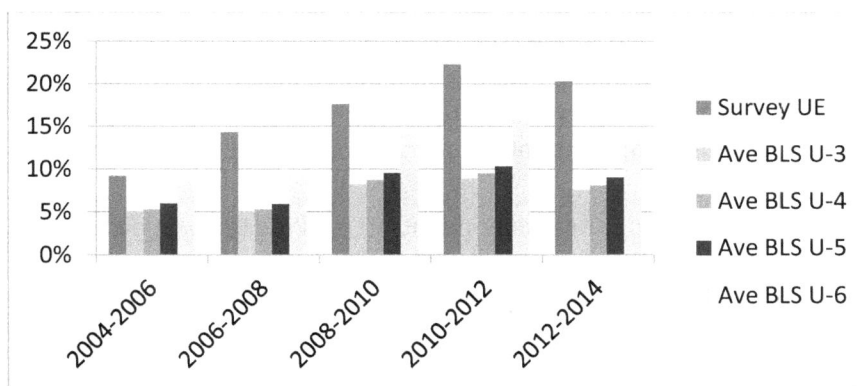

Figure 3. Survey Underemployment Compared to BLS U-3 through U-6.

Respondents' Explanations for Underemployment

Respondents were asked to weigh in on possible explanations for being underemployed. Obviously, the majority of respondents were not economists, but they were certainly the most able to observe and report on conditions surrounding their own situations. However, the design of this study was to attempt to cross-corroborate data across questions and methodologies to insure that the data were not missing something crucial or generating results that were completely off-base. Indeed, survey respondents corroborated the correlation between underemployment and first post-graduate job and underemployment and recession: When asked for the "best" explanation for their underemployment, the most common answer was either a recessionary economy or lack or relevant job experience.

STEM and health care professionals were more affected by recessions, while law professionals were the least affected. Law professionals were more likely to cite "not enough jobs" or "oversupply," which was consistent with their major reasons for professional dissatisfaction. Academic professionals had the highest rate (17.7%) of what I term "relocation" issues, meaning that they might have been able to find an adequate job but were unable to move to more appropriate employment due to family or other logistics associated with relocation. However, all professional groups had some percentage of members who experienced each of these phenomena, and there appeared to be other reasons as well that were not captured by the surveys. Figure 4 illustrates the breakdown of reasons for underemployment by occupational category.

One question asked respondents to provide the best description of their professional or occupational labor market, with six choices representing various economic conditions as well as the choices of "job market changing too rapidly to determine" and "other." The six choices were lay terms (i.e., plain language that did not require an understanding of economics) that described conditions of (a) equilibrium (supply-demand match), (b) undersupply (insufficient number of trained professionals to meet demand), (c) an adequate number of trained professionals with unmet public need (Marx's "poverty in the midst of plenty"), (d) oversupply (too many trained professionals and not enough need or jobs), (e) contingent or secondary jobs, and (f) credentialism.

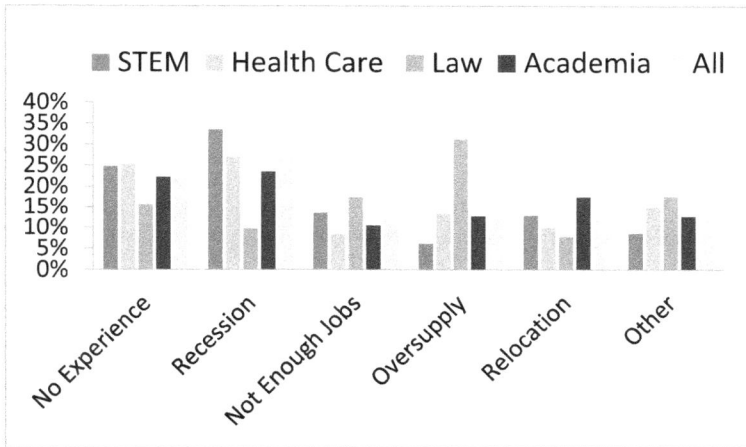

Figure 4. Reasons for Underemployment by Occupational Category

While analyzing the survey responses, there was some evidence suggesting that not all respondents fully understood this question, and the likely default choice was equilibrium. This was indeed the choice cited by most respondents except for law professionals. Law professionals again appeared to be outliers, describing their professional market as being characterized by oversupply (47.3%) or sufficient supply and unmet demand (20.4%). Health care (21.1%) and STEM professionals (18.1%) were the most likely to describe their professional market as being undersupplied, thus lending some support to proponents of the skills shortage crisis. Nearly (or over) 10% of all occupational categories cited some problem with contingent and secondary jobs. STEM professionals were the most likely (9.4%) to say their profession was subject to credentialism. A summary of these results is displayed in Figure 5.

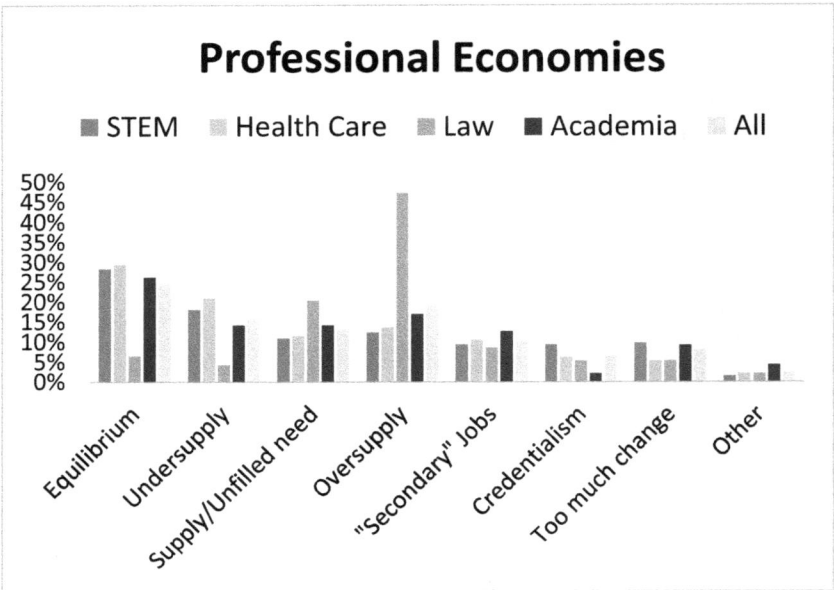

Figure 5. Professional Economies by Occupational Category

Occupational Satisfaction

Although another analysis was specifically directed to factors associated with labor degradation, or alienation, as part of the cross-corroboration strategy, respondents were asked a number of questions about career satisfaction in a more general sense. Rather than simply asking a "yes" or "no" question such as "are you satisfied with your career," this was addressed tangentially, with questions about whether or not respondents would chose the same career if given the opportunity and whether or not they would recommend the same career choice to a young person starting out. Based on these responses, the most satisfied occupational group was health care, followed closely by STEM professionals. Lawyers were clearly the least satisfied. Occupational satisfaction data is summarized in Figure 6.

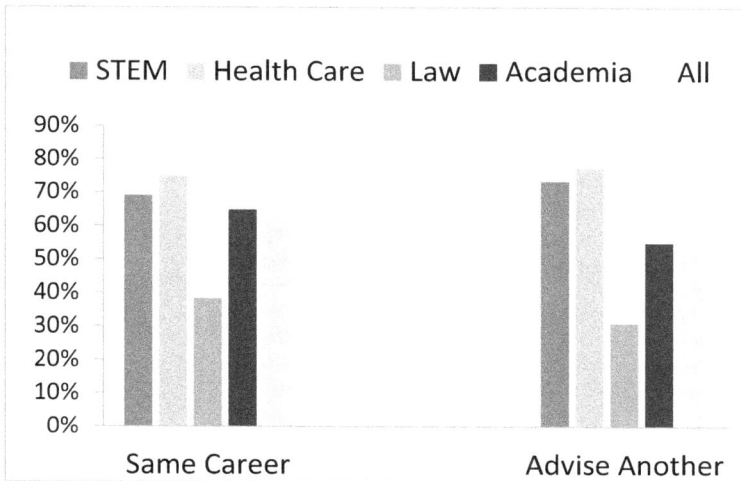

Figure 6. Occupational Satisfaction by Occupational Category

Another series of questions asked respondents to characterize their particular labor market economies as it related to their professional satisfaction. These respondents stated that there were either not enough available jobs, too many others had the same credentials (oversupply), or available labor market information misrepresented the number of jobs. Law professionals were clearly more likely to cite dissatisfaction with the labor market, either an insufficient number of jobs or too many others with the same credentials. Law professionals were also the most likely to be dissatisfied with the quality and reliability of labor market information. Respondents' dissatisfaction with labor market economies and labor market information is summarized in Figure 7.

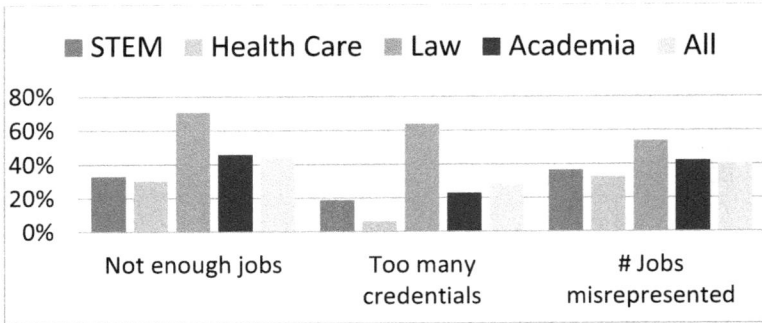

Figure 7. Dissatisfaction with Labor Market Economies and Labor Market Information by Occupational Category

Law professionals were the most likely (44.4%) to cite dissatisfaction with pay in relation to the amount of work, while health care professionals were most likely (42.4%) to cite dissatisfaction with pay in relation to the level of skill required. Academic professionals were the least dissatisfied (6.6%) with pay in relation to amount of work, but significantly more dissatisfied (37.4%) with pay in relation to required skills. Lawyers were slightly more likely than other professionals (37.3%) to state that salaries were being misrepresented. Respondents' dissatisfaction with pay issues is summarized in Figure 8.

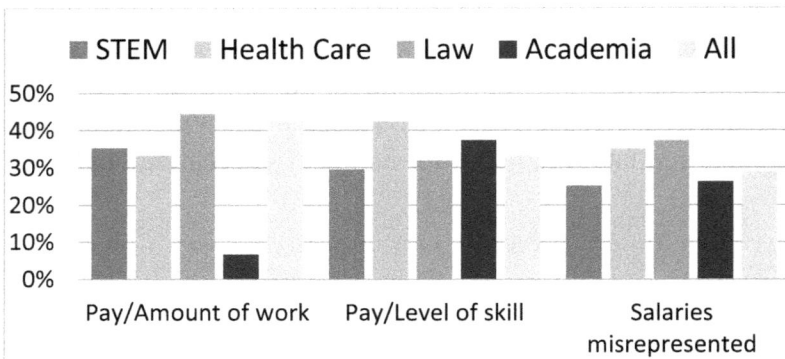

Figure 8. Pay Dissatisfaction by Occupational Category

The analysis of respondents' perception of overeducation is summarized in Figure 9. Although law professionals were the most dissatisfied in general, they were the least likely to identify problems of overeducation or education-job mismatch. This is likely due to the fact that attorneys have the option of opening a law practice (and thus being able to use their educational credentials) in the absence of legal jobs. However, over 20% of STEM and health care professionals said they "don't use all of their education" on the job. Over 20% of STEM, health care and academic professionals cited experiencing some form of job-education mismatch.

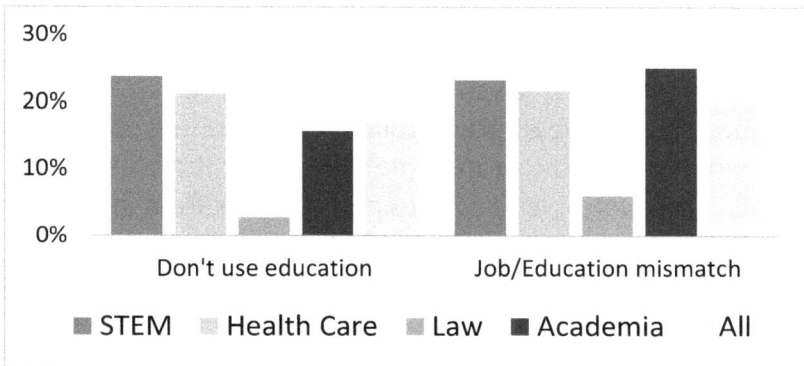

Figure 9. Overeducation and Job-Education Mismatch by Occupational Category

The flip side of the underemployment coin is the paradox of overwork. While some professionals are unable to find work—or unable to find appropriate work—others say they are working so many hours they are unable to have any kind of human "life" outside of work. Health care and law professionals had the highest complaints of issues with overwork and burnout, while STEM professionals had the least. Respondents' reports of problems with overwork and burnout are summarized in Figure 10.

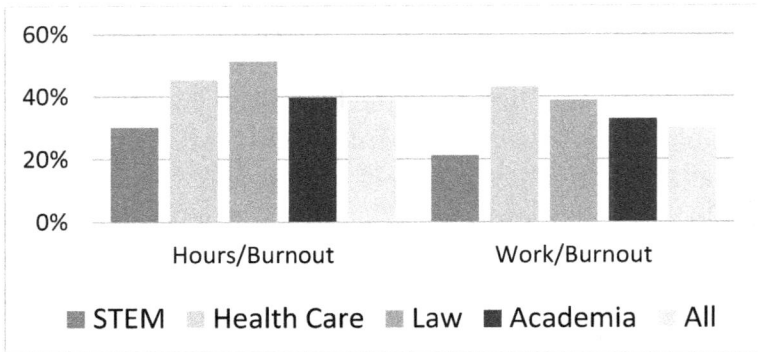

Figure 10. Overwork/Burnout by Occupational Category

Respondents who indicated either that they would not choose the same profession if given the chance to do so so or would not recommend their profession to a young person starting out were given the opportunity to indicate multiple reasons for their dissatisfaction. Other than lawyers, at least 15% of professionals from the other three occupational categories cited a lack of autonomy. Academic professionals were the most likely (30.1%) to say they were spending too much unproductive time on administrative paperwork or production quotas. Other than health care professionals (24.3%), more than 25% of all other professionals cited problems with misrepresentation of job security, with law professionals citing this the most (38.8%). Law professionals were also the most likely (29.95%) to say that their chosen profession was not a good personal fit. This is consistent with more general complaints about inadequate information during the career decision process. Health care professionals were the most likely (35.1%) to say they have no control over the kind and volume of work they are required to do. Academic (30.3%) and health care (24.3%) professionals were the most likely to say that their actual job duties had been misrepresented. These results are summarized in Figure 11.

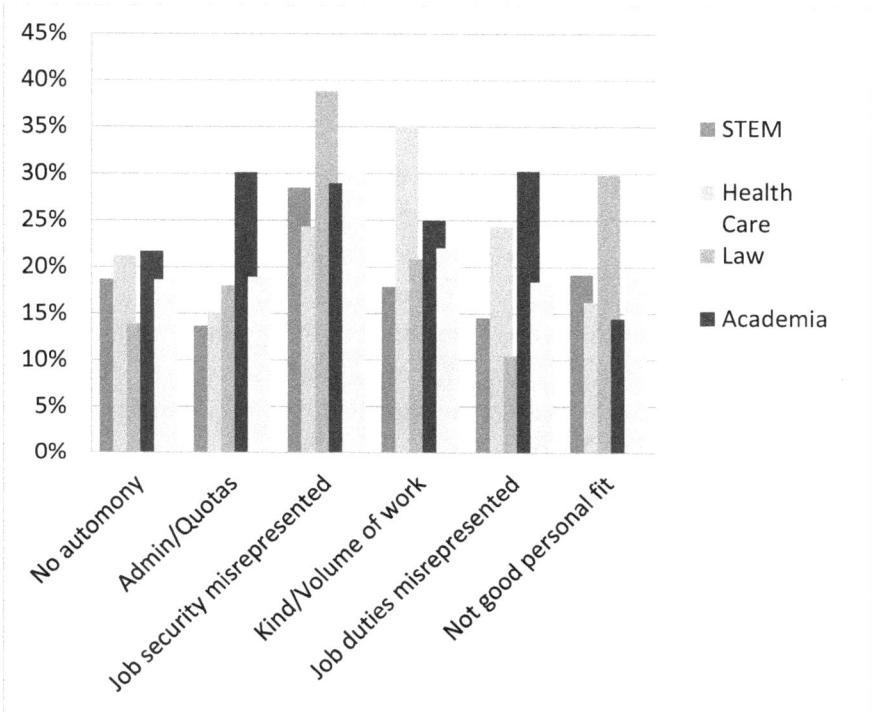

Figure 11. Miscellaneous Sources of Professional Dissatisfaction by
Occupational Category

Labor Degradation Factors

      Labor degradation, like underemployment itself, is a somewhat ambiguous concept that is difficult to define and even more difficult to quantify. For purposes of this study, labor degradation factors were derived primarily from a Dutch study[18] of policy alienation among professional public servants because this study addressed factors that were specific to professional occupations and that negatively impacted professional norms. Because of this focus, the surveys in this study did not quantitatively capture more generalized "bad job" features, i.e., part-time, contingent, insecure and low paid work, that characterizes labor degradation in the general labor force. However, some of these "bad job" features were captured in the qualitative interviews, which will be more fully discussed in the following section.

Unlike the underemployment question, which asked about underemployment over the span of a career, the labor degradation questions applied only to respondents' current job/employer. That is, there was no prior assumption that underemployment and labor degradation would necessarily be correlated. The specific factors that were measured quantitatively were autonomy, agency, role conflict and bureaucratization. Autonomy was defined as the ability to exercise discretion over both specific jobs tasks and work processes (i.e., the amount and kind of work performed per unit time). Agency was defined as the ability to influence the work environment, policies and procedures, as well as the ability to influence outcomes, either for service clientele or with respect to one's own career progression. Role conflict was defined as the extent to which organizational processes interfered with service/relationship with clients and/or reward systems that operated in conflict with professional norms and duties. Bureaucratization was defined as the extent to which rules, regulation, and chain-of-command operated to either make work less efficient or negatively impact client service in some way. The intent of measuring these particular factors was to determine the extent to which organizational processes negatively impacted higher levels of job functions particular to professionals. Respondents were allowed to answer each question with a Likert-type scale of strongly agree, agree, neutral/neither agree nor disagree, disagree, or strongly disagree. The results of this series of questions are displayed in Table 1.

The labor degradation responses were then subject to a series of analysis of variance (ANOVA) testing to determine if there was any correlation between employer size and employer type.[19] This was based on the premise of two hypotheses. The first hypothesis was that labor degradation would be correlated with increasing employer size, since large employers (whether public or private) tend to be associated with top-down, command-and-control bureaucracies more than smaller, entrepreneurial firms. The second hypothesis was that labor degradation would be correlated more highly with private firms as a consequence of profit motivation. Respondents were asked to characterize their current employer as private, public/government or non-profit, and identify the size of their employer by number of employees and geographic scope, ranging from small (less than 20 employees), medium or state level, large (greater than 50 employees or federal level), and global/multinational firms. These results are summarized in Table 1.

STEM professionals were the most satisfied (84.3%) with the level of job task autonomy and academics were the least satisfied (71.3%). Academics had the highest experience of role conflict (46.2%) and law professionals the least (25.5%). STEM professionals were the most likely (61.3%) to indicate discrepancies between organizational objectives and professional standards in performance evaluation criteria, and law professionals cited this problem the least (39.4%). Health care professionals were the most likely (76.8%) to fully utilize their education, skills and training on the job, while academics were the least likely (70.0%) to fully utilize their education, skills, and training. STEM professionals reported the highest rate of ability to influence workplace policies and procedures (74.4%), while academics had the least (57.3%). Academics also cited the most dissatisfaction (67.1%) with limited avenues of upward mobility. Thus, the data suggest that the "academic" professionals, who were primarily female K-12 teachers, experienced the highest levels of overall job degradation.

STEM professionals tended to be employed in larger organizations and were the most likely to characterize their employers as top-down, command-and-control hierarchies. They were also the most likely (50.6%) to express dissatisfaction with unproductive paperwork and approval processes. Paradoxically, STEM professionals also reported the highest rate (74.4%) of having the ability to exercise influence over workplace policies and procedures.

The Great Jobs Deception

Table 1.

Summary of Labor Degradation Survey Questions

Question	Agree or Strongly Agree	Disagree or Strongly Disagree
I am able to fully exercise my professional discretion on the job.	79.04%	10.31%
I have little control over the number or types of cases/projects/clients that form the basis of my typical workload.	52.75%	26.63%
The demands of my employer sometimes conflict with my professional duties to my clients/patients/customers or to the public at large.	38.93%	37.61%
At my workplace, performance evaluation is primarily based on quantitative production or other measures that promote organizational objectives rather than professional standards.	53.91%	21.80%
I am able to fully utilize my education, skills, and training on the job.	73.21%	14.98%
I am able to provide input and influence workplace policies, procedures, rules and protocols that affect my work.	68.06%	16.48%
At my workplace, there are limited avenues to upward mobility.	58.24%	22.30%
My workplace is organized in a top-down, command-and-control hierarchy.	61.23%	11.82%
My workplace is organized as a collegiate of equals or a professional team.	51.25%	25.45%
Although my workplace is generally bureaucratic, professionals (including my own department or office) are able to operate with relative autonomy.	61.23%	13.65%
Professional employees at my workplace spend more time on paperwork, documentation, and/or getting approvals than on productive work.	47.42%	28.95%

182

These results are consistent with Derber's[20] adaptation thesis, in which professionals create separate, semi-autonomous "oases of professionalism" within otherwise bureaucratic and hierarchical organizations.

Not surprisingly, professionals with private (81.3%) and small (80.8%) employers were more likely to be satisfied with their level of autonomy on particular job tasks. Respondents who reported the highest levels of dissatisfaction with role conflict worked for either public/government employers (56.3%) or large (42.5%) organizations. Indeed, role conflict was the only degradation factor that was significantly correlated with employer size, suggesting that larger organizations (both public and private) are more likely to create this specific form of degradation/dissatisfaction than smaller organizations. However, with respect to the specific question about reward systems, employees of private firms were the most likely (56.3%) to say that performance evaluation was based on organizational objectives rather than professional standards, as were employees of large (58.3%) and global (67.4%) organizations. Thus, smaller private employers are more likely to permit greater autonomy with respect to how the job is done, but large private employers are more likely to have reward systems that could potentially conflict with professional norms.

The final quantitative analysis tested the relationship between underemployment and labor degradation, and the results were highly significant.[21] However, this should not necessarily be interpreted that one is either the cause or the effect of the other. In its simplest interpretation, the results suggest that labor degradation and underemployment tend to appear together, which is consistent with empirical logic. However, what the results also imply is that professionals are not immune from the labor market deficiencies and "bad job blues" that affect workers in jobs lower in the occupational hierarchy. This can be interpreted as evidence of the inexorability of the labor degradation process as predicted by Braverman. It also suggests that there are serious deficiencies in the labor market that are not being captured by current labor statistics, particularly as they affect professional workers. In essence, people who invest considerable time and resources to better themselves professionally are not guaranteed a decent place in economic society.

Qualitative Analysis and Findings

Who Were the Typical Respondents?

In the first part of this section, I will summarize the statistical profiles of the typical respondent in each of the four broad occupational categories. In the second part of this section, I will briefly describe the situation of the individuals who were actually interviewed. In the third part of this section, I will discuss the particulars of labor disutility and "bad job" characteristics as experienced by the interviewees.

STEM Professionals. The most common STEM professional was either an engineer (18.6%) or someone in information technology (IT) (27.4%). Typical STEM professionals attended either state flagship (41.6%) or private elite (35.7%) universities and were age 30-40 (28.5%). Stem workers were the most racially diverse: White (69.0%), Asian (13.8%), Black (7.1%), and a small majority were male (52.6%). The sorting factors for STEM interviewees were occupation (engineer or IT), age, and type of school. This generated eleven potential interviewees, seven of them who were underemployed.

Health Care Professionals. The majority of health care professionals identified themselves as nurses (39.0%) or "other health care" (31.6%). Health care professionals were the most educationally diverse, with 37.9% attending state flagship universities, 27.4% attending private elite universities, and 25.3% attending small private colleges. These professionals were overwhelmingly female (72.3%) and 69.2% White. The main age ranges were 20-30 (31.9%) and 30-

40 (21.3%). The sorting factors for health care professionals were occupation (nurse or "other"), female, and age between 20 and 40. This generated eight potential interviewees, six of them who were underemployed.

Law Professionals. Law professionals were the most occupationally and demographically homogeneous group, which could explain why certain labor market patterns were more readily identified. Thanks to the cooperation of the Mississippi and Kansas State Bar Associations, the majority of these respondents were attorneys (74.5%) from a handful of states in the U.S. central South-East. The majority of these professionals were White (81.5%) and attended state flagship universities (45.7%) or small private colleges (28.7%). A slight majority of them were female (54.4%), although their age ranges were significantly more dispersed than the other categories. Law professionals were thus sorted into attorneys and type of school (state flagship and small private), which generated eight potential interviewees with five of them underemployed.

Academic Professionals. The majority of academic professionals were K-12 teachers (53.2%), followed by "other academic professionals" (21.0%). Like health care professionals, they were overwhelmingly female (77.5%). Like the attorneys, the majority of them were White (82.4%), with fairly dispersed age ranges. Most of them attended state flagship universities (43.4%), followed by elite private schools (25.2%). An initial sorting of academic professionals by occupation, gender, and type of school produced a large number of potential respondents. While this group comprised less than a quarter of the entire sample (24.2%), they appeared to have a much greater willingness to participate in interviews. Consequently, this group was further sorted by underemployment, which produced fourteen potential interviewees, all of who were underemployed.

Five persons actually agreed to be interviewed. Two were STEM professionals, two were recent law school graduates, and one was an adjunct college instructor. Of the two STEM professionals, one was an IT worker in the Seattle, Washington area and the second was a research scientist in epidemiology. There were no respondents from the underemployed health care occupation profiles who agreed to be interviewed.

The Interviewees and Their Stories

IT engineer in the Seattle, Washington area. J.C. is an IT engineer located in the Seattle, Washington area, an urban "hub" of global tech industries. J.C. reports that in the Seattle area, ."..just like there's a coffee shop on every corner, there's two IT guys looking for work." J.C. described a number of jobs that were mostly part-time, and all of them were contingent, which required him to cobble together various jobs just to make ends meet. The bottom line was working too many hours for too little pay, "...you can be underemployed and work 60 hours a week, you're just not getting paid what you're worth." Although the Seattle area had an oversupply of tech-trained workers, J.C. said that it was possible there could be localized skills shortages elsewhere. J.C. also described the constant need for retraining in the tech industry, which generated revenues for a local cottage industry of tech certificate providers. J.C. characterized the Seattle area as being subject to boom-and-bust cycles (first with truck drivers, then with aircraft manufacturing, and now with tech workers), where unemployed workers discarded from the previous boom are herded into training for the brave new jobs, which then creates an oversupply for the next employment bust. "It's a vicious cycle, there's huge pools of skilled workers in areas you no longer need."

Ph.D. level research scientist in epidemiology. N.L. is a research scientist (Ph.D) in epidemiology. She reports being underemployed over her entire career (since 1980), which has been primarily due to substandard work assignments and managerial decisions as opposed to macroeconomic structuring of her particular job market. N.L. has worked for private employers over her career, although the majority of research scientists in the surveys (9 out of 14) worked for public or non-profit employers. N.L. partially blamed her situation on her own inability to "horn blow," "brown nose," and "work the system," partially on gender discrimination by supervisors, and partially on managerial ineptitude at the department level. N.L. had nothing but praise for her current supervisor (a woman), but said it was difficult to get motivated after "working so hard for so many people for so many years [and getting] nowhere." Even in her current (better) job situation, N.L. said she did not fully utilize all of her education and training. N.L. also demonstrated the kind of demoralized hopelessness that some researchers have identified in the long term un- and underemployed.

Masters level college/community college instructor. S.D. has been an instructor of English literature and writing at the college level for over 20 years. At one point in the past, S.D. had a full-time job where she also did tutoring, peer assistance and academic advising. However, the majority of her career has been spent in part-time adjunct faculty positions. S.D. described how low pay requires adjuncts to string together classes from several institutions, and they never know which assignments are going to materialize from semester to semester. The adjunct system renders instructors' financial survival tenuous and insecure. This lack of connection to any one institution impacts adjuncts' ability to serve students in ways other than specific instruction, such as academic and career advising.

S.D. alluded to a general lack of autonomy (which was also suggested in many of the extraneous comments from K-12 teachers), although the job she had at the moment provided a "decent amount of autonomy," which permitted her to do "creative things" in the classroom. The biggest frustrations were the total lack of promotional pathways and the attitude of permanent faculty toward the adjuncts' abilities. S.D. described attending professional development classes that she "could very well have presented [her]self." She lamented the institution's failure to give credit for adjuncts' prior service when the (rare) full-time position does become available. S.D. also briefly described the institution's "vociferous" opposition to a recent faculty vote for collective bargaining representation.

Recent law school graduates practicing law in rural and urban markets. Both A.A. and L.W. were recent law school graduates (J.D.s) who described an unrewarding search for regular employment that culminated in both of them opening a solo law practice. Although A.A. and L.W. described similar career dynamics, they work in widely different markets. A.A. practices in a small rural county where there are, at most, 10 other attorneys. Conversely, L.W. works in an urban area that is "glutted" with attorneys. A.A. worked in a non-legal job to make ends meet until she finally decided the only way she would be able to use her law degree was to open her own practice. L.W. described job offers or short-lived legal jobs with small firms that appeared to exploit new law graduates, so he too made the decision to open his own practice.

A.A. described the practice of law as being based on inefficient and outmoded business models. She did not view the problem as one of too many attorneys, but described it as a "distributional" problem of too many attorneys "doing the same thing in the same place." L.W. described the problem as being unambiguously about an oversupply of attorneys. Although both A.A. and L.W. said accurate and reliable information about the legal labor market was not available, L.W. placed a large part of the blame squarely on law schools, with their "vested interest in just turning out lawyers." Both A.A. and L.W. described a system whereby public legal services such as criminal prosecution, public defenders, and even foster care had been converted to outsourced contracts, and these contract assignments were coveted by private attorneys seeking to supplement their marginal practices.

Both A.A. and L.W. also corroborated a phenomenon identified in the surveys: in spite of a sufficient number of lawyers to serve the general population, a large number of potential clients could not afford their services. L.W. described at length the microeconomics of a small law practice, including the efforts he makes to keep costs down while attempting to meet his breakeven point. L.W. also had uncharitable comments regarding his fellow attorneys, stating that, "when the money fell off, they turned on each other...and left [the new attorneys] twisting in the wind.... I like to use the term they eat their young."

In the next step of the qualitative analysis, the interviews were coded for themes. These themes were in part defined by the issues addressed in the quantitative data and in part were defined by issues that emerged in the interviews. Although the qualitative data raised some questions and issues that were not addressed in the quantitative data, none of it was expressly disconfirming. That is, both data types were either confirmatory or supplemental.

Work Dissatisfactions

Time paradox. Time disutility is more complex than a simplistic categorization of part-time jobs: even the Bureau of Labor statistics measures involuntary part-time underemployment. Professional workers seem to experience a paradox of both involuntary part-time work and/or working too many hours, particularly since most (if not all) of them are exempt from overtime pay requirements under the Fair Labor Standards Act. J.C. described the experience of having to work too many hours in various part-time jobs just to make ends meet. L.W. described his law practice as not having enough business to "fill my calendar." Conversely, A.A. described how some of her law school friends who had landed employment at large law firms were working so many hours they were unable to have a life. In the case of adjunct academics, additional difficulties were presented by the unpredictable nature of assignments, and the difficulty in planning and accepting work that was subject to change at the last minute.

Management and leadership issues. There were eleven survey comments that attributed underemployment to individual decisions by management and leadership rather than macroeconomic factors. These were in addition to seven comments that expressly referenced downsizing and layoffs, and four comments that expressly referenced foreign outsourcing (all from STEM professionals), which appeared to be more macroeconomically-based. These "managerial decisions" were described as everything from incompetence of individual supervisors to "state mandates" to "decisions in Washington" to identification of specific political leaders (generally involving public budgets).

Issues of managerial ineptitude only arose in one of the interviews. N.L., the research scientist, described her inability to progress in her career because the better assignments were awarded based on sexism or other non-merit-based reasons. Sexism, or gender discrimination, was a theme that ran throughout N.L.'s interview. These problems were compounded by supervisory inattentiveness, "poor communications between departments," and lack of transparency involving criteria for promotion. Additionally, there were suggestions in survey comments from attorneys that discrimination—in the form of non-merit-based employment decisions—was occurring within that profession as well.

Professional character and ethics. Although the interviewees did not directly implicate a deficient labor market with bad behavior, there was some implication that professional standards were being eroded, particularly in the legal profession. L.W. described some attorneys he had worked with as being "manipulative and selfish," aggravating hostilities in a divorce case to generate increased fees. A.A. did not view the problems so much as a lack of ethics in individual attorneys, but rather the entire profession had become calcified into a professional model that no longer served to fulfill its public purpose. N.L. described the "politics" of advancement in her research field, in which those who got ahead did so by constant self-promotion and expropriating credit for the work of others.

Relocation/personal issues While the focus of this study is on market failures rather than personal reasons for underemployment, it nonetheless acknowledges that professionals—as are all workers—are part of non-work social systems that sometimes take priority over maximization of individual opportunity. Although this career sacrifice burden tends to fall primarily on women, men can experience the same dynamic. Moreover, spouses of professionals or significant others are frequently professionals themselves, and even if one spouse/partner can do better by relocating, the other may not be able to find comparable employment, and so the couple as a unit has to weigh the net utility or disutility of any such relocation.

The surveys specifically defined underemployment as being involuntary, yet five respondents—all of them female—reported that they voluntarily left employment to take care of their children. Two academics and one attorney (all female) were underemployed due to relocations related to a spouse's career or education. One respondent (female) left work because of her own health issues and another (also female) moved across country and took a lower-paying job to care for a sick relative. The interviews of J.C. and L.W. (both male) also revealed how career location decisions are affected by significant others. In J.C.'s case, he had to remain in the Washington-Oregon area to help with caretaking of his grandparents. L.W. acknowledged that he might find more legal work in a neighboring rural county that was not "flooded" with recent graduates of the local law schools, but L.W.'s wife had a long-term stable job in the area and commuting was logistically unfeasible.

Perhaps the reality of dual-income families will necessitate that at least one of them be underemployed because it is stretching the capacity of a local labor market to provide adequate employment for both of them. In essence this suggests that professional labor markets are national in scope, which means that frequent moves for one or both professional job-holders are required for them to maximize a career progression. If this is the case, it has negative implications for the ability of professional families to establish roots in a local community and build a social life that does not revolve around work.

Expectations versus reality. Several attorneys in the surveys as well as both of the attorneys who were interviewed expressed disappointment in the contradiction between what they believed their career would look like and how their career turned out in actuality. This same disappointment was also expressed by the adjunct writing instructor and the research scientist. There was a general feeling that if you did what was required of you—both school and work-wise— you had earned your place in a profession where you could earn a decent living and were respected. Some of them wondered in hindsight whether their expectations might have been unreasonable. All of them expressed dissatisfaction with the completeness and accuracy of career information, and this particular issue will be further addressed in the Chapter 7 discussion about the role of schools in career advising.

Labor Market Deficiencies and "Bad Job" Characteristics

Oversupply or not enough jobs. There was a definite perception of a supply-demand mismatch in the IT and legal professions. However, whether this was due to too many people with credentials or not enough jobs was much more difficult to determine. There also seemed to be some distributional factors at work, meaning an oversupply or lack of jobs in one geographic area might exist with an undersupply of talent or skill in another. In the case of attorneys, an oversupply—or mal-distributed supply—exists simultaneously with unmet public demand for services. In the case of adjunct academics, the problem appears to be not so much a matter of supply-demand mismatch between teachers and students as the replacement of full-time and tenure track faculty with part-time, contingent positions.

Underemployed professionals and unmet public demand (poverty in the midst of plenty). The surveys and the two attorney interviewees corroborated a "poverty in the midst of plenty" phenomenon with respect to the legal profession. That is, there were more than a sufficient number of attorneys at the same time many people could not afford an attorney's services. A.A.'s view of the situation was that it was a distributional problem: there were too many attorneys concentrated in urban areas and not enough in rural areas (like where she practices), and too many attorneys were pursuing specialty occupations rather than general practices. L.W. reported a similar situation of unmet need in an urban market "flooded" with lawyers. However, he identified the problem as being related to the microeconomics of law practice, in which he described in detail the practical difficulties of meeting expenses and earning a living while providing legal services at a cost most people can afford.

Contingent employment. Both J.C., the IT Engineer, and S.D., the college instructor described the tenuousness of the unpredictable employment that represented the majority of available jobs in their occupations. When the short term contract was up, they were back looking for work again, and constantly having to weigh the convenience of one multiple-gig strategy against another. Aggravating the constant insecurity was the low pay—nowhere near anything that could be considered a professional income. S.D. alleged that if even her part-time hours were paid at a pro-rated rate comparable to a full-time professors, she would not be struggling with near-poverty. S.D. and L.W. both commented on the element of "luck" with respect to how similarly educated and experienced persons ended up on the occupational income distribution.

Effects of Long Term Underemployment: Pessimistic Futility

There were a number of comments, both as extended "other" comments from the surveys and in the interviews, which expressed frustration and even a degree of hopelessness, but did not necessarily fit squarely into the other categories.

S.D. laments the wholesale destruction of tenure-track faculty positions:

> *I'm switching gears. I'm not looking at a tenure-track position in English. I'll have the credentials and maybe I can apply for a job or two, but they're so few and far between. I...frankly, I've given up on it.*

Lawyers expressed discontent both with the profession and with other lawyers:

> *LW: The practice of law has turned on itself. Because the money went away, and they all, you know, sort of blamed each other for it, and they really...really turned on the new attorneys and left them just twisting in the wind. I like to use the term they eat their young.*

> *Uninspiring work, lots of attorneys are themselves uninspiring.*

STEM professionals were not immune to pessimistic futility:

> *outsourcing and industry collusion has ruined the pay and availability of high tech jobs in this country.*

One engineer noted the futility of career planning in general:

> *Life long career is fiction.*

Several Ph.Ds. lamented the lack of opportunities for career advancement and having to work within a "rigged" system:

> *NL: But I feel like not having an opportunity for internal advancement is very frustrating...and disappointing. It makes me disappointed in institutions, and also disappointed in individual leaders that allow this to, you know, perpetuate itself.*

> *Under the current insurance system, a Doctor of Psychology barely makes enough to live. All t[sic] kudo's are on pushing drugs for drug companies, and since a Psychologist can't prescribe, he is left out in the cold on all the perks.*

Although no K-12 schoolteacher agreed to be interviewed, they provided many of the extraneous comments on the surveys in this category. Some of these comments expressed both pessimistic futility and lack of professional autonomy:

> *Teachers are under-appreciated and work too hard for the small amount of money they make.*

> *The job has gone far beyond passing on skills to dealing with an ever-growing bureaucracy. Some formerly important training skills have been downsized.*

> *THE EDUCATION SYSTEM IS TERRIBLE.*

> *Teacher expectations for 2014 are unreasonable and unattainable*

> *teaching is no longer teaching—it is more "crowd control"*

> *elementary education has changed—there is little room for creativity*

> *Teachers Unions, over-testing and "Common Core" are ruining the best of our Educational system*

> *There are too many restrictions on teachers in the schools*

> *its hard work with few rewards at times*

Summary and Conclusions

Braverman's theory predicted the "inexorability" of the labor degradation process. That is, the alienating features of work would creep upward into higher occupational levels, and this indeed appears to be happening. Although workers can still better their job prospects (either increasing their average wage or decreasing their likelihood of being unemployed) by gaining education and skills, professional level education is no longer a guarantee of meaningful and rewarding (both personally and financially) work.

For blue collar workers, who in the past were the primary subjects of studies about work alienation, work is something they do to provide for a life. For professional workers, work often is their life, and sometimes even the primary foundation of their personal identity. Professional workers have also traditionally resisted the forms of organization and culture of solidarity more typical of the working class. However, now that they themselves are experiencing many of the same "bad job" features, there has been some indication of willingness to engage in collective opposition. The problem is that the degradation of professional employment takes more varied and complex forms than the Taylorist job deconstruction associated with blue collar factory workers and pink collar office workers. In the following chapter, these finer nuances of occupational degradation will be analyzed.

Notes

1 Orth, C.D. (1965). *The optimum climate for industrial research*. In N. Kaplan, (Ed.), Science and Society. Chicago, IL: Rand McNally, at p. 141.

2 Marx, K. (1844). Economic and philosophical manuscripts. In Marx-Engels *Gesamtuasgabe, Vol. 3*. Berlin, Germany: Marx-Engels Institute (Pub. 1932).

3 Horowitz, I. L. (1966). On alienation and the social order. *Philosophy and Phenomenological Research, 27*(2), 230-237.

4 Blauner, R. (1964). *Alienation and freedom*. Chicago, IL: University of Chicago Press.

5 Nair, N. & Vohra, N. (2009). Developing a measure of work alienation. *Journal of Workplace Rights, 14*(3), 293-309 at p. 299.

6 Tummers, L., Bekkers, V., & Steijn, B. (2009). Policy alienation and public professionals. *Public Management Review, 11*(5), 685-706 at p. 688.

7 *Id.* at p. 689.

8 Aiken, M. & Hage, J. (1966). Organizational alienation: A comparative analysis. *American Sociological Review, 31*(4), 497-507.

9 Miller, G.A. (1967). Professionals in bureaucracy: Alienation among industrial scientists and engineers. *American Sociological Review, 32*(5), 755-768.

10 Tummers, Bekkers, & Steijn. (2009). *Supra*.

11 Mraz, S. J. (2012, Jan. 19). Time for engineers to think about unionizing? *Machine Design*. Retrieved from: http://machinedesign.com/engineering-education/time-engineers-think-about-unionizing

12 Greenhouse, S. (1999, Feb. 4). Angered by H.M.O.s treatment, more doctors are joining unions. *The New York Times*. Retrieved from: http://www.nytimes.com/1999/02/04/nyregion/angered-by-hmo-s-treatment-more-doctors-are-joining-unions.html?pagewanted=all&src=pm

13 Mortazavi, M. (2012). Lawyers, not widgets: Why private sector attorneys must unionize to save the legal profession. *Minnesota Law Review 96*(4), 1482-1543.

14 Hiltzik, M. (2015, August 1). Tech industries persistent claim of worker shortage may be phony. *LA Tmes*, August 1, 2015. Retrieved from: http://www.latimes.com/business/hiltzik/la-fi-hiltzik-20150802-column.html

15 Summary of Chi Square Results:

Variable and Degrees of Freedom (df)	Valid N	χ2	Phi/ Cramer's V	Significance (ρ)
Underemployment & Occupational Category, df = 3	591	2.184	.061	.535
Underemployment and Gender, df = 2	588	.842	.038	.656
Underemployment and Race, df = 8	587	6.770	.107	.562
Underemployment and Age, df = 5	588	3.918	.082	.561
Underemployment and Educational Level, df = 5	591	3.285	.075	.656
Underemployment and School Status, df = 3	591	1.825	.056	.610

16 The high rate of underemployed M.D.s was viewed as an anomaly that received additional analysis. First, there were only eight individuals in this group, and their specific occupations were extremely diverse: one each of computer programmer, university professor, engineer, K-12 teacher, forensic scientist, physician/surgeon, psychiatrist, and "other STEM." These results could have been due to a combination of survey-takers marking their "degree" incorrectly and/or persons who completed medical school and found the profession to be a poor personal fit. For purposes of the study as a whole, these results were considered to be outliers, and the general results are interpreted to be applicable only to the more "typical" health care professionals; i.e., nurses and "other" health care.

17 http://www.bls.gov/spotlight/2012/recession/

18 Tummers, Bekkers, & Steijn. (2009). *Supra.*

19 Summary of ANOVA Analyses

Fixed Factor/ Independent Variable	All Degradation Factors, p, η2	Autonomy, p, η2	Role Conflict, p, η2	Agency, p, η2	Bureaucracy, p, η2
Occupational Category	.033, .015	.026, .016	.020, .017	.003, .023	.398, .005
Employer Type	.003, .020	.001, .022	.089, .008	.034, .011	.001, .025
Employer Size	.391, .005	.182, .008	.027, .015	.728, .002	.515, .004

Values for p less than .05 are considered "significant"; i.e. it permits rejection of the null hypothesis, or a finding that the variables are totally independent. Posthoc tests (Tukey's HSD) were performed on all significant results. Levene's test for equality of variances was nonsignificant for all posthoc tests except for the test between type of employer and bureaucracy.

20 Derber, C. (1983). Managing professionals: Ideological proletarianization and post-industrial labor. *Theory and Society, 12*(3), 309-341.

21 Both ANOVA and t-test produced p values of .000.

Chapter Six
Underemployment in the Four Occupational Categories: Similarities and Differences

IN THIS CHAPTER, the specific forms of underemployment and/or "bad job" features in the four occupational categories will be explored in greater detail. The information is a composite of study interviewees and the academic literature relevant to particular occupations. There is some variation of a bifurcated labor market in all of the occupational categories, which is consistent with Braverman's prediction. This has resulted in a dichotomy of specialized skills shortages in STEM occupations along with job loss from offshoring and cheapening of wages. Information technology (IT) jobs in particular appear to be designed to be part-time, contingent, unpredictable, and insecure. The legal profession is characterized by the "poverty in the midst of plenty" phenomenon of new law graduates unable to secure full-time legal employment at the same time there is a large unmet demand for legal services. Both law and academia appear to exhibit trifurcated labor markets, where there is a group of high-paid and high status professionals (big law firm partners, "celebrity" professors, and high-level university administrators), a much smaller group of "mid-level" professionals (a shrinking number of tenured professors, mid-level university administrators and public/government attorneys), and a growing (in academia) number of low-paid and insecure adjuncts along with recent law graduates engaged in tenuous legal freelance and self-employment.

No health care professional was willing to be interviewed and so this occupational group has the least descriptive data from the study. This is unfortunate, because this group (from the surveys) had the highest rate of underemployment, although most of it occurred post-Great Recession. The rollout of the Affordable Care Act could also have impacts upon health care professionals, but ACA (or any other discrete non-labor market event) impacts were not the focus of this study. Health care professionals themselves attributed their own underemployment primarily to either recession (27.2%) or lack of experience (25.4%). Conversely, health care professionals had the highest measures of professional satisfaction, which was consistent with their primary career motivation to make a difference and help people. Ironically, the major job dissatisfactions for this group was too much work (43.2%) or too many or irregular work hours (45.5%). This suggests that simply hiring more health care workers could possibly ameliorate both issues with underemployment and overwork.

STEM (Science, Technology, Engineering, and Math) Markets

The dichotomy of underemployment and allegations of a "skills shortage" crisis is nowhere more apparent than in the so-called STEM professions. This group comprises engineers, computer programmers, information technology (IT) specialists, and research scientists from all manner of specific fields. The debate about whether there is a STEM skills shortage or oversupply has not abated. The Brookings Institute conducted a study analyzing the length of job openings and found the duration of STEM job openings to be twice that of non-STEM vacancies.[1] Specific "high value skills requested by employers" (i.e., computer skills) were found to be particularly scarce relative to demand.

Conversely, the Center for Immigration Studies found that one-third, or 5 million native-born Americans with STEM degrees were working in non-STEM jobs, with 1.2 million STEM-degreed workers unemployed or not in the labor force.[2] The Economic Policy Institute weighed in with the suggestion that employers were narrowly defining skill requirements and exploiting loopholes in the definition of prevailing wage under the H1-B visa program, resulting in computer science and electrical engineering workers being underpaid by 15-20% of their true market value.[3] The issue of STEM supply and demand is now part of the larger national debate on immigration reform. A somewhat cynical (yet accurate) explanation of this divergence is that whether one finds a STEM shortage or oversupply depends on whether the study is constructed from the viewpoint of employers or that of workers.

The popular media and politicians continually urge the production of workers with scientific and technical credentials based on claims of skills shortages that are being promulgated by corporate CEOs and university research administrators. Yet, the story told by STEM workers themselves is vastly different, and the evidence tends to support this latter reality. Even in 1998, when there was a short-term spike in demand for computer programmers due to the impending Y2K crisis, evidence of an employment shortage of IT workers was mixed, and IT salaries were essentially flat in spite of employment growth.[4] More recently, reports from the National Science Board, the National Institutes of Health, the National Academies and the American Chemical Society found record levels of un- and underemployment, and warn that overproduction of STEM Ph.Ds. is damaging America's ability to recruit its own citizens.[5]

American-born STEM workers have been assaulted by both outsourcing and liberalized immigration. The Institute of Electrical and Electronics Engineers (IEEE) reports that 221,000 computer and engineering jobs were lost between 2000 and 2004, mostly due to offshoring, and that this resulted in the first decrease in income for IEEE members in 31 years.[6] A 2004 report sponsored by the Information Technology Association of America found that 104,000 jobs were offshored between 2000 and 2003, but this number would likely have been higher but for dissatisfaction with Indian employers, who have a tendency to hire young, inexperienced programmers to save costs.[7]

At the same time STEM jobs are being outsourced, Ph.D. level scientists in physics and engineering are being replaced with foreign workers on temporary visas, sometimes even being required to train their replacements. Foreign workers on temporary work visas are prohibited from taking other jobs and thus provide a source of low-cost skilled labor. Between the export of jobs and the glut of imported labor, the wages of tech workers and research scientists have been flat or declining for at least a decade. However, public discourse continues to advocate for more STEM training and liberalization of immigration law while ignoring the voices of un- and underemployed STEM workers. "It is a narrative that has been skillfully packaged and promoted by well-funded advocacy groups as essential to the national interest, but in reality it reflects the economic interests of tech companies and universities."[8]

J.C., the Seattle-based IT engineer, described a situation that demonstrated a combination of skill oversupply, contingent and part-time jobs, and an element of credentialism. Although he surmised that there could be shortages of certain tech skills in underserved rural areas, he described the Seattle tech job market as "...just like there's two coffee shops on every street corner, there's two IT guys looking for work." He was able to survive only by cobbling together a series of part-time jobs, which resulted in the paradox of both overemployment and underemployment: "...you can be underemployed and work 60 hours a week, you're just not getting paid what you're worth." J.C. also described the "constant" need to upgrade certifications "at your own expense," which had given rise to a cottage industry of tech certificate schools in the area.

Health Care Markets

Unfortunately, no underemployed health care professional agreed to be interviewed. The majority of the survey sample indicated they were either nurses (38.95%) or "other health care" professionals (31.58%), and a significant majority of them (72.3%) were female. It is acknowledged that the passage of the Affordable Care Act (ACA) has implications for the health care job market, but these effects will probably not be definitively discerned for some time. Therefore, the main descriptors for health care occupations have been taken from the academic literature focusing on physicians and nurses. Traditionally, males have dominated the occupation of physician and females have dominated the occupation of nursing, although these occupations have seen more of the "opposite" gender joining their ranks in recent years. As of 2015, a little less than half of U.S. physicians are female.[9] According to the U.S. Census bureau, in 2011 the nursing occupation was 91% female. Although male nurses comprise only 9%, they enjoy a "glass escalator effect," earning higher wages than their female nurse counterparts in spite of their fewer numbers and shorter time in the profession.[10] Thus, these occupations are characterized by status sorting/discrimination effects that may be independent of changes in the health care industry as a whole.

The biggest change in the delivery of health care services over the past several decades has been the replacement of traditional fee-for-service with centralized health management organizations (HMOs). HMOs were touted as a means to both control costs and improve quality. Physicians, on the other hand, have typically been suspicious of the market-driven business models imposed by insurance companies, and were equally cynical about HMOs.[11] George Ritzer, the sociologist behind the concept of McDonaldization, describes how rationalized processes have deprofessionalized physicians by exerting greater control over independent medical decisions, creating "McDoctors." Large corporations are gobbling up not just for-profit hospitals, but health insurance firms and medical supply companies. Ritzer predicts that "Those physicians who resist moving into various large-scale capitalistic medical organizations are going to have to be even more entrepreneurial than they have been in the past."[12]

Physicians lament the loss of their decision-making authority as well as a drop in their income, yet over 90% of physicians have at least one contract with a managed care company.[13] The foundation of the managed care model is a primary care physician who serves as a gatekeeper for referrals to specialists. The purpose of gatekeeping is to serve as a rationing function for higher cost specialized services, which may create an adversarial doctor-patient relationship.[14] Moreover, the primary care gatekeepers are never provided an opportunity to gain knowledge in specialties, and, although not expressly "deskilled," are thwarted from growing in knowledge and developing expertise. More cynical analyses suggest that the objective of organized capital is to expropriate the medical sector's "unnecessary share of gross national product"[15] by reducing physician's incomes and status and diverting the excess to the corporate bottom line.

Like labor degradation, rationalization involves the disempowerment of one (usually larger) group of persons with concomitant increased power to another (usually much smaller) group. Rationalization (from Chapter 3) involves replacing independent human judgment with bureaucratic rules and procedures and human labor with technology. Without consulting the literature, most of us can think of concrete examples that demonstrate how this has been happening in the medical profession. Apologists for the managed care revolution agree that physicians will lose their former levels of income, autonomy, and security, but claim that those who find low cost, low-tech interventions and focus on preventive care will thrive, while the cost of health care will be reduced.[16] However, HMOs have not delivered on their promise of either lower costs or higher quality. Although HMOs purport to screen physicians for quality, in practice they will "contract with virtually any physician willing to accept discounted payments in exchange for the possibility of additional patients."[17] On the front end, HMOs limit consumer/patient choice, as plan participants are required to obtain services from physicians participating in the plan network. The traditional (if somewhat romanticized) doctor-patient relationship is now governed by impersonal third party intermediaries.

The nursing profession, like the tech industry, is characterized by the dichotomy of panic about skills shortages along with un- and underemployment of nurses. In 2011, the International Centre for Human Resources in Nursing conducted a survey of 20 nursing associations with international membership to get a better understanding of both the extent and causes of nursing underemployment. The study found that, "Nurse unemployment and underemployment is a hidden problem, because *many countries do not have adequate data to measure it, and often assume that unemployment cannot exist in the midst of a shortage*" (emphasis added).[18] Exploring possible causes, the study found that nurse underemployment was created by three main scenarios: (1) poor working conditions which lead to external migration of nurses (this was usually found in low-income and less developed countries and regions), (2) oversupply, or localized mismatch between supply and demand, and (3) a negative feedback dynamic where poor working conditions and low pay lead to high stress and burnout, and when the overstressed and burned out nurses leave, the remaining nurses are that much more overworked and stressed.

Because this was an international study, there were significant differences in problems of work quality, particularly in less developed countries. Here, nurses faced not just overwork and low pay, but also real physical dangers from disease and war, as well as frustrations from lack of supplies to adequately serve their patients. However, the main theme that carried throughout this study was the definition of "demand," with its acute contrast between actual public need and "demand" as defined by economists, i.e., dollars to pay for it. Supply-demand mismatches appeared to be caused by (in some countries) an educational system that produced more nurses than the labor market could absorb, as well as "inflexible" hours driving many nurses (who also have family responsibilities) out of the market. Other reasons for

207

supply-demand mismatch were financial constraints caused by health care system reform, financial austerity measures, or privatization. In the United States, unemployment was less of a problem than part-time underemployment, which was attributed to employers moving toward "just-in-time" staffing strategies that adjusted to changes in patient volume.

Legal Markets

There is no one-size-fits-all model that describes modern law practice. The majority of attorneys (62% in 2005, according to the American Bar Association) work as solo practitioners, partnerships, or in small firms as they have historically. The remainder of attorneys serve in various capacities as in-house corporate counsel, as public servants (prosecutors, public defenders, city and county attorneys, legislative analysts, etc.), in nonprofit entities, or in large law firms, which primarily serve corporate entities and tend to be modeled after them. Most of the literature about the legal profession describes work in these large law firms, notwithstanding that the majority of attorneys are Main Street lawyers. The large, elite law firms may employ hundreds of attorneys (not counting an army of paraprofessional and support staff) and have offices in a dozen or more globe-spanning urban centers. These firms limit recruitment of new attorneys to top students from elite law schools, and competition for these limited associates' positions is fierce, because they pay six figure salaries. In the middle of the twentieth century, the majority of the work of large firms involved corporate deal-making (IPOs, mergers and acquisitions) rather than litigation, and the firms' attorneys tended to reflect the demographics of its client's CEOs; i.e., white, male, and preferably with connections to old money or socially prominent family.

The increasing complexity of regulation and globalized business practices challenged the fixed fee schedules that law firms had traditionally used when billing for their services. Corporate clients began demanding more transparent billing practices, and so the billable hour was born. The billable hour initially appeared to be a more accurate and legitimate accounting than the typical one-line description of legal services under the former fee schedules, but since the adoption of the billable hour beginning around 1960, new complaints have arisen. Ironically, the source of complaints about the billable hour is from both corporate clients (who allege that firms are "padding" bills with unnecessary work) and new associates, who complain that the demand for a billable hour minimum quota precludes any form of a human life outside of work.

In 1961, a typical billable hour quota was 1,200 annually. By the mid-1980s, annual billable hour quotas at large Wall Street firms averaged 1,800, prompting former U.S. Supreme Court Chief Justice William Rehnquist to compare the treatment of legal associates to one hundred tons of scrap metal.[19] Today the typical requirement is between 2,000 and 2,500 hours.[20] Partners are rewarded based on the number of billable hours produced by themselves and their associates, and associates' prospects for partnership are based on meeting (or exceeding) their billable hour quotas. Associates' salaries have been raised to accommodate the increase in billable hours, with new associates at large prestigious firms earning upwards of $160,000 per year. At a billing rate of $400 per hour, a hypothetical 2,000-hour associate brings in $800,000 per year to the firm, a return of over 400%.[21]

While both billable hours and beginning salaries have gone up, the number of partnership positions has gone down, which has led to a backlash among the high-paid associate indentures, who have recalculated their long-term chances of partnership. Associates are collectively asserting that the billable hour requirements force them to focus on quantity over quality, and prevent them from establishing mentoring relationships, engaging in non-work forms of professional development, and providing the *pro bono* and community service that is encouraged by professional bar associations.[22] Moreover, demands for better work-life balance began to be heard when women entered the labor force, and have accelerated with the entrance of the millennial generation. However, law students and new associates have encountered difficulty in pushing for reforms because they have little information about the realities of work life in large law firms, and the only way they can compare firms is by salary offers.[23]

Law firm billing practices are again being challenged by their corporate clients, who are also pressuring the traditionally white, male law firms to be more demographically diverse. However, the bigger problem is that the distrust between corporate counsel and outside firms has created a new industry of legal bill review and audits. These audits claim to save their corporate clients money by identifying such practices as vague billing entries, unauthorized "lumped" billing (including more than one task in a single billing entry), excess staffing, insufficient delegation (to lower-cost associates or paralegals), excessive time to complete a task, unnecessary legal research and other variations of "unnecessary" or duplicative work.[24] It may indeed be true that the pressure for billable hours results in overcharges to clients, but the advent of billing audits also serves as a form of micromanagement, requiring the legal firm to maintain ever more detailed levels of documentation and institute Taylorist efficiency protocols that have nothing to do with improved service.

The general public tends to have an uncharitable view of lawyers, viewing them as being either primarily motivated by money or willing to manipulate the facts in order to advance their client's interest. However, the lawyers in this survey sample were not much different in their career choice motivations from the other professionals in the sample as a whole. The top three choices (although not in the same order) of career choice motivators among all four occupational categories were the ability to make a difference and/or help people, pride in the work, and job security. Law professionals (62.8%) trailed only academics (70.6%) in stating that the ability to make a difference and/or help people was a primary motivation for career choice. Of all the occupations in the survey sample, lawyers have the greatest opportunity to open a practice and work for themselves, thus liberating them from becoming subjects of labor expropriation. While this did indeed translate to lawyers having the lowest self-reported rate of underemployment, this did not necessarily translate into occupational satisfaction.

Lawrence Krieger, a professor of law at Florida State University, and Kennon Sheldon, a professor of psychology at the University of Missouri, conducted a study on lawyer happiness from the framework of self-determination theory.[25] Self-determination theory proposes that all human beings have psychological needs for competency, autonomy, authenticity, and connectedness with others. One purpose of the study was to debunk the myth that lawyers are characterized by certain (usually undesirable) personality traits that make them different from the general population.

Krieger and Sheldon found that many attorneys arrive at law school with high aspirations to help others and make a difference, but are changed by the process of law education itself, as well as the realities of the job market. Krieger and Sheldon's findings are supported by the surveys in this study, in that the primary career motivators for attorneys were a desire to help others/make a difference and take pride in their work. Corroborating the interviewees, Krieger and Sheldon also found that prospective law students had an unrealistic expectation of earnings.

Krieger and Sheldon divided their attorney population into "prestige" occupations (large law firms engaged in primarily corporate, commercial, and international practice), "service" occupations (prosecutors, public defenders, government agency and legal aid attorneys), judges, and an "other" category, the general practitioners that are associated with neither high earnings nor public service. The happiest attorneys were judges, who have both relatively high salaries and autonomy as well as a public service component, followed by those employed in public service. While these public lawyers had lower salaries than those employed at large, prestigious law firms, their work was more connected to their personal intrinsic values and they tended to have better work-life balance. Indeed, the number of billable hours was the strongest negative predictor of attorney well-being. However, the overworked and overpaid large-firm attorneys had higher ratings of well-being than those attorneys the authors classified as "other."

The interviewees in this study belonged to Krieger and Sheldon's "other" category. It is likely that prestige attorneys—who nevertheless experience particular forms of degradation—did not participate in this study, as highly paid law firm associates struggling to meet billable hour requirements are unlikely to consider themselves underemployed. However, as large law firms are turning to outsourcing, advancement to partnership becomes more competitive, and fiscal austerity dominates the public sector, it is likely that more and more attorneys will find themselves in the "other" category. Although these "other" attorneys have opportunities to "make a difference" for their clients, the economics of a small law practice make daily survival stressful and insecure.

Both A.A. and L.W., the attorney interviewees in this study, were members of Krieger and Sheldon's "other" category of lawyers. Both were recent law school graduates who had unsuccessful searches for legal employment and ended up opening their own private law practice. L.W. clearly viewed the problem as one of oversupply, or too many lawyers, and described his local market as "glutted" with lawyers because of proximity to two law schools. L.W. admitted that there would be less competition in some rural counties "farther out," but they needed the income from his wife's job and the daily commute was logistically unfeasible.

By contrast, A.A.'s practice was located in an "underserved area," where there were, at most, 10 other attorneys in the same county. A.A. described the problem as one of distribution in that there were "too many attorneys doing the same thing in the same place." A.A. also blamed the system of legal service delivery as being "stymied and slow to...change and adapt," suggesting that legal services could be provided at an affordable price if the profession was willing to be creative and move away from a "corporate focus" on the practice of law. Like George Ritzer's independent physicians attempting to survive in a world of rationalized "McDoctors," the independent attorney can survive if he or she is sufficiently entrepreneurial.

A.A. and L.W. both described unmet legal needs in their respective communities. In A.A.s case, "probably 70% of my county lives below the poverty line," and literally have no access to justice. A.A. further described clients who had attempted to "do things themselves" which created a "huge [legal] mess" for them. L.W. went into detail about the microeconomics of his practice, describing potential clients who called every day and could not afford his services "even as cheap as I work." L.W. was frustrated because the people who called him "desperately needed help" but they could not "even afford my breakeven point." Both A.A. and L.W. also reported on the fate of some of their classmates. A.A. reported that "maybe 60% of my graduating class was employed in a job that required bar passage." She also described the situation of a friend who was literally a slave to billable hour requirements and was "constantly working," even on the weekends. L.W. described classmates who had "hung a shingle as a solo attorney" as a last resort and were barely making ends meet. L.W. further reported that "not a week goes by" where he doesn't hear from a classmate who has "taken a job as a financial advisor, or teaching or something...they've basically left the practice of law because they just couldn't hold out anymore."

A graduating law student in Texas, who is in the top third of her class in addition to having law review and other achievements to her resume, describes a futile job search that is strikingly similar to that reported by A.A. and L. W. She also addresses the problem of oversupply and inadequate job market information:

> *This is the legal job market. We do not need to protect new students from it. We need to be honest about it. I do not agree with the current trend of discouraging everyone from going to law school, but schools should start being more open about the market and job prospects, and should provide realistic income expectations from the beginning. I realize that schools may shy away from the truth because it is not very good for business...*[26]

Although this was not the major topic of the interviews, both A.A. and L.W. alluded to a system of outsourced and contract legal work, primarily on the part of local governments. These jobs involved services usually provided by public entities such as prosecution, criminal defense and even foster care. In essence, legal jobs that once were performed by a "public servant" with a regular, full-time job were now subject to a privatized system of contracts and bidding. Although strapped attorneys in private practice would compete for these contracts, L.W. described the "deal" offered in one state in which attorneys were paid by the hour at rates that were set in 1994. According to L.W., "...it'll get you some work and it'll get you some experience, and at least cover your gas to get back and forth to court...maybe buy your lunch, but you'd better have some other way to pay your rent for a year or two..."

Several theories have been offered to explain why so few attorneys choose professions that involve public service. A common theme is the idea that attorneys are simply greedy and gravitate to high income employment in large corporate firms. Another theory is that high levels of educational debt renders the lower salaries at these jobs financially unsustainable. In *The Trap: Selling Out to Stay Afloat in Winner Take All America*,[27] Daniel Brook documents the process by which attorneys (as well as other professionals) abandon their ideals of making the world a better place in exchange for corporate work that allows them to secure a home mortgage and start a family on top of their educational debt. However, the public service "jobs" themselves are being decimated in an era of public fiscal austerity and outsourcing to privatization.

Christa McGill, an attorney who formerly worked at the Social Security Administration and is now in private practice where she represents social security claimants and disabled veterans, has challenged the notion that law students are abandoning public service occupations solely because of astronomical levels of law school debt. McGill rather argues that it is a combination of how students are socialized in law school and how occupational pipelines are constructed that determines where and how students decide to pursue their legal careers. Although the amount of student debt does have a small influence on law graduates' choice of career, the greatest predictors of whether or not a law graduate took a job in the public sector were (a) a pre-existing desire to work in the public sector and (b) opportunities for summer internships in the public sector.[28]

Moreover, McGill also found that public service motivated students were under-represented at prestige firms and over-represented in small firms and "other" categories. McGill suggests that these graduates would desire a public service job, but when such jobs are not available, they migrate to low quality legal employment; or, like A.A. and L.W., they become sole practitioners by default. McGill concludes that, ."..the biggest barrier between students and [public service] jobs may be lack of supply, not the lack of demand by law students."[29] The irony is that public service jobs can help fulfill social needs while at the same time providing employment for law graduates that is both psychologically rewarding and fiscally sustainable, yet in a political climate that expends considerable efforts to disparage the public sector and demands to shrink it, this solution is not likely to be viable in the near-term.

The legal profession appears to be represented by a trifurcated labor market, illustrating the complexity of degradation factors even within a single occupation: highly paid associates in large, prestigious law firms, public service attorneys, and the so-called "others." The group that has received the most attention is the large-firm associates. These positions are generally reserved for top students from elite law schools and are highly competitive. The work of these firms is directed to the preservation and defense of the interests of capital—mergers and acquisitions, global business transactions, tax avoidance, legislative influence, and labor union busting. Although it is difficult to sympathize with the overworked plight of big law firm associates given their huge salaries, when compared to the even huger profits realized by the firms from the work of these associates, it operates as an expensive form of expropriation.

The second group of attorneys—the public- sector attorneys—are the happiest. Although public sector jobs are characterized by alienating factors related to bureaucratic structures, this may be outweighed by their appeal to intrinsic values and public service motivation. The final group—the "others"—may be represented by some combination of the romanticized small-town attorney of the past (think Atticus Finch) and the occupational outcasts who comprise Marx's reserve army. Logic may suggest that this group represents the best hope of addressing unmet legal needs as well as the intellectual freedom to solve social problems, yet it is the most financially unable to do so.

Academic Markets

While employers are bombarding public officials with complaints about an untrained workforce, student enrollments at community colleges and public four-year universities are booming. Faced with the dual pressures of unpredictable enrollment increases and budget reductions, colleges are increasingly hiring part-time contingent, or adjunct faculty. In the early 1980s, about 20% of college courses nationwide were taught by adjuncts, and by 1998 this had risen to 43%. More recent data from the American Association of University Professors indicates that non-tenure track faculty comprised 64% of university faculty overall in 2001, and increased to 70% in 2011.

In earlier decades, adjuncts were generally working professionals who taught a course or two on a part-time basis, either for reasons of personal fulfillment or generation of a side income. Today's adjuncts are more likely to be Ph.Ds. attempting to squeeze out a living by cobbling together courses at a number of scattered institutions. These adjuncts are usually paid a couple of thousand dollars per course, and have no office, no benefits, few opportunities for professional development, and little prospect of a permanent position. Because they spend a lot of time traveling between their fragmented teaching gigs, some have labeled them "roads scholars."[30]

The academic job market has been polarized beyond the split between full-time tenure track and adjunct faculty. As universities become increasingly competitive, they strive to build reputation and prestige by attracting high-profile "celebrity" faculty. These faculty members have not necessarily earned reputations through the usual process of peer review, but have achieved wider national recognition through high-profile business or government positions. Because resources are limited, universities will bid against each other for a handful of high-profile faculty in a few selected departments rather than attempting to improve academic departments across the board, in the hopes that the celebrity faculty will generate a "halo effect" for the rest of the university.[31] In this manner, academia begins to take on the characteristics of winner-take-all markets, with a very small number of celebrities receiving huge salaries and research budgets, a somewhat larger (but decreasing) core of reasonably well paid tenured faculty and administrators, and an army of underpaid adjuncts.

Some studies have suggested that a large number of adjuncts has adverse impacts on the student experience. This is not necessarily because the adjuncts are lower quality instructors. Indeed, a number of studies confirm that the quality of adjunct teaching is comparable to that of full-time professors.[32] In addition to tenuous and underpaid employment, adjuncts do not have access to the larger educational infrastructure. Adjuncts do not have offices or other places to meet with students, and, outside of their own class or subject matter, they are unfamiliar with the college's other offerings or programs in general. Thus, students receive adequate subject-matter instruction from adjuncts, but their overall academic integration is compromised. Adjuncts have been compared to an academic "underclass, [who have been relegated to] a high level of job insecurity, low wages and poor working conditions."[33] Many adjuncts belong to the American Federation of Teachers, which has historically represented public schoolteachers in grades K-12, and in July of 2002, 4,000 adjuncts at NYU joined the United Auto Workers union.[34]

At least one researcher has suggested that the primary conceptual paradox in attempting to describe the "market" of adjunct faculty was whether or not to view non-tenure-track-faculty (adjuncts) as professionals or laborers.[35] Adjunct faculty were found to be more similar to other contingent professionals (computer technicians, nurses, and engineers) due to their level of commitment to work and professional standards. Moreover, they share the traditional professionals' desire for autonomy, adherence to self-governing regulations such as peer review, and a general antipathy toward labor unions. However, adjuncts have been stripped of agency (the ability to form collegial relationships, access resources, and affect institutional outcomes) and the ability to learn and grow by engaging in professional development. Thus, although adjuncts' relationship to their work may be more like that of the professional, their relationship to the organization is more like that of the laborer.

S.D., the academic interviewee in this study, had been an instructor of English composition for nearly two decades, alternating between adjunct and full-time employment. Her current "gig" was comprised of classes for freshmen at a four-year college and an English-as-a-second-language class at a local community college. SD described a desperate scramble every semester to decide whether to commit to classes at University A while awaiting appointments at University B, wherein a wrong guess or a last-minute cancellation would leave her "kicking [myself] and broke." S.D. further reported that at one time she had a full-time position as an academic advisor, and even though such activities fell "outside of contract" (i.e., uncompensated), she addressed these issues with her students because "ethically, I feel like if I have the information I should share it." She confirmed findings in the literature that describe a wholesale destruction of permanent, full-time and tenured faculty positions in favor of the just-in-time adjunct system. S.D. said she would not even mind teaching half-time if they were paid at half a professor's salary, which would allow her some chance of actually making ends meet.

One of S.D.'s biggest disappointments was the total lack of respect and potential avenues to upward mobility. When a rare tenured position did become available, adjuncts were given "no credit for the service" they had already given the institution. S.D. described how the "regular" faculty tended to view the adjuncts as inexperienced, although they had similar credentials and teaching experience. S.D. described "sitting through professional development stuff on how to teach that you darn well could be presenting yourself." As almost an aside, S.D. mentioned a recent vote to establish a collective bargaining unit, which was "vociferously" fought by the institution.

S.D. loved teaching, but lamented that there appeared to be no future. The loss of a future is particularly acute for adjuncts, who are denied access to the "usual" academic support systems such as research budgets and financial assistance to attend national conferences—all of the basic requirements that establish oneself as a scholar. S.D. concluded that where one ended up in academia seemed to depend on "bad luck…due to market constraints, not due to your experience constraints."

Summary and Conclusion

Professional labor markets have thus become "degraded," but not by the same simplistic Taylorist reductionism that characterized industrial manufacturing. The industrial working classes made a Faustian bargain with the capitalist establishment: we will work these boring, repetitive, tiresome and meaningless jobs in exchange for livable wages, reasonable job security, and benefits such as health care and retirement—a bargain that has been unilaterally abandoned. With professionals, the work itself has not so much been deconstructed as work relationships have been rearranged. Academics continue to prepare and teach classes; lawyers advise about legal issues, write briefs and try cases; health care workers diagnose and treat patients; engineers design buildings and bridges; IT and computer programmers solve technical problems. Unlike their blue collar counterparts, professionals maintain a degree of autonomy over their actual work and have not experienced labor degradation as described by Marx and even necessarily by Braverman. However, what has changed is their relationship to the employing institution, most particularly their ability to build secure and meaningful careers.

Critics of Marx and Braverman (and even some of their supporters) believed that professionals would remain immune from labor degradation by virtue of the education, reasoning skills and autonomous decision-making necessary to perform their jobs. Braverman himself, who sometimes suggested that some higher-level occupations might be immune from degraded labor processes, also predicted the emergence of new and more complex labor structures with the goal of increasing profits by making workers fungible and reducing their power and status. The evidence suggests that this is happening, although it appears to be happening in public and non-profit organizations as well as in private, profit-driven ones. This could be a result of a more general trend of organizations to become larger and more bureaucratic (rationalization), or a cultural imperative of efficiency and the urge to make government and public service "more like a business."

David Kusnet corroborates the paradox of this phenomenon in his 2008 *Love the Work, Hate the Job.*[36] Kusnet's work covers the stories of aerospace engineers at Boeing, software testers at Microsoft, and health care professionals in the Seattle, Washington area. Kusnet suggests that modern surveys on work satisfaction may neglect to accurately measure work dissatisfactions because many professionals like and enjoy their day-to-day work. Indeed, Kusnet finds that these workers—including those who went on strike at Boeing—are actually more concerned about the quality of products and services than their employers. In today's workplace, more people are doing work that "challenges them intellectually rather than exhausts them physically" and have, to a large extent, chosen their profession.

Yet, professional workers are finding that their jobs (and even their careers) are part-time, contingent, and less secure. Many of them also worry that cost-cutting and "bean-counting" is compromising the quality of their work as well as their professional norms. Nurses, for example, were "offended by the commercialization of health care" and its negative implications for patients. Software designers (corroborating the infamous "bugginess" of Microsoft product launches) wondered whether programs were being rushed out the door before they had been adequately tested. Teachers and social workers complained of caseloads that prevented them from providing the individualized attention their students and clients needed. In other words, professionals still have control over the discrete decisions and tasks that constitute their individual work, but they lack control over the overall processes and the bigger decisions involving resource allocations and outcome measurement.

Perhaps the most obvious evidence of Braverman's predictions is the bifurcation of professional work. That is, the occupational split is now no longer only about educated persons versus those without education, but a split in which persons with similar or near-identical skills and credentials are split into good-paying, secure jobs and low-paid, part-time and contingent jobs. Kusnet describes an über-credentialed "Norma Rae with an MBA" working at a temporary position at Microsoft, "in the hope of getting a foot in the door for a permanent position." He also describes a veritable caste system at Microsoft, where employees wore badges that identified them as "temporary" or "permanent." In spite of having similar skills and credentials, the temporary employees were paid significantly lower salaries, did not receive the stock options that made some of their co-workers wealthy, and had almost no prospects of upward mobility. As Kusnet explains: "A new kind of class conflict was emerging between professionals and technicians and the people who managed them, outearned them, and lorded it over them, politically and culturally."[37]

Thus, it appears that Braverman's predictions about the inexorability of labor degradation and its manifestation at ever higher levels of occupational skill and standing have come to pass. Kusnet also asserts that professionals (largely because many of them are public employees) are now the most heavily unionized occupational group. Professionals do not join unions for the same reasons that their working class neighbors do, and the unions themselves are finding that they have to adapt to this new (and somewhat counter-intuitive) membership. So far, there have been no signs of revolutionary activism. In spite of the loss of relative pay and status, the majority of professionals remain committed to their work, including professional standards and ideals. But what does it portend when now even professionals, like most everyone else in the work force, are working harder for less and living with increasing economic insecurity?

Notes

1 Rothwell, J. (2014, July). Still searching: Job vacancies and STEM skills. The Brookings Institute. Retrieved from: http://www.brookings.edu/~/media/research/files/reports/2014/07/stem/job%20vacancies%20and%20stem%20skills.pdf

2 Matloff, N. (2013). Are foreign students the 'best and brightest'? Data and implications for immigration policy. Economic Policy Institute Briefing Paper #356. Retrieved from: http://www.epi.org/publication/bp356-foreign-students-best-brightest-immigration-policy/

3 *Id.* at p. 3.

4 Lerman, R. I. (1998). Is there a labor shortage in the information technology industry? *Issues in Science and Technology, 14*(3), 82-83.

5 Benderly, B. L. (2013). It doesn't add up. *Columbia Journalism Review, 52*(1), 54-56. Retrieved from: http://www.cjr.org/essay/it_doesnt_add_up.php?page=all

6 Schneiderman, R. (2005). IEEE cites outsourcing as wages drop and U.S. loses 221,000 jobs. *Electronic Design, 53*(6), 25. Retrieved from: http://electronicdesign.com/archive/ieee-cites-outsourcing-wages-drop-and-us-loses-221000-jobs

7 Matloff, N. (2004). Globalization and the American IT worker. *Communications of the ACM, 47*(11), 27-29. Retrieved from: -and-the-american-it-worker/abstract

8 Benderly, B. L. (2013). Supra p. 54.

9 October 2015 data from the Kaiser family Foundation, http://kff.org/other/state-indicator/physicians-by-gender/

10 U.S. Census Bureau, http://www.census.gov/people/io/files/Men_in_Nursing_Occupations.pdf. Full-time female nurses earn 91 cents for every dollar earned by full-time male nurses.

11 Berenson, R. A. (1991). A physician's view of managed care. *Health Affairs, 10*(4), 106-119.

12 Ritzer, G. and Walczak, D. (1988). Rationalization and the deprofessionalization of physicians. *Social Forces, 67*(1), 1-22 at p.10.

13 Greenhouse, S. (1999, Feb 4). Angered by H.M.O.'s treatment, more doctors are joining unions. *The New York Times*. Retrieved from: http://www.nytimes.com/1999/02/04/nyregion/angered-by-hmo-s-treatment-more-doctors-are-joining-unions.html?pagewanted=all&src=pm

14 Berenson, R. A. (1991). Ibid. at p. 115

15 Chernomas, R. (1986). An economic basis for the proletarianization of physicians. *International Journal of Health Services, 16*(4), 669-674 at p. 669.

16 Pfifferling, J. (1997). The revolution is here. *Physician Executive, 23*(5), 36-38. Retrieved from: http://www.physicianleaders.org/news/journals/plj#JournalArchives

17 Berenson, R. A. (1991). *Supra* at p. 111.

18 Spetz, J. (2011). Unemployed and underemployed nurses. International Centre for Human Resources in Nursing. Retrieved from: http://www.icn.ch/images/stories/documents/pillars/sew/ICHRN/Policy_and_Research_Papers/Unemployed_and_Underemployed_Nurses.pdf

19 Rehnquist, W. H. (1986, Sept. 12). The legal profession today. Dedicatory address before Indiana University School of Law. Also in *62 Indiana Law Journal*, 151, 153 (1987). Retrieved from: http://www.repository.law.indiana.edu/ilj/

20 Bruck, A., & Canter, A. (2008). Supply, demand, and the changing economics of large law firms. *Stanford Law Review, 60*(6), 2087-2130.

21 Harper, S. J. (2013, March 28). The tyranny of the billable hour. *The New York Times*. Retrieved from: http://www.nytimes.com/2013/03/29/opinion/the-case-against-the-law-firm-billable-hour.html

22 Hirshon, R. E. (2002, February). Law and the billable hour. *ABA Journal 88*, 10. Retrieved from: http://www.abajournal.com

23 Bruck, A. & Canter, A. (2008). *Supra.*

24 Abrams, D. L. (2004, January 27). Legal bills review in an era of subtle overbilling. Retrieved from: http://www.metrocorpcounsel.com/pdf/2004/January/27.pdf

25 Kreiger, L. S. & Sheldon, K. M. (2014). What makes lawyers happy? Transcending the anecdotes with data from 6200 lawyers. Pending publication (2015) in *George Washington Law Review 83*, 554-627.

26 Venrick, H. (2014). Will work for...well, anything at this point. *Texas Bar Journal, 77*(3), 224-225 at p. 225. Retrieved from: http://www.texasbar.com/AM/Template.cfm?Section=Past_Issues&Template=/CM/ContentDisplay.cfm&ContentID=25417

27 Brook, D. (2007). *The trap: Selling out just to stay afloat in winner-take-all America*. New York, NY: Henry Holt & Co., LLC.

28 McGill, C. (2006). Educational debt and law student failure to enter public service careers: Bringing empirical data to bear. *Law & Social Inquiry, 31*(3), 677-708.

29 *Id.* at p. 704.

30 McArdle, E. (2002, December). The adjunct explosion. *University Business, 5*(10), 25-29 at p. 25. Retrieved from: http://www.universitybusiness.com

31 Rodden, J. (1998). The scholar gypsies: Academic celebrity in America. *Modern Age, 40*(2), 169-176 at p. 172. Retrieved from: http://www.mmisi.org/MA/40_02/rodden.pdf

32 Roueche, J. E., Roueche, S. D., & Milliron, M. D. (1997). *Strangers in their own land: Part-time faculty in American community colleges.* Washington, D. C.: Community College Press/American Association of Community Colleges.

33 Kimber, M. (2003). The tenured 'core' and the tenuous 'periphery': The casualization of academic work in Australian universities. *Journal of Higher Education Policy & Management, 25*(1), 41-50.

34 McArdle, E. (2002, December). *Supra* at p. 28.

35 Umbach, D. (2010). Theories used to study and understand non-tenure-track faculty. *ASHE Higher Education Report, 36*(5), 19-38.

36 Kusnet, D. (2008). *Love the work, hate the job: Why America's best workers are more unhappy than ever.* Hoboken, New Jersey: John Wiley & Sons, Inc.

37 *Id.* at p. 91.

Chapter Seven
The Dynamics of Career Choice

*"The contempt of risk and the presumptuous hope of success,
are in no period of life more active than at the age
at which young people choose their professions."*

Adam Smith, *The Wealth of Nations,* 1776.

IN THE UNITED STATES, career decisions are made when a student graduates from high school or college, generally between the ages of 18 and 22 years. Although the college-bound have an additional four years before committing to a career, they need to make some preliminary determinations in order to select courses and declare a major. The "science" of career counseling has thus primarily focused on high school and college students, although with the current era of layoffs and job insecurity, some studies have begun to address the needs of mid-career (or career-changing) adults.

In reality, the typical career decision is more of a process rather than a one-time event, as decision parameters shift based on informational feedback and changing circumstances. For example, the pre-med undergraduate that is not accepted into medical school must modify the plan to become a doctor that was made when choosing an undergraduate major. Other decisions are impacted by life events, such as the death of a family member that requires a student to forego school and find immediate employment. Students are faced with a perennial Catch-22 of choosing courses that will somehow help them to develop an as-yet-to-be-determined "career" while not foreclosing alternatives that might turn out to be better. The career counseling literature itself presents a dichotomy of techniques to facilitate a decision while at the same time reassuring the student that failure to make the optimal decision at the earliest possible moment will not result in catastrophic outcomes.[1]

Career Choice and Job Market Information

One hypothesis to explain underemployment is that young people are not provided sufficient labor market information early enough in the educational process. This (hypothetically) leads to poor educational choices which then serve to saddle young adults with educational debt for training and skills that they are unable to maximize in the workplace. However, even if young adults had access to better career information, this would not necessarily optimize their career choices. In a rapidly changing labor "market," skills and occupations that are in demand when a student embarks on a course of study may become saturated with credential-holders by the time of graduation, especially if there is a public propaganda campaign to encourage particular courses of study because of purported skills shortages. There is also evidence that schools, particularly private for-profit schools, are incentivized to exaggerate the benefits of their credential offerings.

Most high schools and community colleges provide some kind of career counseling—a combination of assisting students with choosing courses and majors in addition to identifying potential career prospects. These services frequently include a battery of tests to determine the students' aptitudes, values and interests, and the tests themselves may be fraught with reliability and validity issues. In developing a general theoretical taxonomy on career decision difficulties, one study identified 44 specific difficulties under the general headings of lack of motivation, indecisiveness, dysfunctional myths, lack of knowledge about the career decision process, lack of knowledge about oneself (8 categories), lack of information about occupations (4 categories), lack of knowledge about ways to obtain additional information, unreliable information (6 categories), internal conflicts (7 categories) and external conflicts (4 categories).[2] Thus, it seems like the "science" of career counseling itself is challenged in its own efforts to procure and/or disseminate information that is operationally useful to students and graduates.

Even with the availability of career planning services, recent studies have shown that a fair number of students do not pursue careers consistent with their college or graduate course of study. A survey of engineering undergraduates found that 44% were unsure about pursuing a career in engineering and 14% were definite that they would not pursue engineering.[3] Alternatively, immediate career indecision can lead to plans for further education: A survey of masters-level mathematics students (the majority who expressed a distinct preference for statistics) found that about one-fifth intended to immediately pursue graduate studies, another 32% intended to pursue both graduate studies and work, and 68% intended to pursue a doctoral degree within 10 years of earning their masters.[4] Surprisingly, even among graduates of a surgical training program, 25% had changed to a different surgical specialty, 20% had moved to a non-surgical specialty, and 2% had left the medical profession altogether.[5]

Hypothetically assuming that better career and labor market information could be made available, the job search process itself is highly inefficient. Although workers are theoretically chosen for the best "fit" of skills and aptitude, this is nearly impossible to determine without allowing each individual applicant some short-term opportunity to actually perform on the job. Employers thus create job postings that describe their hypothetical ideal candidate, and job seekers desperately tweak their resumes (both online and off) to make themselves "fit" into jobs they believe might be a good match. The irony is that when there are literally hundreds of minimally qualified (and often overqualified) applicants for each advertised position, employers must rationalize the hiring process both in order to manage the high volume of applications and to mitigate the possibility of illegal discrimination.

Peter Cappelli, a Professor of Management at the University of Pennsylvania Wharton School, makes the argument that a huge glut of qualified workers has allowed employers the ability to demand a "perfect" range of skills and competencies. In essence, the perfect (Capelli terms this hypothetical perfect job candidate the "purple squirrel") becomes the enemy of the good. Employers want to both minimize risk of a failed job candidate as well as insure that the new hire will be able to pick up the work of two or three other employees who were (or will be) subject to layoff (for the same single salary). Cappelli also argues that applicant screening software operates as a brutal sorting mechanism, most likely eliminating many qualified candidates because their application materials are not compatible with the software algorithms on some irrelevant point.[6]

Some studies have attempted to analyze the efficacy of various job search strategies. Many private and public (state workforce development) job search coaches in the U.S. recommend the use of personal networks as a way to circumvent applicant screening software and overwhelmed HR employees. Recognizing a "well-documented" problem that a "substantial portion" of graduates were overeducated, an Australian study examined the effect of job search methods on the incidence of underemployment.[7] This study found that graduates were overeducated both at their entry point into the labor market as well as throughout their working lives, and analyzed whether particular job search strategies helped to mitigate the incidence of underemployment. Graduates who found jobs through public service examinations were most likely to be overeducated.

Graduates who found jobs through social networks and direct employer applications had better qualification matches than graduate job seekers who found work through "formal search channels" (job advertisements and employment agencies). However, the much-touted strategy of "networking" also produced different results for different groups of job-seekers, suggesting the implication of status sorting phenomena: Older males who found jobs through networking

230

were less likely to be overeducated, which the authors attribute to their access to the "hidden job market." However, personal networking had no advantage over job advertisements for young graduates or older females.

Recently, a Russian study (a country that is not known for being open about its shortcomings or permitting publication thereof) admitted that high un- and underemployment among professional workers threatened a "second wave of crisis" for workers who were barely recovering from "the mass layoffs of 2008."[8] In Russia, the State plays a much greater role in both subsidizing education as well as rationing it than in the U.S. The author reports that only about 30% of university graduates are finding jobs in their academic specialties, and the State has already imposed reductions in funded education slots for some of these specialties. Although Kuz'min's state-mandated solutions (affecting both schools and subsidized students) would be inappropriate in a market economy, he did propose that the State provide better long-range demand forecasts for professional specialties, as well as insure that this information was available to "every young person who is about to choose a life path."[9] The Kuz'min study implies that even in a planned economy, it is difficult to maintain and disseminate adequate labor market information, either for purposes of labor policy planning at the state level or career decisions at the individual level. It also suggests that, as Russia has adopted Westernized practices over the past several decades, it too is experiencing professional underemployment, which further suggests that underemployment is not an exclusive phenomenon of capitalist economies.

One study has found a positive correlation between the number of available formal job information sources, perceptions of person-job fit, and work outcomes.[10] In the case of public employment, reasonably adequate salary and employer information is available through freedom of information requests or other public databases. In the case of private employment, such information is frequently subject to confidentiality, business necessity or trade secret protocols, so information is compiled based on individual job announcements and then aggregated by public workforce development agencies or private job search services.[11] Thus, there is some evidence that the quality of a career choice is improved with information, but there are questions about how much of the plethora of available job information is accurate and reliable.

In the real-life world of the career decision process, the majority of people do not behave in the manner of economists, scouring job information and dispassionately analyzing various labor markets. Rather, this process is usually a circuitous journey of determining one's own interest and aptitudes in course selection, and only later figuring out where these might lead to a career. Dissertation survey respondents who indicated sources of career information other than those presented in the survey choices tended to fall into one of two categories. The most common were the do-it-yourselfers. These responses ranged from "self-analysis" and "self-study" to "gut feel," "prayed to God," "my heart," and "decided things for myself." The second most common response was consultation with personal networks such as friends, family members, professors, "job shadowing," high school counselors, and career fairs. Nine survey responses were coded under the category of "regrets." These individuals either blamed themselves for insufficient effort in researching careers or otherwise expressed a lack of information in general. One survey respondent stated, "...there was no way of knowing what I needed to know at the time."

In the dissertation surveys, thirty-five respondents indicated some form of intrinsic motivation for their career choice, with many of them using terms like "enjoy," "love," and even "passion." Respondents who were not pointed to careers through their own interests or aptitudes tended to arrive at them somewhat serendipitously. In these cases, they followed the recommendations of a friend, or otherwise just "fell into" a particular field. The interviews echoed these themes around non-directional pursuit of specific courses or majors that led to careers:

> *SD: I majored in English just because I liked it years ago. I went to grad school just because I wasn't sure what to do, and there I stumbled onto teaching because that funded my graduate study. And it was through teaching that I discovered I liked teaching, and further I really liked teaching writing. My original graduate degree was in English literature, and I really enjoyed composition and rhetoric.*

> *AA: I had a...my undergrad is in psychology and I couldn't decide whether I was going to go on in psychology or go to law school. And the LSAT came first, so that's what I did. And I scored well enough to get into either one of the schools in my state...so, I went in that direction. I ended up in family law just because it's the area that has, in my mind, has the most flexibility, and is the most well-suited to my personality.*

> *NL: This goes way back to undergraduate. I really didn't know what I wanted to do or be, but I was good at technical writing, and I was good at statistics, and I majored in psychology with a minor in biology, and so the epidemiology just seemed to fit very well for me.*

> *LW: I had a long...I'm not a young man. I became an attorney at 52 years old. I'm 53 now. I had a long and diverse career, and at 45 years of age I had back surgery, and the company I worked for would not let me go back to work because I could not meet the heavy labor requirements that they basically added to my job right about the time I went out to have surgery. And I had long term disability insurance through my job and I qualified for that, so I went back to school. When I first went back, I thought I'd be a school teacher, but I didn't...it didn't take long to decide I really didn't want to be a schoolteacher. And I had a friend that was an attorney, and he said, you know, yeah, they would love to have you in law school. I applied and was accepted, and here I am. I wanted something I could do for the rest of my life. I've worked all my life, and just...you know, drawing a check from age 45 on was just not an option for me.*

Students, graduates, and even career-changing adults thus do not exclusively base their long-term career plans on formal job market information. However, when they do consult this information, there are issues with reliability and trustworthiness. In the dissertation study, survey respondents were asked a number of questions about their perceptions of the reliability of labor market information at the time they made their career decision and whether they believed information that was generally available to jobseekers today was reliable. Except for law professionals, nearly or greater than 80% of respondents in the other three occupational categories believed the information they accessed during their career decision process was both sufficient and reliable. Law professionals were clearly the most dissatisfied with labor market information as well as the most likely (58.51%) to believe that colleges and universities make false and misleading statements about job prospects in order to induce enrollments. However, a sizeable minority of the other respondents (between 37% and 46%) also believed that colleges were promulgating false information about job prospects. Lawyers again had the least confidence (31.91%) in the reliability of labor market information that was generally available. STEM professionals had the most confidence in the reliability of general labor market information at 60.97%. These results are summarized in Figure 1.

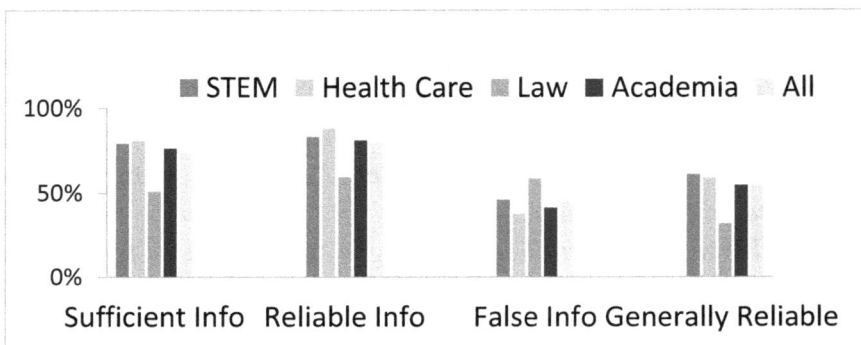

Figure 1. Quality of Labor Market and Career Information

In addition to "Yes" or "No" answers, respondents were also given the choice of "Don't know or unsure" for answers to questions about labor market information. This was to capture doubts about this information that may have prevented either an unqualified "yes" or "no" (i.e., the respondent could not state with certainty that information was either reliable or not). When allowed to express qualified doubt, over 19% of respondents in all occupations expressed uncertainty as to whether colleges were deliberately misrepresenting information, with academics expressing the most doubt (28.7%) followed by health care professionals (25.3%). Academics (21.7%) and law professionals (20.2%) were the most likely to express doubts about whether labor information was generally reliable. These results are summarized in Figure 2.

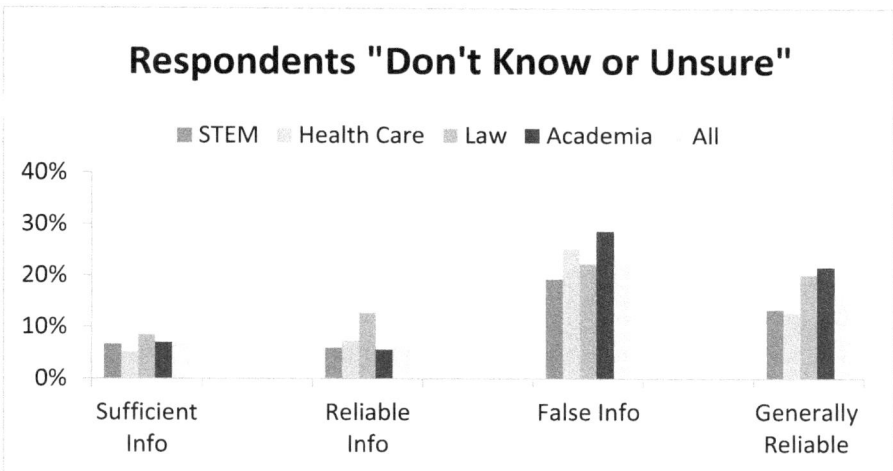

Figure 2. Doubts About Reliability of Labor Market and Career Information

Among all respondents, the most frequent source of career information was friends and family (49.1%), followed by college career offices (40.9%) and online resources (39.3%). The least utilized resource was public labor market databases (10.8%). Law professionals were the most likely to consult with friends and family (59.6%) and nonrelative members of the profession (40.0%) when making their career decision. STEM professionals were most likely to use their college career office (45.7%) and online resources (43.1%). Respondents who expressed dissatisfaction with the reliability of labor market information were then asked to identify these unreliable sources. Law (50.0%) and STEM (44.0%) professionals were the most likely to identify college career offices as unreliable. Health care professionals were the most likely to identify online resources (43.5%) and friends and family (39.1%) as unreliable. While dissatisfied STEM professionals gave public workforce development agencies a 27.6% unreliability rating, none (0.0%) of the dissatisfied health care professionals identified these agencies as an unreliable source.

The interviewees, particularly J.C. (IT engineer) and the two lawyers, provided greater detail about how unreliable information played into their decision to pursue credentials. J.C. admitted that he was to some degree led by the hype about the market demand for IT as well as its potential for a financially rewarding career. A.A. described an inability to determine what the micro-market in her geographic area was for attorneys, implying a greater need for localized detail rather than a broad national aggregate of the legal labor market. L.W. placed the blame squarely on law schools, who were incentivized to keep the pipelines of students full regardless of their potential job prospects. Although he said he did not believe there was some "malicious conspiracy," he did believe that law schools engaged in manipulation of data to make the numbers appear more positive. For example, so long as a law graduate was employed somewhere "requiring a bar admission," the individual was included in the overall job stats, even if he or she was barely making ends meet. According to L.W., "Law schools have had a vested interest in just turning our lawyers...it's in their best interest...which is not the same as the student's interest...to keep a steady flood of candidates coming through."

In the case of N.L (research scientist) and S.D. (college instructor), even if they had perfect information at the time, there was really no way for them to predict what the reality of their job situation would look like some years hence. In the late 1980s and early 1990s, S.D. observed "a very graying, aging, soon-to-retire population of English professors. So, I thought I was making a practical choice." What she did not predict was the wholesale destruction of full-time, tenure track positions and their replacement with low-paid, part-time and contingent adjuncts. N.L. did not experience so much a radical change in the "market" of research science, as workplaces that were characterized by gender discrimination, managerial ineptitude and a combination lack of transparency and research ethics (who gets credit versus who actually does the work) that resulted in her inability to be awarded the "better" assignments and move up in her career.

In essence, although better job market information could definitely help young adults, there are some things that either cannot be predicted, or do not constitute the "usual" information contained in job statistics (such as organizational culture, favoritism, etc.). Fortunately, there has been the advent of Internet sites such as Glass Door, which aggregates employee reviews of companies as places to work. These reviews cover more than simply job title, salary and benefits, but also cover issues such as management practices and workplace culture. However, such sites are still relatively new, and they depend upon voluntary (and sometimes subjective) submission of information.

Motivations for Career Choice and the Utility Maximization Model.

Economic models are based on the behavioral premise of utility maximization. That is, people make choices based on self-interest, which has alternatively been described as the satisfaction of preferences. Classical economists tended to view these preferences as being fairly fixed and predictable, and so utility maximization predicts that people will choose careers to maximize income, security, or prestige. However, even assuming that educational and career decisions are based solely on self-interest, this "interest" is a composite of numerous factors and complex interrelationships. Consequently, some economists[12] constructed alternative models to expand the concept of "self-interest" and explain empirical observations that could not be accommodated by Becker's original model of human capital.

The career decision process itself is influenced by prevailing cultural norms, personality differences,[13] and even one's position in the social hierarchy.[14] Moreover, students and workers are members of social systems outside of school and work, and these social systems exert influence over career and educational decisions beyond the usual considerations of individual preferences.[15] For example, a student with a parent who is an engineer or attorney may be pressured to choose these occupations (with financial support contingent thereon) regardless of her own ability or inclinations. Married workers with families must balance the needs for their own self-actualization with the needs of children, disabled family members, and often another working spouse, which has generated a subfield of so-called gender-space studies that examine how women's career options are limited by a primary earner spouse.[16]

One part of the dissertation study was a test of the utility maximization theory as it applied to persons making decisions about professional careers. Survey respondents were asked two questions with respect to their choice of professional career. The first question asked for the primary reason they chose their profession. For this question, respondents were permitted only one choice. The second question asked respondents about factors that influenced their choice of career or profession, and respondents could mark multiple responses. The choices in both questions were: (a) To make as much money as possible, (b) To enjoy status and prestige, (c) To be proud of what I do, (d) To have job security, (e) To be able to work for myself/own business, (f) To make a difference/help people, (g) For intellectual challenge, (h) Someone in my family is a member of this profession and encouraged me, and (i) Other.

Except for STEM professionals, the most frequent primary choices were to make a difference/help people and pride in the work. STEM professionals were the most likely to be motivated either by money (15.2%) or intellectual challenge (17.5%). While health care professionals had the highest need for job security (16.8%), over 10% of all professionals cited job security as a primary motivating factor. STEM (10.0%) and law (9.6%) professionals were the most likely to list the ability to work for oneself as a primary motivating factor. These results are summarized in Figure 3.

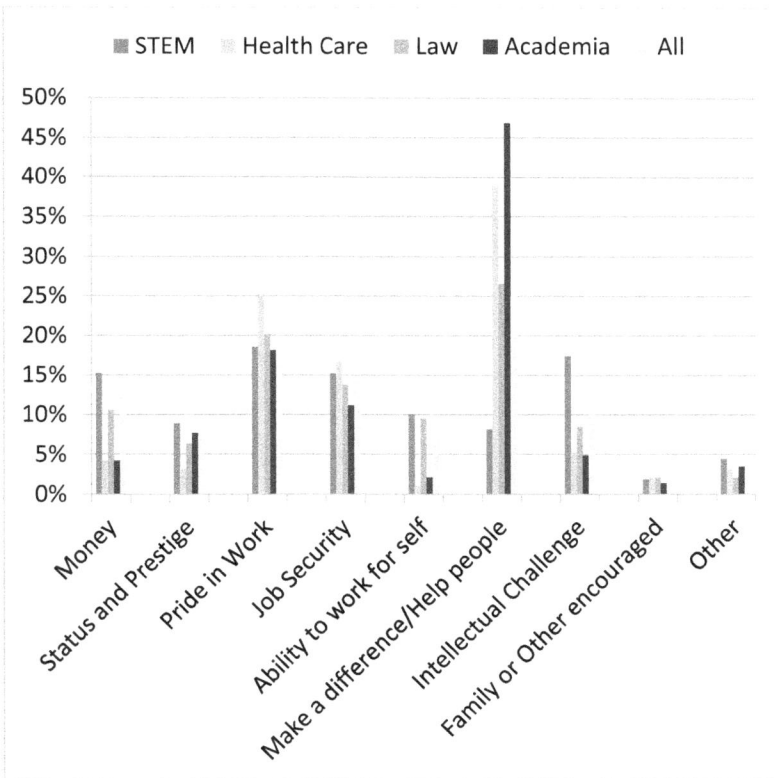

Figure 3. Primary Reason for Professional Career Choice.

Responses to the second question (in which respondents could select multiple choices) were not radically different. The most frequent choices for most categories were pride in work, job security, and making a difference/helping people. Academics again led with a desire to help people (70.6%) followed by law professionals (62.8%). Law professionals pulled ahead of STEM in citing money and intellectual challenge as a motivating factor (44.7% and 37.7% respectively). Except for academics (31.5%), over 40% of all other occupational categories said that job security was a motivating factor in professional choice. Over 50% of all professionals indicated a need for pride in their work, with law professionals marking this choice the most (62.8%). When considered as a motivating factor rather than a primary factor in occupational choice, law professionals were the most likely (44.7%) to cite money, followed by STEM (38.8%). This same pattern was observed for status and prestige (29.8% of law professionals and 26.1% of STEM professionals). These results are summarized in Figure 4.

In the 1990s, Indiana University Professor James L. Perry caught the attention of public administrators with his research on a phenomenon he terms "Public Service Motivation," or PSM. Perry defines PSM as a "predisposition to respond to motives grounded primarily or uniquely in public institutions."[17] Early studies identified three theoretical bases of PSM: (1) rational-based, which arises when individuals are committed to a public program, serve as advocates for it and personally identify with it; (2) norm-based, which arises when individuals are motivated by a duty to serve the public interest, often in the form of patriotism or civic involvement, and (3) affective, which is grounded in an emotional desire and willingness to help others. For public hiring managers, the promise of Perry's work is that citizens who are motivated to serve others could also be motivated to apply for work in federal, state and local governments, notwithstanding a climate of fiscal austerity and bureaucrat bashing.

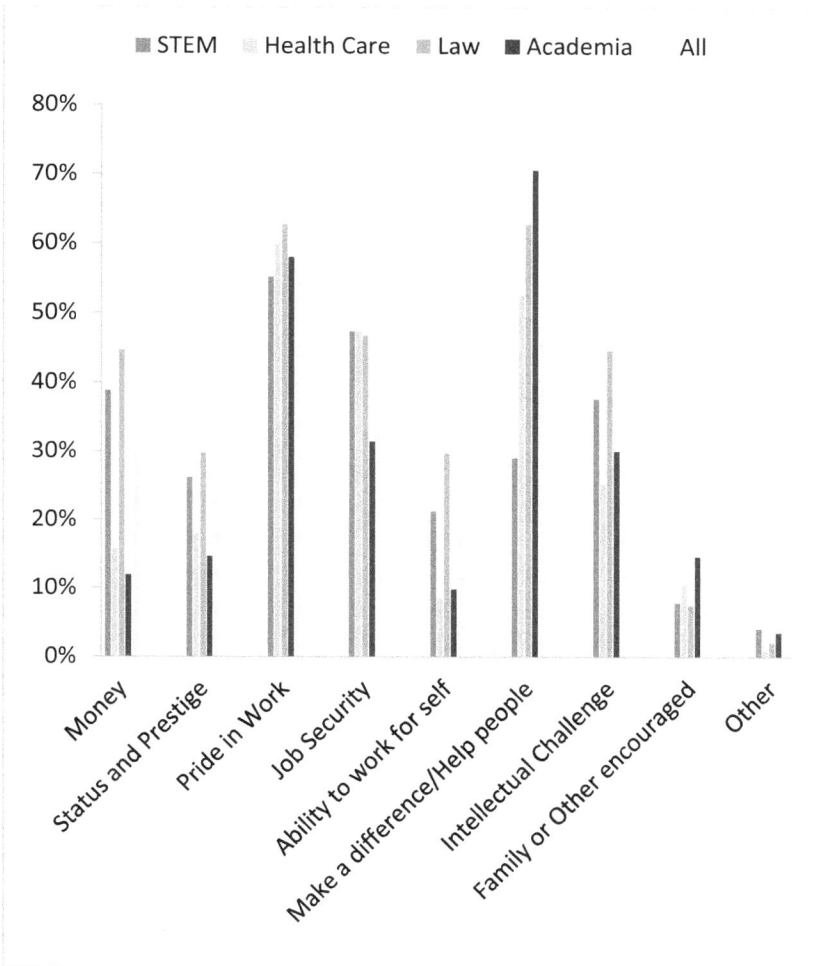

Figure 4. Factors that Influenced Professional Choice

In a subsequent study, Perry attempted to determine to what extent individuals are predisposed to perform public service as opposed to PSM being environmentally induced, i.e., created by socialization and culture.[18] That is, to what extent do "socializing institutions" determine how PSM values are inculcated. Perry used a self-administered survey to correlate parental socialization, religious socialization, professional identification and political ideology with the PSM constructs identified earlier. Perry's findings had a number of counter-intuitive surprises. Professional identification was negatively related to attraction to policy making, which Perry suggested might be associated with professional disdain for politics. Also a surprise was the negative relationship between church involvement and PSM. Perry suggests this may be either because church involvement leaves less time to devote to civic activities or as a consequence of "fundamentalist" rejection of worldly activities. Higher income also negatively correlated with commitment to public interest and civic duty. While Perry's study finds that there are no "bright line" relationships and simplistic explanations, his findings suggest that experiences with family, schools, profession and other socializing institutions have some influence over subsequent development of PSM.

Perry criticizes the neoclassical paradigm of economics and psychology which regards individual choice as an overly simplistic rational calculus of utility maximization, and the purpose of his research was to develop a theory of motivation that serves as an alternative to the self-interest "rational choice" theories that dominate current motivational theory in organizations.[19] He contends that motivation is a complex, interconnected confluence of socio-historical context (environmental variables that shape individual preferences and motives), motivational context (situational factors that influence behavior), and individual characteristics such as abilities, self-confidence, and behavior. Perry suggests that behavior ultimately results from a process of self-regulation, which influences motivation only to the extent that the individual is judging his or her behavior against a set of internal standards.

Building on Perry's work, later researchers[20] applied Q-methodology sorting on a sample of 69 federal and state employees[21] and found four individual conceptions of PSM: (1) Samaritans, who personally identify with the underprivileged and are emotionally moved to help people in distress, although they do not necessary have self-sacrificing tendencies; (2) Communitarians, who are motivated by sentiments of civic duty, associate public service with government service, and maintain a sense of pride and elitism; (3) Patriots, who are motivated by causes larger than themselves and possess a unique sense of loyalty to duty and high degree of self-sacrifice; (4) Humanitarians, who are motivated by a strong sense of social justice and fairness. Like Samaritans, Humanitarians are compassionate in their concern for those who lack political and economic resources, but they take a broader, societal perspective. While Communitarians and Patriots exhibit motives of self-sacrifice and civic duty, Patriots are greater risk-takers. Brewer further states that these employees may be "difficult to manage" because they believe that their primary responsibility is to the nation or the public at large and not to the organizational hierarchy.[22]

The explanatory value of the utility maximizing educational and career decision model is therefore likely to be inadequate because it fails to acknowledge the complexities of human motivation, the influence of workers' relationships with non-work social systems, the influence of inherent personality traits as well as environmental influences on the development of internal values, and the impact of insufficient or unreliable information. An uncertain and unfavorable job market itself can affect the decision process. Some career counselors have shifted the emphasis away from career planning and management to the creation of opportunity or leveraging of serendipitous events.[23] Others have found that heightened anxiety increases career indecision,[24] thus suggesting that decisions made in a constrained, hypercompetitive, anxiety-provoking environment are not likely to be good ones.

Conclusion

Most anyone who has looked for a job recently will likely agree that job market information could be improved. However, even better information will not be able to solve the underlying problem of inadequate jobs. This is more than just an inadequate number of jobs, but inadequate job quality in terms of pay, hours, opportunity to learn and grow, and some reasonable expectation of stability. It also seems that there is what economists term "pent up demand" in the form of opportunity to serve others and make a difference in society. While pay and benefits are certainly important, both the surveys and the interviews suggested a latent longing for livelihoods that not only provide a decent standard of living, but also make use of natural skills and talents in the service of others. The attorney, A.A., expressed disappointment in her education's failure to inform students how to "do the practical day-to-day things that being a lawyer requires" as well as "how to go about creating a meaningful career and...what that might look like." This raises the issue as to how well colleges and universities are serving the professional students who continue to pay rising tuition costs for ever-diminishing returns. It is to this educational piece that we next turn our analysis.

Notes

1 Lewis, R. A. & Gilhousen, M. R. (1981). Myths of career development: A cognitive approach to vocational counseling. *Personnel & Guidance Journal, 59*(5), 296-299.

2 Gati, I., Krausz, M., & Osipow, S. H. (1996). A taxonomy of difficulties in career decision making. *Journal of Counseling Psychology, 43*(4), 510-526. Retrieved from: http://www.apa.org/pubs/journals/cou/index.aspx

3 Lichtenstein, G., Loshbaugh, H. G., Clarr, B., Chen, H. L., Jackson, K., & Sheppard, S. D. (2009). An engineering major does not (necessarily) an engineer make: Career decision making among undergraduate engineering majors. *Journal of Engineering Education, 98*(3), 227-234.

4 Piotrowski, C., & Hemasinha, R. (2012). Career path decisions of master's–level mathematics students: A comparative review. *College Student Journal, 46*(4), 823-828. Retrieved from: http://www.questia.com/read/1G1-285532018/career-aspirations-of-undergraduate=mathematics-majors

5 Richards, J. M. J., Drummond, R., Murray, J., Fraser, S., McDonald, A., & Parks, R. W. (2009). What proportion of basic surgical trainees continue in a surgical career? A survey of the factors which are important in influencing career decisions. *Surgeon, 7*(5), 270-275.

6 Cappelli, P. (2012). *Why good people can't get jobs: The skills gap and what companies can do about it*. Philadelphia, PA: Wharton Digital Press.

7 Carroll, D., & Massimiliano, T. (2013, February). Job search as a determinant of graduate over-education: Evidence from Australia. University of Bonn, Forschungsinstitut zur Zukunft der Arbeit [Institute for the Study of Labor]. IZA Discussion Paper No. 7202 at p. 2.

8 Kuz'min, E., Ia. (2014). The market of labor and professions for young specialists. *Russian Education and Society, 56*(1), 13-18 at p. 13.

9 *Id.* at p. 17.

10 Saks, A. M., & Ashforth, B. E. (1997). A longitudinal investigation of the relationships between job information sources, applicant perceptions of fit, and work outcomes. *Personnel Psychology, 50*(2), 395-426

11 Indeed, some private employers (who are not subject to Constitutional guarantees of free speech or open records requirements) expressly prohibit their employees from discussing salaries with each other.

12 Stoikov, V. (1977). On some models of the educational decision. *Kykos, 30*(1), 74-87.

13 Pearson, C. S. (1991). *Awakening the heroes within: Twelve archetypes to help us find ourselves and transform the world*. New York, NY: HarperCollins.

14 Toit, D., & Coetzee, M. (2012). Archetypal values of science and engineering staff in relation to their career orientations. *South African Journal of Industrial Psychology, 38(*1), 1-14.

15 Duffy, R. D., & Dik, B. J. (2009). Beyond the self: External influences in the career development process. *Career Development Quarterly, 58*(1), 29-43.

16 Hoogstra, G. J. (2012). Gender, space and the location changes of jobs and people: A spatial simultaneous equations analysis. *Geographical Analysis, 44*(1), 47-64.

17 Perry, J. L., & Wise, L. R. (1990). The Motivational Bases of Public Service. *Public Administration Review, 50*(3), 367-373.

18 Perry, J. L. (1997, April). Antecedents of Public Service Motivation. Journal of *Public Administration Research and Theory, 7*(2) at p. 181.

19 Perry, J. L. (2000, April). Bringing Society In: Toward a Theory of Public-Service Motivation. *Journal of Public Administration Research and Theory, 10*(2), at p. 471.

20 Brewer, G.A., Selden, S. C., & Facr, R. L. (2000, May/June). Individual conceptions of public service motivation. *Public Administration Review, 60*(3), 254-264.

21 The participating states were Arizona, California, Georgia, New York, Oklahoma, Texas and Utah.

22 Brewer, et al. (2000). *Supra* at p. 263.

23 Mitchell, K. E., Levin, A. S., & Krumboltz, J. D. (1999). Planned happenstance: Constructing unexpected career opportunities. *Journal of Counseling and Development, 77*(2), 115-124.

24 Campagna, C. G., & Curtis, G. J. (2007). So worried I don't know what to be: Anxiety is associated with increased career indecision and reduced career certainty. *Australian Journal of Guidance & Counseling, 17*(1), 91-96.

Chapter Eight
The Rationalization of Education and Its Role in Underemployment

Everyone is a genius.
But if you judge a fish by its ability to climb a tree,
it will spend its whole life believing it is stupid.

Attributed (without proof) to Albert Einstein.

THE PURPOSE OF EDUCATION is to prepare people for citizenship. In this respect, it is required to serve a multiplicity of functions. The most elementary is to impart basic communication (reading and writing) and numeracy skills so that the student has the ability to continue learning even after formal schooling is complete. On a secondary level, school is ideally supposed to impart socialization skills. Combined with the educational "basics," the student who completes the educational process should have the skills to be a productive citizen and fully participate in civic life. Education has also traditionally been associated with democratic ideals and meritocracy, providing social mobility for anyone willing to make the effort.

The essence of human capital theory is that through a combination of increased knowledge, skills, and socialization, educated citizens can better provide for themselves and their families and more effectively participate in civil society. Under traditional notions, it is presumed that education systems serve the mutual interests of both citizens and the state: education provides opportunity for individual advancement, and society benefits from an educated citizenry. Human capital theory forged an enduring link between education and increased GDP. Broadening access to education thus became the panacea both for slow economic growth and socioeconomic inequality. Indeed, Becker's own view was that education was to increase public welfare as well as individual and public wealth. In his Nobel lecture, Becker states, "Along with others, I have tried to pry economists away from the narrow assumptions about self- interest," and argues that "behavior is driven by a much richer set of values and preferences."[1] Some scholars argue that the process of education—where "people are made better and not better off"[2]—itself serves to form and shape preferences. Indeed, they even propose that the very purpose of education is to encourage people to transcend their self-interest in order to further social cooperation.[3]

There is evidence to suggest that the primary purpose of education today is to make workers "job ready" by conforming students into fungible technical skill sets for rationalized corporate jobs. When corporate interests realized that if they captured the education piece they could model schools to not only train workers (at taxpayer expense) for those precise skills required for technocratic production, but also produce workers who were appropriately inculcated into passive, obedient behavior that was submissive to organizational hierarchy. Hence, the ideology of the "knowledge economy" and a constant crisis of skills shortages was born. However, decades of near-constant and ever-changing educational "reform" initiatives appears to have resulted in a citizenry who is civically disengaged and lacks the capacity for critical thinking. It thus seems that schools have abandoned the objective of helping students to find their true calling and make them better members of society.

The existence of overeducation (or underemployment) appears to challenge the notion that a rising tide of education lifts all boats, as well as the foundation of human capital theory. Over the past several decades, a combination of falling real wages for those at the bottom of the labor market (as well as for many in the middle), dramatic increases in the cost of higher education, and decreases in public subsidization of education for low-income families renders those least able to afford post-high school education squeezed out of (ever fewer) decent jobs. On the opposite end of the educational continuum, overeducated individuals are left with no recourse but to take lower level jobs from the less educated (who may themselves be qualified for these jobs), if only for the purpose of paying their student loans.

To further confound this paradox is a seemingly constant need for "retraining" solely to maintain survival in a constantly changing job market. This constant retraining usually has to come out of the workers' own pockets, but yet they never seem to realize corresponding gains—caught in the treadmill of adding to individual knowledge and skill sets, yet always ending up working harder for less. Thus it appears that education is not paying off (or is producing diminishing returns) for most of us either as individuals or as a society. But it is obviously paying off for someone—and that someone is the educational establishment.

The Purpose of Education and the Premise of Educational Reform
Like all social institutions, schools are creatures of the societies that create them, and may operate to serve certain interests at the expense of others. The educational reform movement that followed publication of the 1983 *A Nation at Risk* (National Commission on Excellence in Education) was premised on the need to maintain economic competitiveness, with "reform" being equated with efficiency, standards, and productivity. This reform movement ushered in an era of increasing "partnerships" between schools and business. Consequently, many schools were presented a solution to the demands for efficiency by the introduction of numerous pre-packaged, corporately produced curricula of "narrowly-defined and technically based courses" that failed to address real-world problems or examine their relationship with the dominant political economy.[4] Other critics of educational reform allege that it removes the traditional role of schools in fostering civic education, political

democracy and social justice by insinuating the ideologies and agendas of elite corporations and the military-industrial complex.[5]

Samuel Bowles and Herbert Gintis (both now associated with the Santa Fe Institute) first made the argument in 1976 that the real, but unacknowledged, function of schooling was to reproduce status hierarchies rather than (as propagandized) provide more equally accessible avenues to upward mobility.[6] According to Bowles and Gintis, schools occupy ground zero in the conflict between the rules of the marketplace and democratic society. In a capitalist system, schools serve to produce both a sufficient level of aggregate skills to comprise a "reserve army" of low-cost labor and also to produce "psychologically appropriate workers" by replicating a system based on dominance and subordination. Schools influence cultural models to which children are exposed and immerse them in a structure of external rewards and sanctions.[7]

Schools do more than simply reproduce the hierarchical power relationships and reward structures of the workplace, but inculcate social traits that are valued by employers: "It is essential that the individual accept and, indeed, come to see as natural, these undemocratic and unequal aspects of the workaday world."[8] Schooling itself was to serve as an apologetic for the characteristics of work in a capitalist bureaucracy: hierarchical lines of authority, job fragmentation (efficiency) and unequal pay (pseudo-meritocracy). On a more sinister note, schools were expected to depoliticize the "potentially explosive class relations of the production process." The mission of schools increasingly became more about the inculcation of technocratic work skills than the morals of citizenship.

When Bowles and Gintis originally published *Schooling in Capitalist America,* they made the argument (heretical at the time) that an individual's socio-economic status was more dependent on the socio-economic status of the person's parents and not solely the result of more education. Obviously, there are a lot of interrelated factors that could be interpreted either way: parents occupying the higher socio-economic ranks usually have both higher IQ and more resources to spend on education, both of which pass advantages along to their children. Bowles and Gintis were aware of this and so used a variety of mathematical controls to determine which of these factors had more impact on outcomes. They also have made regular updates to their original research over the years, to see how much their original findings have held up over time. Even controlling for these inter-related variables, parents' socio-economic status had more influence on economic and job market outcomes than years of schooling or score on a standardized IQ test, and the findings suggested persistently high levels of fixed intergenerational economic status.

The promise of expanded education, particularly higher education, was that working and middle class people would have access to avenues of upward mobility that had previously been out of reach for them. However, the expansion and greater equalization of education has not produced a corresponding equalization in incomes or opportunities. Bowles and Gintis attribute this to the fallacy that universal education cannot solve inequality by "fixing people," while doing nothing to change the social structures that regulate people's lives. Workers in essence must live their lives in a totalitarian economic system embedded in a formally democratic political system, where the livelihoods, freedoms, and security of masses of workers are controlled by a small minority of managers and owners.[9] Thus, schools represent the perfect merger of the promise of equality of opportunity with social control: Education is something that is both "done for the poor and to the poor."[10]

This is not to say that all advocates of school reform have ulterior motives. The desire to provide universal education presents a genuine problem of affordability. If the state is to make education universally available regardless of individual ability to pay, the need to efficiently deliver education to the greatest number of people requires the adoption of large-scale service delivery and standardized instruction. In order to justify the expenditure of public funds, a means to measure public benefits must be adopted. Because it is difficult to measure actual "learning," educational accountability is typically measured in terms of course or program completion rates. The need for public accountability measures thus transforms the traditionally organic and individualized process of education and the creation of knowledge into a rationalized process of credential production.

The rationalization of education has been accomplished not only through top-down dictates of school reformers, but also by voluntary actions of schools themselves, particularly in higher education, who are increasingly required to compete in an educational "market." Academics have noted (and complained about) how institutions of higher education have adopted corporate-style models of competition and entrepreneurship, often at the expense of the welfare of the institution as a whole.[11] Public funding has been restructured to accommodate consumer choice, so funding follows the students and research grants are project-based, rather than funds being allocated to the institution specifically. Thus, institutions of higher education are incentivized not to compete for the best students, but to enroll the most students. Even academic research is increasingly required to have income-producing potential (e.g., in the form of patents). Consequently, colleges and universities must use more of their revenue to market degree offerings, recruit large numbers of students, and "pitch" research proposals to grant funders.

David Dill, a professor of Public Policy at the University of North Carolina, suggests that, instead of decreasing costs and increasing choices and quality, competition for college students has actually increased average tuition as well as increased stratification between colleges in student admission scores and variance in quality. When colleges and universities must compete for students, some of them tend to focus on the nebulous concept of "prestige." Prestige-based institutions invest in factors that bolster their image, such as admissions selectivity and on-campus student services, which may or may not be associated with student post-graduate outcomes. Academic institutions "invest" in either reputation or prestige as "a means to buffer themselves from competitive forces."[12] These "investments" are directed at things calculated to increase student enrollment (if not necessarily graduation rates) such as celebrity faculty, attractive facilities and revenue-generating research grants, which may or may not have direct implications for student learning. Teaching is relegated to a method of cross-subsidizing research, and institutions compete for public grant-matching research funds and attracting research faculty. A subset of copycat "prestige-seeking" institutions attempts to duplicate the infrastructures of prestige institutions rather than being innovative or addressing student demand. Dill also discusses the inability of consumers (students) to differentiate between a genuine reputation and the more nebulous prestige, thus perverting the rational operation of consumer choice.

Dill admits that "prestige" can confer benefits in the job market unrelated to actual skills and talent. Students with personal networks formed among alumni of selective institutions are more likely to end up with better jobs and salaries.[13] As such, it serves the system as another form of status-sorting device. However, Dill suggests that market forces operate like advertising, in that needs and wants are created to induce people to spend money (tuition) on goods or activities that will not produce a corresponding real benefit. Dill expresses concern that competition for students will result in a "positional arms race" among both public and private universities, increasing the drain on the public treasury to the point that, like health care, cost increases in education will greatly exceed any aggregate social gains.[14]

The interview of S.D., the college instructor, provided insight into how schools have adopted business practices, including the language of competition and markets. The result of this worldview is that students become a form of commodity, in which schools are motivated to drive large numbers of students through their doors without regard to student outcomes in the job market. S.D. expressed concerns about how schools are moving toward corporate-style models of competition and entrepreneurship:

SD: Several years ago, maybe 15 years ago, I was reading articles where students were referred to not as students but as customers or clients. And that freaked me out, and still does. I don't think it's healthy for students. I don't think it's healthy for the enterprise, [inaudible] of teaching and learning. I just don't think it's a good thing for human development. But that's it. In retail, they talk a lot about, you know...and in real estate...curb appeal...getting people in the door, in the door. And that's where a lot of those are seeing money going, to things like residence hall expansion and facilities...and classrooms being, you know...just not dealt with [laughs]...so, the facilities and the look of things. Yeah, I guess this non-profit enterprise is starting to be run like a for-profit enterprise. And again, especially since I'm in a region of the country that's getting older and not younger, and where institutions are competing...competing for students. And even just using words like competition...kind of drives...disappoints me.

Perhaps the most counterintuitive irony is that the expansion of education has not operated to broaden economic opportunity, but may indeed have facilitated an increase in socioeconomic inequality. The increasing scale of the educational enterprise "intensifies information trade-offs and shifts the structure of rules," which directs the content of instruction toward the universal (least cost) rather than the particular (higher cost).[15] Real opportunities for students to develop their unique talents are being pushed higher up the educational ladder, and "the knowledge that allows access to high paying jobs in the occupational structure is rapidly shifting upward to graduate education."[16] This operates to increase the cost of knowledge that allows students to compete for middle-class jobs by requiring students to purchase ever more schooling, resulting in the benefits of expansion being disproportionately distributed to those who enter the system from the most economically advantaged starting point.[17]

The Transformation of Education into a Pipeline for the Corporatocracy

Rationalized education has thus transformed not only how education is delivered and how outcomes are measured, but also what information is imparted and the inculcation of social values and mores. In order to accommodate the costs of expanding public access to education, this larger system requires standardization, efficiency, logical structures, planning and control; i.e., rationalization. Management of this larger scale of information necessitates a degree of uniformity. This results in instruction that is "based on a narrower range of skill and knowledge (less information) that requires most of these students to compete, not on the basis of their strengths, but on weakness—competition within the institution forces students to climb a narrow path up the ladder of educational attainment."[18] So, while more students complete the curriculum, the curriculum itself is directed toward an ever narrower range of human talents and skills.

Dr. Edward Berman has written about the influence of corporate values on philanthropic foundations as well as on educational reform. Berman argues that school reform has been led by institutions and groups that are "inextricably linked to the American system of state capitalism,"[19] whose main purpose it to "mold schools increasingly to the requirements of the corporate state."[20] Consequently, an increasingly "corporatized curriculum" has "reduced the educational process to little more than an exercise in the accumulation of discrete facts divorced from any larger socioeconomic or political context."[21] Couched in the language of efficiency, standards, and productivity, a "technicist logic" reduces instruction to those things that can be easily quantified, which avoids the instruction of complex or potentially controversial material.[22] The "essence of good teaching [becomes] the ability to manage large

255

numbers of children" and the objective of school reform is to produce "uncritical workers who will contribute to increased economic activity."[23]

More than the inefficiencies and inequalities, perhaps the biggest threat to educational reform is its cultural transformation.[24] When the goal of the educational system is to produce obedient, technocratic automatons to serve the accumulation of profits, what is lost is the ability of those caught within the system to critique it, let alone do anything to change it. The American Bar Association, as well as numerous state bars, has been active for years in an effort to increase "civics education," because the schools have been so woefully deficient. Although bar associations tend to focus on the role of courts and lawyers and the importance of an independent judiciary, they at least provide students an understanding about the third branch of government. However, if not in schools, where are students supposed to learn about the institutions that govern them— not only the mechanics of how a bill becomes a law, but which voices get heard in the legislative process and how issues get introduced into the policy agenda. Obviously, the less "We the People" know about how governance works, the less likely we will be able to challenge a system that no longer serves our best interest.[25] Not surprisingly, the corporatized curriculum must be designed to exclude any material that could be perceived as "leading to the empowerment of disadvantaged groups," as such would be "dysfunctional to the purposes of harnessing the school to the engine of increased economic productivity."[26]

The Commodification of Education and the New Poverty of Knowledge.

The rationalization of education has been analogized to the process of commodification. Commodification involves the transformation of ideas, knowledge, practices and even the self into something that can be assigned a value and exchanged in a commercial marketplace. Paradoxically, the commodification of education has not been limited to capitalist market economies. A Russian study[27] documents how rationalization is turning knowledge itself into a commodity, which is altering how education is organized. "By the early 2000s, the university had begun to resemble a transnational corporation, a technobureaucratic structure…[and] as aspects of professional life become subordinate to administration, the administration process represents the most rapidly expanding area in attracting resources, rather than research and teaching."[28] The "logic of the market" regards the educational institution as a supermarket and the students as customers or consumers, as "The reformers do not want citizens, they want obedient consumers" and workers.[29] Knowledge itself thus becomes another commodity subject to production and consumption functions, while losing its traditional purpose of socialization and the development of moral character.

Yihui Su, a graduate sociology student at Peking University, was courageous enough to publish a paper denouncing the practices of Foxconn Technology,[30] a multinational corporation and the largest Chinese contract electronics supplier to U.S. companies such as Apple, Dell, and Hewlett-Packard. Su investigated the conditions leading to 17 suicide attempts (13 of them successful) among the "student-interns" at Foxconn and subsequent protests. Su traces a history where the state (Chinese government) had instituted a system of "combination of learning and working" (gong xue jie he) in which students learned skills from technical schools while working in related occupations in state industries. As these students developed higher level skills, they became the instructors for future groups of students. Su describes this as an arrangement of reciprocity in which neither the schools nor the state-run enterprises gained profit. However, when the state instituted "'economic reform" (i.e., neoliberal marketization), the labor market was no longer able to absorb the large numbers of skilled workers graduating from the technical schools.

Su describes Foxconn production as "Taylorized:" that is, production was "deskilled," which created a demand for unskilled, cheap labor. As enrollments in the technical schools decreased (because students were aware of the likelihood that they would be joining a skilled reserve army without a job), the technical schools worked a deal in collusion with Foxconn and the blessing of the state. The schools would provide cheap labor in the form of student interns in exchange for equipment, trainers and funding from Foxconn. The students were assigned many hours in these low-paid internships, often at the expense of their studies. Moreover, the work the students performed was meaningless and monotonous, frequently with no connection to their course of study, notwithstanding that their work shifts at Foxconn were "required" to receive an academic credential. Because the students were not legally "workers," they had no labor rights and no protections against industrial injury or illness. The conditions endured by these "interns" resulted in exhaustion, alienation, and a fragmented social life (from unpredictable and irregular hours of work) that left many students feeling lonely and helpless. Even in the undemocratic People's Republic of China (PRC), the protesting students were able to frame their experience under the Foxconn empire as a "crisis of moral legitimacy," allowing them to build sufficient public support (mainly via the Internet) to end the enforced internship practice.

It should come as no surprise that the PRC has enjoyed phenomenal economic growth over the past several decades. It combines the corporate Holy Grail of a (quasi)-market economy with a top-down, totalitarian, command-and-control government. Oppressive regimes that have no qualms about suppressing internal dissent make such countries attractive locations for corporate offshoring of jobs, and many American companies have taken advantage of this. There is no need to concern oneself with starry-eyed American ideals about individual liberty and messy, inefficient democracy that could potentially disrupt the production of profit. Any government that is willing to run down its own people with tanks has proven its ability and commitment to keeping the lower orders in their appropriate, subordinate place.

The combined commodification of education and labor implicates a complex interrelationship of feedback effects and externalities that will be difficult to correct. The traditional, simplistic economic view of overeducation as a temporary condition of "oversupply" that will eventually be corrected by the natural operation of free markets does not seem to offer a viable solution. "Rather than assuming an unproblematic or automatic link between educational institutions and the labor market, overqualification research makes the relationship between them an empirical problem."[31]   That is, overeducation serves both to create reserve armies of skilled labor and a steady supply of tuition to the educational pipelines, providing a self-perpetuating symbiosis of exploitation.

Richard Bates makes the argument that the increased rationalization of society, the emphasis on vocational education, and the "redefinition of the student and professional as worker rather than citizen" has actually operated to deskill the professions.[32] Notwithstanding the greater inculcation of technocratic skills that serve corporate production and efficiency, as a people we are losing our higher-level critical thinking skills and thus the ability to solve the increasingly complex social problems that confront us. Even an older generation appears to have lost the ability to discuss difficult and contentious policy issues in a logical and civilized manner. The United States Congress, probably the most homogeneous collection of America's elite upper classes outside of country clubs, cannot even bridge the fracture of its own partisan divide.

A group of researchers at the Mount Saint Vincent University in Halifax, Nova Scotia have also critically examined the modern educational establishment in the context of a "globalized knowledge economy."[33] This so-called "knowledge economy" has been constructed to serve the interests of capital and operates to produce

259

economic disenfranchisement under the guise of education. Learning, "like taking vitamins and stopping smoking, is...unproblematically assumed...to be a good thing...[but] what exactly the term 'learning' actually refers to is left eerily undefined."[34] In these authors' views, the so-called knowledge economy is designed to "...provide competitive access for certain privileged social groups to the highly concentrated flows of wealth of global capitalism, ...[but] do[es] little to challenge the overarching exploitative and wealth concentrating structure of the knowledge economy."[35] The irony is that the system actually thwarts forms of everyday learning capacity that people might find useful in building livelihoods (i.e. community action and self-provisioning activities). However, the "dominant economistic paradigms and power structures make critical reconsideration [of education in the knowledge economy] very difficult."[36]

Michael Apple, an educational theorist and political activist who has criticized the rationalization of education for decades on the basis that it has not delivered on its promises, nevertheless argues that education may actually offer the only way to solve the increasingly urgent challenges before us, including the rationalization, cost cutting, privatization, and political demonization of schoolteachers that affect education itself. [37] In theory, education can provide a path to the betterment of individuals and society, as contained in the promise of human capital theory.

However, market-based competition in the provision of education (which even many neoclassical economists admit is a public good rather than a private commodity), especially if it is based on rationalized production models, can subvert the benefits of education and render even consumer choice meaningless. This process presents a threat to democratic ideals when educational policies are dictated by employer demand for particularized discrete skills (rather than more complex skills such as problem-solving and critical thinking) to produce a workforce comprised of fungible, cheap, and obedient labor. Moreover, education is a primary foundation of cultural values, morality, and development of the whole person, which are destroyed when it is converted to commoditized information. Yet, the irony is that in a world of deskilled jobs, overeducated workers, and underemployed professionals, we are going to have to learn how to construct a better society. So, if more education is going to be part of the solution, it needs to first undergo some critical reformulation.

Notes

1 Becker, G. (1996). The Economic Way of Looking at Behavior—The Nobel Lecture. Stanford, CA: Hoover Institution on War, Revolution, and Peace, Stanford University. Retrieved from: https://searchworks.stanford.edu/view/3224007

2 Gilead, T. (2012). Education and the logic of economic progress. *Journal of Philosophy of Education, 46*(1), 113-131 at p. 125.

3 Gilead, T. (2009). Human capital, education and the promotion of social cooperation: A philosophical critique. *Studies in Philosophy and Education, 28*(6), 555-567.

4 Berman, E. H. (1988). Civic education in the corporatized classroom. *Theory Into Practice, 27*(4), 288-295 at p. 292.

5 Finkelstein, B. (1984). Education and the retreat from democracy in the United States, 1979-1987. *Teachers College Record, 86,* 275-282. Retrieved from: http://eric.ed.gov/?id=EJ313005

6 Bowles & Gintis, (2011 Ed.) *Schooling in capitalist America—Educational reform and the contradictions of economic life*. Chicago, IL: Haymarket Books.

7 *Id*. at p. 13.

8 *Id*. at p. 104.

9 *Id*. at p. 54.

10 *Id*. at p. 29.

11 Servage, L. (2009). Alternative and professional doctoral programs: What is driving the demand? *Studies in Higher Education, 34*(7), 765-779.

12 Dill, D. D. (2003). Allowing the market to rule: The case of the United States. *Higher Education Quarterly, 57*(2), 136-157 at p. 148.

13 *Id*. at p. 152.

14 *Id*. at p. 152.

15 Loomis, S., & Rodriguez, J. (2009). The individual-collective problems in education: the special cases of John Dewey and human capital theory. *Oxford Review of Education, 35(*4), 509-521 at p. 520.

16 *Id*. at p. 518.

17 *Id*. at p. 510.

18 *Id*. at p. 517.

19 Berman, E. H. (1988). *Supra* at p. 290.

20 *Id*. at p. 291.

21 *Id*. at p. 291.

22 *Id.* at p. 291-292.

23 *Id.* at 293.

24 "The representatives of capital, wrapping themselves in the rhetoric of disinterested public concern, have made a significant impact in determining what values the nation's schools impart." *Id.* at p. 294.

25 Giroux, H. (1987). Citizenship, public philosophy, and the retreat from democracy in the United States. Civic education is "no longer structured around the interests that promote the development of citizens who possess the social and critical attributes to improve the quality of public life." In E.B. Gumbert, (Ed.), *In the nation's image: Civic education in Japan, the Soviet Union, the United States, France and Britain*, 61-84 at p. 74.

26 Berman, E. H. (1988). *Supra* at p. 286.

27 Karpov, A. O. (2013). The commodification of education. *Russian Education and Society, 55*(5), 75-90.

28 *Id.* at p. 79.

29 *Id.* at p. 81.

30 Su, Y. (2010-2011). Student workers in the Foxconn Empire: The commodification of education and labor in China. *Journal of Workplace Rights, 15*(3-4), 341-362.

31 Vaisey, S. (2006). Education and its discontents: Overqualification in America, 1972-2002. *Social Forces, 85*(2), 835-864 at p. 835.

32 Bates, R. (1992, September). Barely competent: Against the deskilling of the professions via the cult of competence. Paper presented at the Seminar on Competency and Professional Education, Centre for Research in Professional education, University of Canberra, Australia at p. 6. Retrieved from: http://files.eric.ed.gov/fulltext/ED353635.pdf

33 Plumb, D., Leverman, A., & McGray, R. (2007). The learning city in a 'planet of slums.' *Studies in Continuing Education, 29*(1), 37-50.

34 *Id.* at p. 43.

35 *Id.* at p. 4l-42.

36 *Id.* at p. 37.

37 Apple, M. (2013). *Can education change society?* New York, NY: Routledge.

Chapter Nine
Suggestions for Workforce Policy Reform

" Is...improvement in the circumstances of the lower ranks of the people to be regarded as an advantage or as an inconvenience to society?...What improves the circumstances of the greater part can never be regarded as an inconveniency to the whole. No society can surely be flourishing and happy, of which the far greater part of the members are poor and miserable."

Adam Smith, *The Wealth of Nations,* 1776.

IT IS AXIOMATIC that one cannot write about a problem without proposing some type of solution. Before addressing specific policy proposals, I am going to address the larger issues—those things that may be more difficult, but necessary, to resolve before any proposed policy changes can be successfully implemented. Perhaps the most inextricably problematic issue is that those in policy power positions must first disabuse themselves of the fallacy that what's good for Wall Street and multinational corporations is good for everyone. Then there is another issue of terminology. How we discuss and describe things can affect our reaction to them no matter how much we may pride ourselves on logic. For example, the very term "workforce development" itself implies a technocratic agenda and a view of workers as some fungible aggregate that can be conformed to the dictates of the market.

In order to address problems of labor disutility and "bad jobs," we as a society are going to have to arrive at some consensus on common values. In order to do so, this will necessitate the development of alternative language and terms to discuss what is happening to our work life in a way that engages, rather than alienates, the population at large. Both Adam Smith and Karl Marx (or in more modern times, Gary Becker and Harry Braverman) have something useful to tell us about labor markets, but we have to see past the ideological divide. The "free enterprise" and human capital schools argue that work should, if not be fulfilling, at least be socially useful and bind people to their communities, rather than operating to fracture civic and social life. The Marxist-based schools argue that work relations cannot be examined outside the context of hierarchical power structures, which poses a threat to our democratic ideals and possibly our moral values as well. Rather than discussing these issues using the clinical terms of "human capital," "labor degradation" and "alienation," we may prefer to frame these discussions in terms of meaningful work and sustainable livelihoods.

Before addressing specific labor policy proposals, there should be a more comprehensive discussion about the objectives of public policy. This type of inquiry involves a more philosophical approach and requires some sort of consensus as to what kind of society we wish to be. Do we truly want to have a hypercompetitive, dog-eat-dog, everyone-for-himself society in which success is determined by how much one can extract from everything and everyone else? Alternatively, do we want a completely rationalized society in which success is determined by maximum efficiency, squeezing the most out of every available resource, and decisions that are made based on algorithmic logic alone? Or, do we prefer a society which aims to maximize the well-being (however this is measured) of the most of its members? Until we can achieve some general consensus on what the ultimate objectives of workforce policy should be, specific reforms may be nothing more than wishful thinking.

In one of its most rousing and historically significant statements, the United States Declaration of Independence declares that all human beings have God-given rights to life, liberty and the pursuit of happiness. Indeed, these rights are so "inviolable," it is the duty of governments not only to refrain from violating these rights themselves, but to protect these rights from violation by others. But what, exactly, is this elusive concept of happiness? From the standpoint of economically dominated thought, can money buy happiness?

The answer from research is yes, money can indeed "buy" happiness, up to a point. However, once people have enough to maintain a minimum level of subsistence, comfort, and security, more money does not necessarily make them happier. To illustrate this more graphically: Everyone needs to eat, but, while quantities and food preferences may vary, there is a point beyond which people are unable to eat any more. In the terms of economics, money does buy happiness, but there is a point of diminishing marginal returns. Because there is a point of diminishing marginal returns for income at the individual level, this suggests that a similar dynamic could exist at the level of national GDP. But to even suggest such a thing in modern capitalist economies is to brand oneself as a heretic.

Fortunately, research can tell us something about what makes people happy. In defining "happiness," researchers prefer to focus on more long-term satisfaction with life generally—what they term "subjective well-being"—rather than on the more short term "hedonic happiness," which behavioral science defines as the attraction to pleasure and the avoidance of pain. In individualistic societies such as the U.S., recommendations revolve around individual behaviors found to be correlated with higher life satisfaction such as mindfulness, gratitude, generosity, and forgiveness. The benefit of these recommendations is that they involve attitudes and behaviors over which most of us can exert some kind of control. What this approach lacks is an examination of the societal effects on individual happiness/well-being. For this perspective, we turn to research from Europe, particularly the Nordic countries, which have a tradition of concern for the collective welfare.

The countries that typically score highest on levels of citizen happiness are Denmark, Norway, Finland, Sweden and The Netherlands. The Happiness Institute is a research think-tank located in Copenhagen, Denmark, whose mission is to specifically identify those factors that happier societies have in common. The Danish Happiness Institute has identified the following factors that help make Denmark a happy society, although with the caveat that "the list should not be regarded as the complete and definitive answer."

Trust. Happy societies have a high level of social trust. The Danes have the highest level of trust, with three quarters of them believing they can trust most people. This compares to a trust level of one quarter for most other people. Indeed, visitors to Denmark are often shocked when they see Danish parents leave their children unattended in strollers outside coffee shops. By contrast, here in America, trusting strangers is tantamount to insanity. We need to own guns—lots of them—because even the police cannot be trusted to protect us (and sometimes are the "enemy" themselves). Elites wall themselves off from everyone else behind gated communities and hire privatized security while they argue for decimation of the public sector (which pays for the cops that protect the rest of us). Anyone who leaves their purse/wallet/child/home unwatched/unlocked/ unguarded/undefended is likely to be subject to "blame the victim" lectures when a crime is committed.

Security. A strong social safety net, along with relative (to other developed countries) income and wealth equality, has been correlated with high levels of happiness. A sense that everyone is "in this together" keeps Danes freer from the angst and anxiety that they are only an illness and job loss away from economic ruin. Moreover, the social safety net allows unemployed Danes to keep looking for more suitable work rather than accept the first job that they can get in order to survive, which likely keeps their rate of underemployment lower.

Wealth. As discussed earlier, higher levels of household money income does correlate with increased happiness. Research has also shown that relative income (how much one has compared to everyone else) can be more important than absolute income. However, there are countries that are wealthier than Denmark, but less happy, so this correlation is not absolute. The research in this area warns against the dangers of the "hedonic treadmill," in which the satisfaction of wants leads to the creation of additional wants, leading to a continual striving for the next acquisition. The research also suggests that the ability to spend extra resources to help others increases happiness because it strengthens social relationships.

Freedom. Not surprisingly, freedom is a foundation of a happy society. This is more than just the freedoms we typically associate with democracy, but the ability of people to affect what happens in their lives, the ability to control outcomes, and access to opportunity regardless of their gender, race, or socio-economic status.

Democracy. This also is no surprise to anyone living in a democratic society. The Danes have an enviable 88% participation rate in election turnout, which is among the highest in the world. However, again, there are "quality" factors that impact electoral participation that go beyond the existence of democratic institutions. Studies have found that decentralization and direct democracy, i.e., systems and processes which provide average people the ability to impact decisions regardless of their wealth and social standing, have a positive effect on happiness. Truly democratic systems also have appropriate accountability mechanisms that permit popular "correction" in the case of corruption or other breach of public trust.

Conversely, the U.S. has the lowest election turnout among most other democracies, declining from 64% in 1960 to a low of 48% in 1996 (although by the 2004 election participation had risen back to around 58%).[1] A February 2014 Pew survey[2] found that only 24% trust government in Washington always or most of the time. In a

269

September 2015 Gallup Poll,[3] 49% believe U.S. government is a threat to rights and freedoms of ordinary people. When asked whether they believe that "government is run by a few big interests," about 29% of Americans agreed with this statement in 1964; nearly 70% agreed in 2004. Similarly, about 35% agreed with the statement "public officials don't care about what I think" in 1964, while about 65% agreed in 2004.[4]

In 1998, 75% of respondents believed that "Congress is largely owned by special interest groups and our present system of government is democratic in name only."[5] Between 1980 and 2008, the percentage of citizens who believed government benefits a few big special interests as opposed to everyone ranged from 61% – 76%. Those who indicated that "quite a few" government officials are crooked ranged from 30% – 52%. The percentage of citizens who agreed that people don't have a say in what government does ranged from 29% – 56%, and those who believed that public officials don't care what people think ranged from 31% – 66%.[6] This cynicism about whether or not public officials truly serve "we the people" has increased in a post-Wall Street bailout and *Citizens United* world. Thus, there is a continuous negative feedback loop in which public mistrust of officials leads to greater disengagement, resulting in elected officials being responsive to ever narrower subpopulations, which furthers the disconnection between elected officials and the public at large.

Civil Society. This is defined as the quality of human relationships and social cohesion that go beyond civic and political participation. Researchers emphasize that this is more than just having 500 "friends" on Facebook or building our "networks" on LinkedIn so we can be ready to find a job when the inevitable layoff hits. Social cohesion can often be determined by the level of volunteer work and the number of people we personally engage with on a day-to-day basis.

Robert Putnam's popular *Bowling Alone: The Collapse and Revival of American Community,* (2000), as well as numerous social and academic studies have documented a decline of civic engagement in the forms of organizational membership, club and neighborhood meetings, and attendance at religious services, as well as electoral participation. Putnam terms these connections "social capital," and finds that connections in the workplace and among family and friends have also declined, while lamenting the disappearing rituals of nightly family dinners and neighborhood get-togethers. A deficit in social capital is correlated with increasing levels of crime, suicide and depression. In analyzing possible explanations, Putnam found that financial anxiety and a "changing workplace" may account for up to ten percent of the decline in social capital.

Work. Although some people may fantasize about a life of leisure without the necessity of working, unemployment is associated with stress, loneliness and depression above and beyond the effects of financial anxiety. We need to work, because it (ideally) provides us purpose, meaning, identity, and connection to others. The Happiness Institute found that, for the most part, Danes were thriving in their workplaces. On the variables of interest, Danes ranked highest on overall job quality, which was further parsed into wages, working hours, job content, and future prospects. Danish workers ranked fourth in terms of wages and second in future prospects and working hours.

Balance. As most of us can intuit, too much work can negatively impact happiness as much as not having enough work. The Danes work on average 1,522 hours per year, in contrast with an OECD average of 1,776. By contrast, the average work-week in the U.S. is 46.7 hours, which translates to (using a 50-week year) 2,335 hours annually. According to a 2014 Gallup poll, 21% of workers report that they work 50-59 hours per week, and another 18% report that they work over 60 hours per week.[7] In the European Union, the legally required minimum amount of paid vacation is 20 days (on top

271

of legal paid holidays), and in some countries it is as much as 25-30 days. Over 130 countries have some form of mandatory paid vacation. The U.S. is virtually the only developed nation without mandatory paid vacation, joining such countries as Kiribati, the Federated State of Micronesia, and the Kingdom of Tonga. For those Americans who do enjoy paid vacation, the average is 16 days–which also includes paid holidays. A sad irony is that even those workers who do get paid time off are simply not using it.

Tony Schwartz is a management consultant who earns a substantial livelihood finding ways for corporate managers to squeeze more out of employees, so he is certainly not someone you expect would be sympathetic to workers. However, Mr. Schwartz is practical, as well as surprisingly humane for someone who earns such a living. In *The Way We're Working Isn't Working,*[8] Schwartz asserts that the workplace imperative of "more, bigger, faster" ignores fundamental human needs for renewal, security, self-expression and significance, which actually serves to impede productivity.

According to Schwartz, the first enemy of productivity is lack of sleep. Sleep deprivation is dangerous because it "both prompts cognitive defects and negatively influences our mood, a combination that undermines our judgment, especially under pressure." Sleep deprivation has been causally associated with such infamous disasters as Three Mile Island, Chernobyl, the January 1986 space shuttle Challenger explosion, and the Exxon Valdez accident. Schwartz further asserts that, "…much as we are sleeping less, we're also taking less time off. On average, Americans now fail to use 439 million paid vacation days a year. In 2008, 1/3 of Americans said they intended to take no vacation at all. Another 33% planned a vacation of seven days or less. Only 14% scheduled a vacation of at least two weeks during 2008…."

Sleep deprivation, along with constant multi-tasking and high anxiety "hurry up" demands, results in high levels of the stress hormone cortisol. Cortisol is associated with the fight-or-flight response, and medical studies have shown that recurring high levels of cortisol are also associated with so-called "lifestyle" diseases such as high blood pressure and diabetes. The ultimate consequence of juggling too many tasks is overload—a condition where employees feel they are no longer able to "think straight" and may even exhibit symptoms of ADHD.

Schwartz cites research that found additional stress triggers when employees feel devalued—when they feel they are not being heard, not being appreciated and not being treated fairly. An accumulation of stress operates to shut down the prefrontal cortex, which negatively impacts reasoning power and critical thinking— skills which employees increasingly need to be able to operate effectively in an environment of high demand and uncertainty.

Schwartz's recommendations at the micro level are obvious: Design workplaces to accommodate the basic human needs he identifies by providing (and encouraging) regular periods of rest and renewal, increasing employees' perception of being valued, and decreasing task overload. The macro solution is also obvious: If we take into consideration all the people who are doing the work of more than one employee and created jobs so that everyone was only doing the work of one employee, it would help to alleviate the unemployment problem as well as the work overload problem. However, how many of Schwartz' high-paying clients are actually going to follow his recommendations? His book suggests that, although some have done this, many of them have not.

The good news is that in 2012 the U.S. National Academy of Science established a panel to examine how happiness measures identified from research can be incorporated into the policy development process. Because of the lack of public trust and (to some extent, justified) belief that government does not serve the best interest of the people, it is imperative that changes be instigated from the bottom-up, rather than by top-down regulatory dictates. Anything that is so much as perceived to be a pressure valve for dissent or a way to squeeze even more out of working people will likely not be successful. However, this is not to say that government has no role to play at all, particularly local governments. Governments can serve to build a new way of working by establishing rules and structures that encourage innovation and allow the bottom-up solutions to flourish.

Uniting Politically Polarized Citizens

As the recent (2016) U.S. election has so painfully demonstrated, a sense of unity and common purpose among Americans appears to have been lost. If there is consensus anywhere as to the source of this polarization, most pundits point to "the economy"— citing everything from globalized trade to outsourcing to almost any phenomenon that can be tied to a loss of jobs—and the failure of the political establishment to address it. Now even professionals share some features of typically working class angst and the "bad job" blues. In essence, the lack of jobs—particularly the lack of decent jobs—appears to offer common ground from which to bridge the political divide.

A British economist named Guy Standing has proposed a nascent new class that he has termed the Precariat.[9] The Precariat, which is growing, has been created primarily by the loss of stable, good-paying jobs through globalization and the new "flexible" labor force. Members of the Precariat are not necessarily impoverished, and may even secure good-paying work occasionally. However, what the Precariat lacks is any sense of stability or predictability. No longer appropriately a "middle class," this is the class that occupies the rung just above the working poor on the hierarchical social ladder. The defining feature of the Precariat is both precarious income and precarious personal security. Their vulnerability "goes beyond...money income," but is compounded by the decimation of social insurance and the lack of community created when one has to constantly be on the move in search of work. Thus, the Precariat has no sense of solidarity with the traditional working class, along with a broader feeling of alienation and lack of trust.

Standing divides the Precariat into three subgroups. The first subgroup are those who have "dropped" out of the old working and middle class. This subgroup relates their deprivations to a lost past, including (in America) a lost national supremacy and threats from immigrants. This subgroup is the most likely to respond to messages from the far right. The second subgroup, ironically, is the immigrants and minorities that are feared by the first group. This second subgroup is the most likely to be politically disengaged because they fear retribution from the dominant population. The minority and immigrant subgroup occasionally explodes into rage when they believe their basic survival is threatened, which leads to authoritarian backlash from the dominant society. The third subgroup is the overeducated and underemployed. They have made some effort to better themselves but yet are still stuck in insecure and dead-end employment. However, they are also suspect of old-style laborism, as they view it as co-optation by a corrupt system. This group is the most likely to join leftist movements like Occupy Wall Street. It is also (according to Standing) the group most likely to spearhead real transformation.

At the present time, Standing's Precariat lacks occupational and political identity. What all of these subgroups have in common is their low probability of ever building a career or a secure material life. Unfortunately, they tend to blame the other subgoups for their predicament, viewing them as usurping competitors for increasingly fewer opportunities for personal progress and upward mobility. Convincing these subgroups that they have a common interest will be no easy task. But, assuming that Precariat subgroups could be united around their shared dissatisfactions with how most of us must earn a living in a rationalized, technocratic society, there lies the potential of a significant and transformative political force.

As has been so painfully demonstrated in this study as well as many others—and in spite of growing GDP and the ballyhoo on Wall Street about economic recovery— the "job market" is not serving us. It is not serving us as individual workers and it is not serving us as a civil society. Indeed, as the research cited by Tony Schwartz suggests, it may even be killing us. More than just our physical welfare, the job market—in its current iteration of rationalized expropriation—poses threats to our democratic ideals, our civic and social life, and possibly even our moral foundations as well. It is not something we can expect to change in the near term, and change may well need to be incremental, especially in the beginning. It will involve changing the way we work as well as changing how and what we learn. However, in order to know if what we do is heading us in the right direction, we must first change what we measure.

What We Measure

Although academics have noted the existence of overeducation/underemployment for decades, national measures (i.e., the Bureau of Labor Statistics and the Census Bureau) must take a broader view of labor underutilization. Measures must capture more than simply whether one is or is not working full time. These measures should also capture more than credential underemployment, or persons working in jobs that do not require their highest educational credential, but should also encompass skill and experience under-utilization. This would include persons with years of experience who have been laid off and then had to find employment in an entry-level position, even if this position requires a similar credential. In essence, anyone who must take work that pays less than a previous job is underemployed on some level. More particularized under-employment data could assist young people in their career decisions, as they would have a better idea of the lifetime utility of a particular credential or course of study. Most importantly, by identifying the full extent of underemployment, this data can "find" sources of untapped skills, knowledge and experience that can then drive job creation efforts. This essentially changes the paradigm from attempting to conform workers to jobs that have been designed to extract profit to finding ways to utilize existing skills that serve communities and meet unmet needs.

Conversely, additional measures can take into account the amount of excess work hours and determine where these might overlap with underemployed skills. Policies could then be developed to encourage job-sharing, or find ways to increase penalties for unpaid overtime, so work could be more consistently distributed and thus avoid the paradox of underemployment and overwork. Official labor market statistics should also strive to include those factors identified by academics as "bad job" features in order to better inform labor policy. For example, studies[10] have shown that irregular and unpredictable work hours, especially when combined with irregular and unpredictable pay, increases stress on working families, rendering it nearly impossible for them to either manage their families in the present or plan for the future and attempt to better themselves. Expanded survey data could also address non-economic issues such as meaninglessness and obstacles to pathways of learning and growing, which can give policymakers a better understanding of how jobs are not serving either workers or the larger society.

How We Work

The very concept of what a job should be would be re-examined. The new paradigm would be based on the premise that people are engaged in livelihoods rather than a "job." That is, work should be an activity that is not only economically productive for the worker, it should also benefit the community at large as well as provide meaning and social connection. Muhammad Yunus, who was awarded the Nobel Peace Prize in 2006 for the creation of microfinance and development of social entrepreneurship, proposes that people should become job creators rather than job seekers—even if the only job they create is their own.[11] These new forms of work could include provisions for continuous learning and skill building, except that these skills would be oriented toward fulfilling real needs in the community rather than solely oriented toward the generation of profit. Economic productivity would not necessarily be abandoned altogether, it just would no longer be the sole purpose of livelihoods.

Indeed, there is a new paradigm being developed at the international level for the alleviation of poverty that is based on a "sustainable livelihoods" framework.[12] Sustainable livelihoods are defined as the ability to make a decent living and survive system shocks without jeopardizing the livelihood options of others. The sustainable livelihoods framework is a holistic approach that addresses the complex interrelationships between economic, political, and social systems. The argument for a sustainable livelihoods framework is that existing policies, institutions and processes have been unable to correct social problems created by dysfunctional markets, unresponsive financial systems, inappropriate regulatory frameworks, government corruption, and a lack of political will to address these problems. Much of the sustainable livelihood research has been about policies designed to alleviate urban poverty in unregulated urban settlements. The theory is that even impoverished urban settlements contain assets in the form of a local knowledge base and existing social networks which can be leveraged to develop workable solutions. This is even more so in the context of un- and underemployed professionals.

Recommendations in a sustainable livelihoods framework include expanding dialogue, creating a critical mass for engagement in the process, building truly egalitarian partnerships with stakeholders, insuring inclusiveness and empowerment, making information accessible by eliminating information brokers and intermediaries, and promoting regulatory objectives that keep the cost of land and infrastructure affordable. For example, even well-intentioned regulations (e.g., requirements for minimum dwelling size, zoning regulations and licensing requirements) can create affordability barriers to home and community-based businesses. This can negatively impact not just inhabitants of urban slums who seek to earn income from their homes and neighborhoods, but also un- and underemployed professionals whose only realistic option for employment is to offer their services on a freelance basis.

So-called sustainable livelihoods themselves would be measured by the extent they fulfill all levels of human needs. Many of us may remember the diagram of Abraham Maslow's hierarchy of needs. On the bottom are the physical needs for the basics of food, water, shelter and rest. The next level represents "safety" needs, which also includes security. Thus, jobs in which workers are in constant fear of a layoff would not satisfy Maslow's second level (and many jobs, even those in developed economies, barely satisfy the first level). The third level is belongingness, which involves family, friends and relationships. In modern times, this third level need is often referred to as "work-life" balance. Ideally, work should also facilitate connection by being socially meaningful. The fourth level is esteem (both of self and others), which would require a job to, if not fully utilize the workers skills, at least not grossly underutilize them. It should also provide opportunities to learn and grow. The top level in Maslow's hierarchy is self-actualization. As a practical matter, any job—even a good one—will likely not be able to provide this. However, at a minimum, work should serve the pursuit of self-actualization rather than hinder it.

How and What We Learn

Education needs to return to its roots of helping students find their talents and vocational calling for purposes of building a better civil society, rather than an exclusive focus on technocratic skills and "job readiness." As it is now, students are processed through a system where they are imbued with skills so they can "find a job" upon graduation, yet most of them graduate without any idea what a meaningful career looks like. The concept of "teamwork" can be expanded beyond the corporate emphasis on getting disparate groups of people together to work on a short-term project to longer-term concepts that involve the strengthening of networks and community-building. As many state bar associations are advocating, schools should develop a robust curriculum of civics education. These should not just inform students about how government works, but how all of our social systems work—governments, markets, economics, the non-profit sector, and how even our culture affects—and is affected by—such institutions. Most importantly, education should provide students with the knowledge and leadership skills to impact these systems and bring about social change. Courses in complexity theory could be offered along with courses in citizen activism.

Although the so-called "skills shortage" crisis may be to a certain extent manufactured for the purpose of cheapening labor or externalizing training costs, there is a genuine issue with lack of particularized knowledge that negatively impacts plans for civic progress. The City of Leander, Texas offers an example of this "missing" knowledge. Leander is a small but growing city approximately 30 miles northwest of Austin, and serves primarily as a suburban bedroom community for Austin workers. Although Leander is known for good schools and relatively low rates of crime and poverty, city leaders have been attempting for over a decade to bring more (and better) jobs to Leander, as well as foster greater civic engagement and sense of community.

In 2005, Leander designated a 2,300 acre tract of land as a Transit Oriented Development (TOD) area. The goals of the TOD are to provide a mixed-use, pedestrian friendly space where people can live, work and shop in a compact area that promotes a sense of community. There are active plans to also include a branch of the local community college. The TOD is governed by SmartCode, a form-based code that focuses on how the space works together—sidewalks, plazas and streetscapes—rather than on specific uses that characterize more conventional zoning codes.

However, ten years after the TOD was approved, except for a park-and-ride commuter plaza that connects suburban workers to Austin, the TOD remains undeveloped. Although the Great Recession dried up capital financing for a time, there is a more pervasive issue of developers either not wanting, or not having the skills, to build to the SmartCode. Because the TOD does not provide facilities for big-box retailers and acres of parking lot, one business broker says developers "look at me like I'm crazy" and accuse the city of being "anti-development."

In the Austin metro area, it seems the only building "skills" are for shopping malls, big box stores, downtown luxury high-rise apartments (which working and middle class people can barely afford) and cookie-cutter McMansions on quarter or half-acre lots in the suburbs (which working and middle class people can barely afford). Indeed, the City Director of Development Services laments that, if Leander had not already invested millions of dollars into the TOD, it "would be easier to let go of the vision."[13]   The story of the Leander TOD illustrates the difficulty and the long-term nature of reversing the current human-unfriendly course. Not only will we need to build a vision and a consensus around it, we will also need to learn how to actually "build" communities (and workplaces) that support civic and social life.

Constitutionally Protected Job Property Rights

The writings of America's founders are replete with references to life, liberty and property. It was the job of government to not only refrain from infringing these rights itself, but to protect citizens from infringements of these rights by others. While life and liberty were paramount, the infringement of property rights has the potential to impact the former two. In the early days of America, a man's property consisted (for most persons) of a homestead, tools for self-provisioning, and possibly a small shop. That is, "property" is what allowed citizens to provide for their physical needs, earn a livelihood and gave them a place in the community. In modern times, the main form of "property" available to most citizens is income from a job. For those who do not inherit such things, this is the only income that will allow them to purchase a home and acquire other capital assets. Thus, loss of job income can potentially result in more significant losses, such as loss of home, loss of family (divorce), and even loss of life (from disease or exposure due to untreated illness or homelessness). The irony of our society today is that corporations—which are created by human beings—are protected by the Constitution and the Bill of Rights, while workers in the private workplace—who are created by God—have no such rights.

One can already hear the howling from the Corporatocracy that granting constitutional protection to jobs will render it impossible to fire underperforming employees. However, public employees already have such protections.[14] The Constitution does not guarantee anyone a job, but it does insure that before someone loses a job they are afforded due process--a right to a fair hearing before a neutral decision-maker. Unionized workers, although not constitutionally protected, have many such due process rights as a consequence of their bargaining agreements. While it may take longer and be more complicated, government and unionized employees are ***not*** immune from termination for cause. Indeed, nearly every Constitutional right is circumscribed in some way by Supreme Court decisions or acts of Congress when deemed necessary for the public welfare.

Among workers, there are wide variations in beliefs about whether they have Constitutional rights at work or not. Several decades ago, I encountered highly educated people in the private workforce, including one VP, who were incredulous that they had no Constitutional rights in the private workplace. Today, many more people are aware of their lack of rights and the consequences of so-called "right-to-work" laws. However, at least one study[15] found that when workers believed they had some form of property right in their jobs, this resulted in benefits to both the employers and the workers. For the employer, workers who felt more secure demonstrated increased job commitment, longer tenure (less turnover), decreased absenteeism, and more positive organizational citizenship behaviors. For the workers, they enjoyed an increased sense of control over their work and they were more willing to sue for wrongful dismissal. Thus such a proposal potentially offers a win-win situation for both workers and employers, but expect to see much protest and squawking from the corporate Chicken Littles.

The Role of Government

The intractable problems of a defective labor market and decline in civil society cannot be solved by governments operating alone. We cannot solve the problems created by top-down, technocratic, command-and-control bureaucracies with more of the same. That is, the involvement of government must insure that the process does not degenerate into technocratic delivery of development "programs" that actually perpetuate marginalization rather than transform power structures. Most of the "solutions" are going to have to be small-scale and locally based. However, governments can help to construct a new social order by building platforms of stability, mitigating externalization and risk-shifting, and facilitating connectivity that assists innovation at the local level. That is, governments can provide the infrastructure that supports a sustainable livelihood framework and constitutional property rights.

Governments are already involved in so-called "economic development" activities, in which tax dollars are used for various projects intended to boost local economic growth. The problem with these projects is that they typically are directed toward a small group of high-growth firms or developers who target an affluent clientele. Although the popular conception is that high-growth firms are small, they are more likely to be younger, newer firms, but not necessarily smaller. Moreover, the jury is still out as to whether these firms generate a sufficient return to the community, with many critics (particularly libertarians) saying that government should not be in the business of "picking winners and losers." Local politicians are more likely to tout their "winners," while the "losers" literally get lost in the accounting, particularly where economic development dollars are exempted from freedom of information disclosures. Additionally, economic development dollars often require so-called "flexible" labor policies, which tend to create jobs that are less secure and lower in quality.

Notwithstanding the fact that many economic development projects never pay off for the majority of citizens, some academics in the public policy field nevertheless argue that expanded entrepreneurial policies have the potential for broader benefits.[16] Some of these recommendations include policies that are targeted toward specific populations, such as women, minorities and other persons who tend to be under-represented or excluded from fair share of economic gains. Other policies can be targeted toward specific activities, such as social entrepreneurship. Social entrepreneurs are those whose purpose is to address social problems, particularly those created by market and government failures. These policies will involve strategies to broaden both public input/dialogue and access to capital.

In essence, the public-private partnerships involved in economic development must be expanded beyond the usual participants, whose primary objective is to extract wealth from the community rather than contribute to it. Economic development dollars should likewise be directed to smaller and more locally-based businesses. While these do not have the "job creation" caché of a Walmart or a Google, they are more likely to be bound to the community through personal connection and less likely to abandon it at the first offer of a better deal from another jurisdiction.

In the beginning of this transformation of work, the primary function of governments at the federal and state levels may be one of research and data collection; that is, developing expanded measures of underemployment, the General Social Survey Quality of Work

Life, and other measures of how people are working and how work is affecting well-being. This research itself must be designed to be inclusive and accountable. Early pilot projects that show promise can then form the basis for specific programs and the development of macro policies.

From a more immediate practical standpoint, labor policy can be more effective by simply better enforcing laws that are already on the books. That is, enforce workers' rights to safe workplaces free of discrimination as well as overtime and minimum wage laws. Workers who must work for corporations should be guaranteed the right to organize and bargain for terms and conditions of work. Indeed, the biggest fallacy of labor markets today is the presumption of equality of bargaining power between workers and employers.

Some local jurisdictions have already taken action to alleviate labor market disutility. A growing number of state and local jurisdictions are passing minimum wage laws that are higher than the federal minimum. Contrary to the dire predictions of corporate employers, such raises in the minimum wage did not result in massive rates of unemployment and economic recession. Additionally, Vermont, Montana and the City of San Francisco have passed laws that give workers rights with respect to work hours and scheduling changes, which wreak havoc on both family budgets and caretaking arrangements. Federal, state and local governments could impose fines and/or taxes on businesses based on the number or percentage of their employees on public assistance. This would offset drains on the public treasury as well as provide a source of revenue for building alternative economies. These funds could be used either to strengthen the social safety net or bolster employment in the non-profit sector.

While not related to work issues *per se,* efforts to create sustainable communities, particularly with respect to work-life infrastructure and transportation alternatives can help workers exercise a broader range of work options. Local efforts to provide affordable housing and public transportation can help workers by providing them decent and safe places to live and an affordable way to access livelihoods. Even middle class and professional workers benefit by having more work-housing options and shorter commutes. The millennial generation is already demonstrating a shift away from automobile purchases and driving.[17] Putnam's[18] exhaustively researched decline in social capital found that it was negatively impacted by even a ten-minute addition to a daily commute, citing urban sprawl and suburbanization as possibly accounting for up to 10% of the decline. Research has also found a correlation between length of commute and divorce rates.[19]

With respect to professional underemployment, perhaps the biggest challenge is putting the excess skills, knowledge and experience to socially beneficial use. Many underemployed professionals keep themselves engaged by volunteering, although this "solution" has limited long-term sustainability. Professional organizations such as state bar and medical associations have many sub-programs where they sponsor pro bono work by members in their communities (for example, free dental exams or attorneys that represent foster children or veterans). Many professional schools also have partnerships with public service organizations (governments or non-profits) that provide some form of educational loan forgiveness to professionals working in underserved geographic areas or populations. These programs permit professionals with large student debt loads to accept work that might otherwise be financially unworkable. However, the sponsoring organizations must still have sufficient budget resources to pay some kind of salary, even if it is a reduced one.

In the Austin, Texas area, an innovative program called Leap to Success connects un- and underemployed professionals attending area job clubs with non-profit organizations that need particular expertise and/or assistance with projects they cannot fund. Through the Leap to Success program, underemployed professionals are able to keep their skills sharp and fill in those "gaps" on their resume, and the non-profit entities receive skilled assistance they could not otherwise afford. The only down side is that these volunteer professionals are frequently "lost" in mid-project when they finally secure paying employment, which sometimes requires re-establishment of a project team. While the non-profit continues to receive free services from a new and never-ending "batch" of newly unemployed professionals coming into the job clubs, this ad-hoc and transient system frequently operates to interrupt and delay projects. The professionals who participate in Leap to Success projects appreciate the opportunity to make a difference while they are unemployed, but as a practical matter cannot do unpaid work long-term, no matter how much the non-profit organization needs their services. If anything the Leap to Success program has shown is that there is plenty of socially useful work to be done, just no way to pay for it.

Local city and county governments can assist both themselves and underemployed professionals with similar arrangements, possibly with the assistance of state and federal grant money. Instead of giving away tax dollars in the form of corporate relocation incentives (which only poach jobs from elsewhere), these "economic development" dollars can be used to grow and support small and local businesses, including freelancing professionals. The local government can provide rent or tax-free places to live and work for un- and underemployed professionals in exchange for their expertise and work on "wish list" projects that could not otherwise be funded from the regular budget. When subsidized professionals have established a sufficient level of business or paying clientele from other sources, they can serve as mentors to the next generation of city or county-supported entrepreneurs. This will make communities stronger not only economically, but also through building and deepening of connection.

Building more worker-friendly workplaces and more human-friendly economies will not happen overnight. These efforts will likely start out small-scale and local, and there will likely be as many failures as successes—at least in the beginning. Public leaders who initiate these projects will need to both temper expectations as well as develop performance data to determine what works and what doesn't. These data should be tied to local demographic, economic, and cultural conditions so that other jurisdictions who are analyzing results can determine to what extent the results may, or may not, be generalizable to their own situation. The early pioneers in new ways of living and working will have to be patient, but they can serve as the role models upon which others may follow.

Maybe there will come a day in the future when every judge, before he or she issues a ruling in a case or crafts an opinion that will guide the direction of future law, first asks, "How will this affect the people who work for a living?" When every president, governor, or mayor, before he or she signs legislation into law or issues an executive order, first asks, "What impact will this have on the people who work for a living?" The day when every federal and state legislator, and every county commissioner, and every city councilperson, when confronted by the well-heeled lobbyists and other members of the social and economic elites who are constantly in their offices with "proposals," demands an explanation of how such proposals intend to (or will) benefit the people who work for a living. And if these answers fall short, the opinion is revisited, the law is unsigned, or a bill does not get submitted. Some may say that such a vision is not possible in the current state of affairs. Indeed, it may not be, until We the People who work for a living demand it.

Notes

1 Dye, Thomas. (2006). *The irony of democracy.* Belmont, CA: Thomson Wadsworth, pp. 224-225.

2 http://www.people-press.org/2014/11/13/public-trust-in-government/

3 http://www.gallup.com/poll/185720/half-continue-say-gov-immediate-threat.aspx

4 National Election Studies, The Polling Report for 2004

5 The NES Guide to Public Opinion and Electoral Behavior, 1995-2000.

6 American National Election Studies 2012 Guide to Public Opinion and Electoral Behavior. http://www.electionstudies.org/nesguide/gd-index.htm#5

7 https://www.washingtonpost.com/news/on-leadership/wp/2014/09/02/the-average-work-week-is-now-47-hours/

8 Schwartz, T. (2010). *The way we're working isn't working: The four forgotten needs that energize great performance.* New York NY: Free Press (a division of Simon & Shuster, Inc.).

9 Standing, G. (2011). *The Precariat: The new dangerous class.* London, England: Bloomsbury.

10 Economic Policy Institute Briefing Paper #394, Irregular Work Scheduling and Its Consequences, April 9, 2015.

11 Yunus, M. (2017). *A world of three zeros: The new economics of zero poverty, zero unemployment, and zero net carbon emissions.* New York, NY: Public Affairs/Perseus Books, LLC, a subsidiary of Hachette Book Group, Inc.

12 Majale, M. (2002, April). Regulatory guidelines for urban upgrading: Towards effecting pro-poor change. Intermediate Technology Development Group. Warwickshire, UK.
http://r4d.dfid.gov.uk/PDF/Outputs/Urbanisation/R7850_Majale_RGUU02.pdf

13 Burnett, S. Leander considers changes to TOD. *Community Impact Newspaper,* June 2014.

14 However, these rights are increasingly under assault at both federal and state levels by well-funded groups such as the National Chamber of Commerce and the American Legislative Exchange Council, along with decisions by an increasingly pro-corporate Supreme Court; e.g., the recent (July 2018) decision in *Janus v. AFSCME.*

15 Kelloway, E. K., Barling, J., & Carroll, A. E. (1998). Perceived causes and consequences of property rights to jobs. *Journal of Business and Psychology,* *12*(4), 505-513.

16 Terjesen, S., Bosma, N. & Stam, E. (2016). Advancing public policy for high-growth, female, and social entrepreneurs. Public Administration Review, *76*(2), 230-239.

17 https://www.washingtonpost.com/news/wonk/wp/2014/10/14/the-many-reasons-millennials-are-shunning-cars/

18 Putnam, R. (2000). *Bowling alone: The collapse and revival of American community.* (2000). New York, NY: Simon & Shuster, Inc.

19 Sandown, E. (2013). Til work do us part: The social fallacy of long distance commuting. *Urban Studies*, August 7, 2013. http://usj.sagepub.com/content/early/2013/08/06/0042098013498280

Index

291

G

H

I

J

K

L

Perry, James L., 240, 241, 242
person-job fit, 52, 231
pessimistic futility, 194
political polarization, 274
Ponthière, Gregory, 48
positional arms race, 253
post-educational skills, 81
post-graduate degrees, 167
poverty in the midst of plenty, 92, 131,
 173, 193, 201
preferences
 neoclassical economics, 87
prestige-based institutions, 252
Principles of Scientific Management, 92
Prisoner's Dilemma, 88
privilege, 28, 31, 78, 144
productivity of labor
 defined, 96
professional
 underemployed, 59
professional organizations, 157
professional oversupply, 192
professionals, 10, 11, 12, 31, 40, 45, 98,
 110, 156, 165, 168, 177, 184, 185,
 194, 198, 215, 235, 240
 and part-time underemployment, 44
 autonomy and agency, 180
 overwork and burnout, 177
 relationship to work, 158
 share ideology of higher status, 62
Protestant Reformation, 20
PSM, 240, 241, 242, *See* Public Service
 Motivation
public education, 28
public service jobs, 215
Public Service Motivation. *See* PSM
Putnam, Robert, 271, 286

R

rational investor, 79
rationalization, 10, 74, 107, 108, 156
 justification, 107
Rationalization, 9, 206
Reagan, Ronald, 13, 121, 127

Rehnquist, William, 209
reliability of job market information,
 234
relocation and family issues, 191
rent seeking, 97
research epidemiologist, 186
Ritzer, George, 108, 205, 213
role conflict, 46, 180, 181
Royal Holloway University of London,
 125
Russian study on underemployment,
 231

S

Sattinger, Michael, 145, 146
Sawchuk, Peter, 104
Schooling in Capitalist America, 250
Schwartz, Tony, 272, 273, 276
scientific management, 92, 100, 117,
 136
Scientific Office Management, 92
screening hypothesis, 86
self-provisioning, 23, 24, 27, 51, 75, 77,
 96, 281
Servage, Laura, 133
Sheldon, Kennon, 211, 212
Shulman, Beth, 106
skill-intensity, 101
skills mismatch, 51, 52
skills shortage, 2, 6, 11, 16, 39, 80, 121,
 122, 124, 126, 134, 173, 202, 280
 manufactured crisis, 127
skills-jobs mismatch, 50
slavery, 24, 26
sleep deprivation, 272
Smith, Vicki, 7, 8, 9, 17, 21, 26, 70, 71,
 72, 74, 75, 106
social capital, 88, 133, 271
social safety net, 285
social trust
 and happiness, 268
sociologists
 deskilling of academics, 111
Standing, Guy, 274, 275

www.ingramcontent.com/pod-product-compliance
Lightning Source LLC
Chambersburg PA
CBHW071534200326
41519CB00021BB/6490